NANONOMICS 2.0

MODERN SOCIAL INVESTMENTS

SECOND EDITION

JENS HAGEN

remedy books

Library of Congress Control Number: 2021922515
ISBN: 978-0-9839510-8-7

Author: Jens Hagen, MSFA, CPA

Has worked for some of the top investment and accounting firms in the nation. Has passed six professional examinations in various areas of business, including the Certified Public Accountant exam and Level II of the Chartered Financial Analyst exam. Holds a master s degree in financial analysis, a program of study that provides detailed training on how to conduct business valuations.

TABLE OF CONTENTS

RICH GET RICHER

A research paper published by Emmanuel Saez in 2015 calculated the income distribution across historical time periods. For the 30 years after WWII, the top 1% held roughly 10% of this nation's wealth, but all that changed in the 1980s with Reaganomics. The rich started to become exceedingly richer compared to the middle class. Nowadays, depending on the state of the stock market, the wealth held by the top 1% has roughly doubled since Reagan's presidency compared to the middle class' holdings. As an example, the wealthiest 1% enjoyed an 11% growth in income during the economic recovery occurring between 2009 and 2011 while the bottom 99% saw a 0.4% reduction.[1]

The National Bureau of Economic Research later published a paper attempting to downplay the exact nature of wealth accumulation among the country's top 1%, noting how low- and middle-income workers receive tax credits and public assistance, as if social programs are an appropriate subsitute for wages.[2] Taxpayers may be frustrated over money going toward social programs, but political leaders have barely lifted a finger since the 1980s to fight for higher wages as a way of ending this need for government aid. Hard-working Americans are increasingly overworked and underpaid, causing them to rely on public assistance, all for the benefit of corporate profit margins and mega wealth accumulation among the top 1%.

The chief executive officer (CEO) of a Fortune 500 company earned roughly 20 times more than the average worker in 1965. News reports cite that the ratio had ballooned to where CEO compensation among the country's largest companies equaled 296-fold the average worker's pay by

2013.[3,4] A global survey asked participants what they felt an appropriate CEO-to-worker pay ratio would be; the average responses ranged from a low of 2:1 in Denmark to a high of 8:1 in Australia. Participants were then asked to estimate what the ratio was in their country, and people in the United States thought CEOs made about 30 times more than the average worker—roughly 10% of what the ratio actually is.[5]

In many cases, CEO pay has morphed into extravagant stock options worth millions of dollars causing the full compensation package a CEO receives to far exceed a ratio of 1,000:1.[6] Disney CEO Bob Iger received $65.6 million in total compensation in 2018, including special stock awards. That full compensation package equaled 1,424 times the median Disney worker.[7]

Senator Robert Menendez pushed for the inclusion of Section 953(b) of the Dodd-Frank Wall Street Reform and Consumer Protection Act passed in 2010. This part of the bill mandates the calculation and disclosure of the ratio of CEO pay to the median worker salary. The Securities Exchange Commission (SEC), the government agency in charge of administrating Section 953(b), delayed implementation over the next seven years and only specified firms would need to report the CEO-to-Worker Pay Ratio rule starting in 2018.[8] Disclosure of this rule has many shortfalls because the rule only involves employees whereas many of the larger multinational firms outsource to third-party manufacturing firms. In addition, U.S. firms can also attempt to treat employees as independent contractors, leading to distortions in the CEO-to-Worker Pay Ratio.

Countless examples exist of companies trying to classify workers as independent contractors to save money. Now, there's even more incentive because independent contractors are not included in the calculation of the CEO-to-Worker Pay Ratio. Anyone relegated to independent contractor status must file a business tax return, pay 15.3% in payroll taxes, and self-fund healthcare premiums while simultaneously being denied labor laws, union protections, and company benefits.[9] An independent contractor falls outside the scope of labor laws meant to protect workers against discrimination, sexual harassment, unlawful termination, and unfair wages.

The ride-sharing company Uber Technologies, Inc., based in San Francisco, California, escaped payroll taxes, human resource laws, and healthcare benefits, because it was treating drivers as independent contractors.[10] No wonder a driver for the company was caught on camera arguing with Travis Kalanick, former CEO of Uber Technologies, Inc., about excessively low payments.[11]

The company settled a lawsuit in 2019 to the tune of $20 million over this issue of worker classification, but the settlement allowed Uber Technologies, Inc., to continue treating workers as independent contractors despite this large settlement.[12] California passed Assembly Bill 5, or AB5, to overturn this ruling and ensure gig workers are classified as employees, but companies spent milllions convincing voters to overturn AB5 through Proposition 22, which is now tied up in the courts despite passing.

The news media may cite a low CEO-to-worker pay ratio based on Bureau of Labor Statistics (BLS) data. However, as many as 80% of small businesses have zero employees, and 10% of companies only retain one to four workers.[13] BLS data downplay the general CEO-to-worker pay ratio because of how the agency views business ownership, whereas more than half of all workers in the United States work for large multinational corporations in which CEO pay far exceeds what the average worker makes.[14] Among large multinational firms, the ratio is close to 300:1, showcasing the disconnect between what CEOs make and what the median worker earns.[15]

Economists have studied the compensation packages of upper managers only to discover a weak relationship between stock options and company performance. Studies have confirmed that a large disparity between CEO pay and the general workforce results in diminished productivity.[16] Corporations offer lavish stock plans as part of CEO compensation but this stock only incentivizes excessive risk taking.[17]

In reality, everyone can elevate to a higher wage level as long as productivity gains allow for higher output and CEOs share this increased value with all workers. If CEOs were to engage in innovative practices instead of depending on cheap foreign labor to boost stock prices (and their own compensation), the increase in value could translate into higher wages for the entire workforce. The CEO could earn more, the mid-level manager could earn more, and the entry-level employee could earn more.

Pundits will argue that pay among CEOs is justified because they create firm value, but should top corporate managers be rewarded for ransacking the domestic labor force and outsourcing production to China, Vietnam, or Mexico as a way of employing foreign workers for less than $30 per day? Has the CEO created value through innovation or merely unearthed a scheme to sidestep worker compensation and environmental protections?

Firm "value" should not be based on labor exploitation, stock buybacks, and excess short-term risk taking.

An entrepreneur should be rewarded for advancing the innovation of products, services, and processes. Giving a reward to entrepreneurs who exploit foreign labor does a huge disservice to the overall economic system. Tax policy should favor companies that retain employees in the United States, government contracts should only extend to companies with a predominate U.S.-based workforce, and consumers must make a conscious decision to choose high-quality products made in the USA over lower-quality products manufactured overseas using exploited labor.

Everyone deserves to share in the wealth a company generates because the entire economic system has exposure to the risk of a company. Corporations enlist insurance firms to share in the risk of an unforeseen disaster. Taxpayers bear the ultimate risk of bailing out systemic failures unable to be insured. Nothing exemplifies taxpayer liability better than what happened in the aftermath of Lehman Brothers' collapse. The investment firm went bankrupt and sent shockwaves through the global economy in 2008. Hard-working employees at this firm received pink slips and saw their pension benefits slashed. American taxpayers received a multibillion dollar invoice to bail out what was considered a "too big to fail corporation."

An entrepreneur no longer takes on all the risk of a venture. In today's world, business ownership is a complex mix of venture capital, private equity, investment banks, and commercial banks—it's a long list. Funding for a venture comes from employee pension funds, consumer bank deposits, public grants, and government contracts. Institutional stock ownership by large investment firms and pension funds makes supervision of top managers more difficult, and undeserved stock compensation often falls in the hands of poorly performing managers.

Modern multinational corporations are not started and owned by one person anymore. The days of an entrepreneur pulling up bootstraps to create a successful business empire are long gone. These so-called bootstraps are now funded by taxpayer-supported banks with manufacturing in SE Asia and tax havens spread across Europe. The American public participates to a large extent in the risk pool—as much as 80% through direct and indirect stock ownership.[18] The bootstrap analogy is a farce the ultrawealthy use to distract disenfranchised workers who struggle to regain a grip on living wages and labor protections.

One-third of today's billionaires inherited their money and never rose to success launching an original enterprise.[19] Even then, many of the billionaires who started successful businesses had family support of some kind. As an example, Mike Bezos worked for Exxon Mobil and gave his adopted son Jeff almost $250,000 to start Amazon.[20] Where would Jeff Bezos be today without his father?

It's insulting to the hard-working Americans who live the reality of social stratification to assert that billionaires deserve to accumulate abundant wealth. Soon after graduating with my master's degree in financial analysis, I tracked the portfolio well-being for some of this nation's richest individuals. The portfolio sizes ranged between $10 million and $3 billion. Half of these wealthy elites were sons and daughters who inherited their money. The kids and grandkids of yesteryear's entrepreneurs did not take the initial risk or work hard to build an empire. These multimillionaires simply had the incredible fortune to be born into a family with extreme preexisting wealth, and that wealth escapes taxation through a web of convoluted tax laws, trusts, and grants.

I worked harder than many of these wealthy clients who sat atop multimillion dollar portfolios, and despite earning a starter salary, I paid a higher combined payroll and income tax rate than these multimillionaires. I bore witness first hand to the hypocrisy of a system that lets the ultrawealthy enjoy lower overall tax rates than an entry-level worker. Notice how politicians focus on lowering income or capital gains tax rates but they always ignore holding a conversation on lowering payroll taxes assessed on employee wages.

American culture supports the accumulation of wealth as the fair result of hard work. The problem is that wealth accumulates in the hands of family members over many generations if sophisticated tax provisions can be accessed. Today, there are people throughout the United States who inherited huge sums of money without needing to work for it, and they've lobbied Congress to provide generous tax loopholes to ensure the money remains with future generations.

POOR GET POORER

An examination of the historical U.S. economy shows that productivity was much greater in the 1950s and 1960s, and wages kept pace with those innovation gains. The real growth in compensation levels, after an adjustment for inflation, lost its connection with productivity levels in the early 1970s. U.S. productivty gains began to slow in the 1970s as well as the U.S. manufacturing sector began representing a decreasing portion of the economy.

Up until the 1980s, the workforce consumed anywhere from 63%-67% of America's total output. Workers helped innovate products and shared in roughly two-thirds of consumption, granting the middle class a high standard of living. That percentage of economic participation has steadily fallen to 58% as of 2012.[20] Even though companies are producing a higher volume of goods, workers are not benefitting as much from their output, and pay has not remained in line with production either.[21]

The Federal Reserve's Survey of Consumer Finances published in 2016 showed the dire economic state of middle-class households. The bottom fifth of households saw their net worth decline by 22% over the preceding two decades. The next rung up—the so-called lower middle class—experienced a sharper decline of 34%. Today, not only do the majority of Americans own fewer assets but they owe almost 60% more in debts. This wealth divide worsens for people living in a rural setting.

Meanwhile, household wealth for the top 10% rose 146% over this same timeframe.[22] Among the top 0.1%, representing 16,000 families in a country of 320 million people, their share of this nation's wealth swelled from 7% in the 1980s to 22% today.[23] The middle class is unraveling before our eyes, if you can even call it a "middle class" anymore.

Economic theorists claim that productivity gains should drive positive compensation growth but wages for middle- and low-income earners have stagnated. Amateur economists contend that the microeconomic concept of supply and demand will drive wage growth but that usually only takes place when labor conditions are unusually tight. Such tight labor conditions too often will spark excess inflation and force the Federal Reserve to slow the economy. Wage growth is largely the result of productivity gains at the macroeconomic level—not strong micro labor demand. Meanwhile, income among the ultrawealthy has outpaced productivity measures,[24] which is not possible without a transfer of wealth from low- and middle-class workers—call this Robin Hood in reverse.

Of the 35 nations with robust economies considered industrialized, only two of those countries have a greater portion of low-income households than the United States. Can workers remedy low pay by looking for a new job? Switching jobs becomes extremely difficult when a spouse, child, or other family member needs to remain in a specific location for school, work, or medical treatments. This pattern of accumulating skills through an employer and quitting (or being laid off) creates tremendous inefficiency for the economy as a whole. Countries with robust manufacturing sectors seek to retain workers and assist with skills accumulation.

High employee turnover reflects weak job security as opposed to some abstract market power to land a higher-paying job. The United States ranks dead last in terms of job protections among industrialized nations. Only one other industrialized country, Slovakia, spends less on a per-capita basis to help unemployed persons get back into the workforce.[25]

Allowing workers to share in a company's wealth goes far beyond simple fairness. A protected, well-paid employee takes strides to work in a more productive manner, providing enormous benefits to a company's bottom line and greater output to raise the standard of living for all members of society. A 2015 study found that workers who maintain control over job functions even live longer.[26]

A Gallup Poll suggests that a high percentage—around 70%—of employees are disengaged at work.[27] Employees who feel underpaid or underappreciated tend to call in sick more often and perform job duties with minimal effort. No one derives an incentive to work hard via low pay, absent vacation time, and lackluster retirement benefits. Companies must invest more in skills if they wish to boost productivity gains but low wages usually overlap with an absence of training opportunities. In short, most Americans seek higher incomes but workers are not being rewarded, even when they do innovate. So why innovate?

It might make immediate sense to believe that productivity will increase if employees work longer hours. When running as a presidential candidate in 2015, Jeb Bush claimed that the United States could grow GDP by 4% per year if more people worked.[28] The sad reality is that U.S. workers already face dramatically long workweeks, and an increasing number of people bring work home or answer emails during personal time.

At the height of tax season, I would leave work around 1 a.m.—no one can call me lazy. A colleague would end her day around the same time. One evening, while working late, I asked how many hours she worked in the previous week upon which she stated 110. This number has stuck in my head all these years because this person, who had just worked 110 hours, was also eight months pregnant. The American workforce cannot be called lazy by any measure; workers should be adequately rewarded. Laziness is best reflected by the business managers who outsource jobs to reduce costs as opposed to making investments in the American workforce.

Later, I went to work in the investment industry. My manager overloaded me with accounts to the point where stress was making me ill. She forced me to use personal vacation time to see a doctor instead of sick leave. Up to a quarter of bankruptcies occur because hard-working Americans fall ill.[29] The workload at this job required me to toil far beyond 40 hours per week. Long hours above 40 per week rarely translate into greater output levels because workers burn out and become less focused—such was the case in my situation.

A highly productive worker needs education, incentives, and management support to take a limited amount of resources and use technology to maximize hourly output. An accountant with an abacus could prepare the books for one company each day. Give that same accountant cutting-edge software, a fast computer, and incentive pay, and this worker might now have the ability to prepare the bookkeeping for 10 companies per day; plus, the software helps protect the data's integrity.

Overworking employees can lead to burnout and quality-control issues. Economic output is maximized through using technology, refining processes, and automating tasks. Agriculture production in the United States did not increase exponentially because of an 80-hour workweek. We invented the tractor and invested in transportation infrastructure. For too long, multinational companies have foregone investments in worker productivity and instead simply outsourced to cheap-labor nations.

The primary goal of an economic system consists of taking limited resources and converting them into quality goods and services. Workers tend to innovate and uphold high work standards when treated well at an appropriate pay rate. Exploiting the labor pool leads to low-quality output and inefficient production methods. In the end, precious resources are wasted and consumers lose access to quality goods and services.

There is a myth that Henry Ford increased worker pay so that his employees could afford the cars they were building. In reality, Ford wanted to recruit and retain top talent and realized that higher wages would do the trick.[30] He was not looking for a new class of consumers. He wanted top-notch employees who could boost productivity, which would empower the Ford Motor Company to increase the volume and quality of cars while decreasing costs per unit. This opened the door to car ownership for a broad swath of American consumers—not just his employees!

Noting how better pay helps improve product quality, it's little wonder why the more profitable industries in the United States offer above-average pay. Software, biotechnology, and professional service firms generate high rates of return despite employees receiving high wages. Many business managers believe that high employee costs are the reason for low profitability, but at the same time, the investment world pours a disproportionately higher amount of money into Silicon Valley.[31] Here is an area of the United States with a high cost of living, high taxes, and high employee wages, but it's also where companies generate the highest profits.

A CEO in Seattle, WA, made headlines after encountering a disgruntled worker who could barely make ends meet due to the city's high cost of living. Dan Price, CEO of Gravity Payments, decided to institute a novel wage experiment where everyone, including himself, would eventually receive a wage of $70,000. An initial wage foundation set at $50,000, on course to the eventual wage goal, led to a surprising upsurge in profits and productivity.[32,33] Of course, the corporate news machine attempted to denigrate this experiment as a political stunt, but when does paying people a living wage become an issue of political debate?

U.S. business culture must respect how employee innovations, good customer service, and brand loyalty lead to strong profitability. If expenses cause the demise of corporate profits, then why not eliminate all expenses? End the office lease and operate in a tent. Stop spending money on marketing, administration, and office equipment. Companies could forego corporate cars and have sales personnel ride around town on bicycles or mopeds. Offering high wages and modern benefits like paid leave for childbirth create an engaged, productive workforce. Adding more job control, skills training, and incentive pay in the mix drives innovation, which converts into strong revenue gains and enhanced profit margins.

Corporate media, political pundits, and policy think tanks pound into our heads this notion that wages must be low or else businesses will not be able to compete globally. The American public has been led to believe that the United States must outsource because high labor costs undermine profitability, but that is false. Well-educated, highly paid workers surrounded by computers, automation, robotics, and modern logistics have the potential to outproduce cheaper forms of labor.

The United States blames its multibillion-dollar trade deficit with Mexico on the fact that our southern neighbor maintains a cheap labor pool, but Germany ran an €7 billion trade surplus with Mexico in 2018 despite very high labor costs at home.[34] German manufacturing workers earn 12% to 34% more per hour than their U.S. colleagues, while other Northern European countries pay manufacturing workers even more.[35] European firms do not flood production into Mexico or China despite high tax rates, robust compensation, and tight regulations inside the European Union.

German society invests in producing the world's foremost engineers and vocational trade workers. German manufacturing firms invest heavily in offering apprenticeship positions and lifelong skills training.[36,37] Over half of German workers possess a formal means to bargain collectively,[38] compared to just over 10% in the United States, translating to higher compensation and more personal leave.

A look at gross domestic production (GDP) growth reveals that the U.S. and Germany averaged about the same, or 1.6% annualized, since 1980.[39] You might conclude that taking better care of the workforce does not matter until realizing the United States has relied more heavily on long work schedules to drive GDP growth. Comparing GDP to total work hours per person tells a different story. German workers have one of the shortest workweeks in the European Union, and GDP per hour grew at 1.72% compared to 1.56% in the United States.[40] This divide may not seem like much but stretch this across four decades of accumulated productivity gains. You start to realize why the German middle class earns higher wages and receives more time off than its American counterpart. It's not about working harder to drive GDP growth; America must work smarter.

The cornerstone of German manufacturing is the network of Fraunhofer-Gesellschaft institutes, which connects companies to regional consortia of technical consultants. A Fraunhofer office will house workers with various technical skills to help modern, high-tech manufacturing firms conduct research. Each Fraunhofer office then links into regional universities to expand the country's research potential.[41] All told, German manufacturing firms thrive in an environment where social investments have been made in education, vocational studies, apprenticeships, and the Fraunhofer research system.

Companies remain in Germany because they achieve substantial productivity gains amid these various economic investments, and the productivity gains permit higher compensation, shorter workweeks, and more profit. In the end, the entire global community receives a benefit from German innovation in terms of better forms of healthcare technology, security equipment, consumer goods, and so forth.

If congressional leaders kept their wages stagnate with inflation since the 1980s, alongside American workers, they would be earning a little less than $100,000.[42] But of course, congressional leaders now earn $174,000 with full benefits including a retirement package and health insurance.[43] Why have American workers lost the wage battle? We must deflate misconceptions tossed around by political talking heads and move away from this power structure that demands we work longer hours with fewer benefits. In a democratic society where voters have a means to influence and even kick out congressional leaders, why do people keep refilling the halls of Congress with officials who enact laws that favor billionaires?

REBOOTING PRODUCTIVITY

In the aftermath of America's Great Depression, the venerated British economist John Maynard Keynes studied wage rates in the United States and reached the age-old conclusion that infusion of money into the economic system and real wage rates move together.[44] Since then, economists have discovered how wage rates respond to productivity gains, disproving this notion that microeconomic labor demand is needed to drive up wages.

The word *productivity* has a specific definition in the world of economics. A productive venture will maximize output from a set of resources such as employees, raw materials, and capital (money). A worker does not have to work hard to boost productivity in modern times if companies employ the right technologies, software, and logistics systems. As a person works longer hours and becomes increasingly tired and unfocused, productivity can begin to suffer. Companies that exploit cheap manual labor in Southeast Asia, Mexico, or South America also fail to invest in productive innovations.

In an effort to maximize innovation, investment money must fuel the use of modern facilities, equipment, and workforce skills. An economy does not make appropriate investments when money accumulates among the top 0.1%. Tax policy that allows the megarich to sit around with inherited wealth does not lead to productive gains. If every single person shows up to work knowing that improving processes, defending product quality, and researching new technologies will result in incentive pay, bonuses, and wage raises, then the entire economic system benefits from the resulting advancements in output per hour. Instead of one entrepreneur making mild gains in productivity from personal efforts, the same business can achieve a much higher rate of success from the entire workforce's contributions.

A greater volume of output per hour with a focus on precision translates into increased standards of living for everyone. We all take home more high-quality products at a lower price as a result of innovative practices. Managers can increase profit margins and pay higher wages when following a modern set of human resource principles.

- » Link wages, benefits, and bonuses to productivity levels.
- » Provide opportunities to develop skills and communicate ideas.
- » Base job advancement on the contribution to innovation.
- » Invest in business resources that help employees innovate.

The American dream has made us believe that productivity comes from hard work. This antiquated mindset has been perpetuated via a sense of martyrdom wherein people feel inclined to sacrifice their well-being in order to prove their worth to managers through long work hours. The end result may be an underperforming economy since, between the Industrial Revolution and the Internet Age, productivity has shifted from long factory hours to intelligence-based tasks centering on processes, computers, automation, and logistics.

At my first accounting job during college, this manufacturing firm staggered start times so that one coworker started 30 minutes before me. I would arrive second in the day always to catch my coworker playing mahjong on the computer. It did not take long before I became addicted to playing the game as well, and I had a 30-minute window before the next person arrived.

Long work hours won't lead to productive output if people are sitting all day in front of a computer screen wasting time on games or social media. Plenty of employees fill time with unnecessary tasks as a job security measure. It was in my best interest to waste the first 30 minutes playing mahjong because I could look busy when the managers finally arrived.

Productivity reflects useful worker output that will eventually benefit the consumer. To increase levels of output, employees must insert new technologies into processes, rework systems, and uphold quality standards. Companies need employees to generate increasingly higher amounts of output within the normal workweek.

The most successful approach to date involves rewarding employees for their innovations. I could spend 30 minutes working or use that time to play video games. Either way, I was paid the same amount. A compensation package should include incentive-based pay that rewards employees for thier innovation instead of lowballing workers with basic pay packages meant to reduce costs. This pursuit of low-cost production is lazy management that tends to result in low-quality production, inefficiency, and reduced revenue.

I enjoy asking my economic students this question: "Do you work in an environment that rewards new ideas?" Almost across the board, my students confirm the opposite. If they suggest a new innovative approach or highlight a new idea, management paints a target on their back. Instead of being seen as innovative, my students are afraid that bringing forth ideas will upset precious management egos.

An annual survey organized by the magazine *Area Development* asks upper managers at more than 100 companies what factors they find most important for success. In the 2015 survey, 94.4% of respondents listed access to highways as either "very important" or "important," while availability of skilled labor had a respective score of 89.9%. More than half the firms raised concerns over the lack of strong literacy and vocational skills among U.S. workers. Corporate taxes, state taxes, and local incentives sat in the number 5 spot, highlighting how tax issues often rank low on these surveys.[45] Social investments are a critical element in economic models used to explain wage growth and economic strength. Economists do not draw a relationship between low taxes and economic expansion.

Corporate managers may see taxes as a burden and modify decisions based on tax rates, but what political leaders fail to grasp is how crumbling, outdated infrastructure and underskilled workers place a much greater burden on companies. A 2016 survey of 60 large U.S. manufacturing firms with average revenue of $7 billion revealed how the major barriers to business success were pricing issues, market conditions, and costs, but higher wages and tax policies ranked low among cost factors. These same manufacturing firms reported a high rate of opportunity to innovate, implement new technologies, and improve the customer experience,[46] which all require an investment in a company's cost structure.

The *Global Competitiveness Report 2011-2012* examined 142 global economies to determine 12 key pillars in maintaining productivity growth.[47] A sound judicial system topped the list as investors refuse to put money into an economy in which legal rights are unprotected. There is no sense in buying a factory only to watch as government authorities confiscate it without remuneration. Transportation infrastructure has long been ignored as part of the American economic system despite the critical need to move goods and services swiftly and cost-effectively from factories to consumers. A growing body of economic research points to how government budget deficits—the kind the United States currently runs—drag down investment markets and instill fear in the minds of investors. Fourth and fifth on the list, a society must invest in healthcare and education in order to maximize the ability of the workforce to innovate. The remaining seven economic pillars can be found in Figure 2.1.

Figure 2.1
Twelve Pillars of Economic Success

1. Sound legal system
2. Government stability
3. Transportation infrastructure
4. Healthy workforce
5. Educated workforce
6. Competitive pressures
7. Workforce retraining
8. Investment markets
9. Technology adoption
10. Marketplace size
11. Intellectual capital
12. Research innovation

It's dangerous to overlook the importance of all these critical investments, which make an economy run efficiently, but do you really want to pay higher taxes? No one wants to pay higher taxes. That's akin to wanting to pay more for a dental procedure. It's understandable to complain about taxes and second-guess the need for government services. No one will ever want to pay taxes into a system for haphazard reasons, especially if tax money is inefficiently misdirected to pork projects or wasteful government contracts.

As a democracy, we should make an effort to understand the needs of a marketplace and work through political channels to exert an influence over how tax revenue is spent. But failure to invest in the social fabric of an economy means that consummating economic transactions becomes increasingly difficult, which eats away at our standard of living. An economy will drag along inefficiently without proper investments. Consider four key forms of social investment: education, transportation, communication, and legal system.

A. The modern workforce handles many technical matters for which skills training is vital. To a large extent, this technical know-how requires vocational training during high school years, community college programs, or university degrees related to science, technology, engineering, or mathematic (STEM) fields.

B. The modern logistics system requires seaports, airports, trains, and freeways to deliver products across the entire globe. An investment in public transportation, even when provided as a gratuity to commuters, helps free up bottlejammed infrastructure for commercial interests. A toll anywhere along this system acts as a barrier that will reduce product delivery or retail shopping.

C. Companies need the ability to communicate all across the supply chain, including with customers. The common phone lines have given way to fiberoptics and internet connections. Fast WiFi service encourages online shopping and enables commercial data transmission. The postal service offers companies a way to ship physical products and paper correspondence.

D. A modern economic system needs a robust set of legal codes to follow and enforcement to protect intellectual property, safeguard consumers, and secure a money supply. A well-structured court system is used to clarify the legality of actions according to the code.

Political leaders claim they must amass government debt instead of raising taxes in order to keep the economy moving forward. As U.S. dollars pour into Mexican factories, Saudi Arabian oil facilities, or Chinese manufacturing firms, the foreign investors at the head of these entities turn around and invest those dollars back into the United States via acquisition of real estate, land, stocks, and bonds. It's little wonder why roughly 30% of U.S. government bonds are owned by foreign investors. As taxpayers dip into their wallets to pay the interest on these bonds, an accumulated transfer of wealth overseas has occurred to the tune of $6 trillion (and rising).[48] That is $6 trillion that could have been put toward critical investments inside the United States.

A team at the University of Massachusetts Amherst gathered data on government debt levels for 20 countries since World War II and compared the percentage of debt to gross domestic product (GDP) growth. The optimal amount of government debt is zero, and average GDP growth can decline as much as 1-2% as government debt climbs to the level experienced currently by the United States.[49] Politicians refuse to raise taxes, saying it will drag down the economy, but the accumulation of high debt—now surpassing 100% of U.S. GDP—weighs upon the economy more heavily. Instead of funding education, taxpayers send interest payments to China, Japan, Saudi Arabia, and the United Kingdom, as well as to the U.S. multinational firms holding U.S. government debt in offshore tax havens.

Experts are unsure of causality when it comes to debt levels. Does high government debt directly weigh down an economic system—perhaps because it can crowd out the private market for bonds—or are high debt levels merely a sign that political leadership is irresponsible, failing to invest properly in the economic system?

The U.S. political system is increasingly toxified with big money coming from foreign entities and multinational corporations. Elected officials direct government contracts to these large financial donors and write favorable tax policy for them, creating an environment in which resources are pooled among a few ultrawealthy families. Anyone siding with the conservative philosophy of fiscal responsibility should be aghast at how American political leaders irresponsibly push wealth toward the top 1%.

The American public is not served when political leaders deregulate industries and let multinational corporations run amok without regard to labor rights or environmental protections. Opening markets to international trade increases competitive pressures. Then the same political elites who opened up these markets in a haphazard, thoughtless manner in order to access cheap foreign labor insist that labor costs must be reduced because of increased competitive pressures. It's enough to make your head spin.

Multinational corporations open the proverbial competitive floodgates into foreign markets and then later seek to maintain profitability via exploiting cheap labor in those same markets. This economic formula was used a century ago to convince the nation that tipped wages and child labor were an economic necessity. The British Empire fought to maintain the slave trade for decades citing similar economic pressures.

Corporate elites have coined the term "job creators" to perpetuate a myth that large corporations deserve to pay almost no taxes because they create jobs. These so-called job creators are not giant altruistic benefactors aiming to support the middle class. Companies ask hard-working Americans to sacrifice their health and family to work 50 or more hours per week. These companies want to squeeze every ounce of effort from employees before tossing them aside as soon as they fall sick. Meanwhile, no one seems to realize that payroll expenses serve as a tax deduction that always lower a company's taxable income. Taxes are levied after taking into account all payroll expenses, not before. That means high tax rates do not bear upon a company's ability to pay workers—revenue from satisfied customers give companies the means to pay workers, and payroll costs will always lower the resulting tax liability directly.

Revenue levels will flounder miserably and profit margins will be ripped to shreds when corporations operate under the guise of deregulation, low wages, and thin cost structures. If we fail to keep a marketplace safe, then the system begins to stagnate as consumers fear making purchases. Imagine trying to find a suitable residence but a failure to invest in regulations exposes people to the risk of asbestos or black mold. Or, what if when you go out to eat, a lack of government inspection means that you have zero trust in the sanitation of the food? An economy will see business transactions languish if consumers remain fearful of products and services.

Would you be more likely to purchase items online with slow WiFi or fast fiberoptic internet? You may tap a button to make an online purchase, and this event seems straightforward, but the ease at which that transaction has occurred comes with multiple layers of government oversight and investment. Taxpayers helped fund the technical education of software engineers who designed and implemented the online platform. Movement of data packages instructing the company about your purchase run along expensive communication infrastructure. Depending on where your product was manufactured, the logistics system requires interstate roads, seaports, and airports to bring the delivery right to your door.

No one can form a complex and robust company without investment in equipment, marketing, and technical skills. To the same degree, America cannot form a modern economy without critical investments in education, transportation infrastructure, communication lines, and a legal system. Personally, I don't want to travel along cramped roadways to buy an unregulated product subject to safety concerns. These conditions may sound absurd, but billions of people in underdeveloped nations live amid disorganized, unregulated economic systems. These conditions persist because of a failure to raise taxes and maintain proper government services.

An economy is not a linear set of events that permits an individual to become successful directly through hard work. An economy exists as a robust system of supply chains, consumers, infrastructure, and resources. To maximize our success, working hard is an important ingredient but we must ensure that money becomes invested in productive tasks. We cannot pump blood through clogged arteries or shriveled veins, and we cannot pump money through an unskilled, unregulated, and unstructured economic system. We perceive wealth as the immediate upshot of work, but plenty of people in developing nations work hard without securing wealth.

An economy is not defined by wealth held inside the investment account of one person who started a company. Money does not fall out of the sky and land in an entrepreneur's hands randomly. The real economy is rooted in daily transactions of goods and services taking place among billions of people. An economic transaction involves one party handing money over and the other party providing a product or service. An intelligent entrepreneur assesses the strength of a company's cost structure and makes targeted investments where the rate of return is highest. Costs faced by companies must be assessed using financial data to find a point of optimization, but one common theme is consistently true: Costs are indeed required to advance a company and generate a high rate of return. There will always be a cost of doing business.

COLLECTIVE BARGAINING

Congress passed the National Labor Relations Act (NLRA) in 1935 to advance unionization efforts and formalize collective bargaining rights.[50] Referred to also as the Wagner Act after Senator Robert Wagner (D-NY), the Act allowed workers to form bargaining units and established a labor board to help employees settle disputes with their respective management.

Formal membership in a union is not a prerequisite for exercising many of the rights extended to workers by the NRLA.[51] The NLRA permits two or more workers to "engage in concerted efforts" to undertake bargaining actions or appoint a representative to perform the same. These employees can stage a work strike without fear of management retaliation, but nowhere in the NLRA does it establish resources or infrastructure to help employees organize.

In order to exercise formal collective bargaining rights under the NLRA, employees must vote on forming a collective bargaining unit with over 50% being in favor. Here's where the workforce runs into a major obstacle. The NLRA does not clearly define who is part of an employee bargaining unit, giving company management the power to define the collective workforce in a vague manner, which then obstructs unionization efforts. As workers attempt to organize into a bargaining unit, upper management can redefine job roles, split up departments, or expand overseas outside the reach of the NLRA.

Two employees may not have the capacity to take on a multinational corporation with its team of lawyers, or employees may lose power if the company retools the business in a way that undermines informal bargaining efforts. Concerted activities and unionization efforts might hit a wall if companies consolidate, merge, and expand across multiple states.[52] Even small companies might have a satellite office with only a few employees.

Today, more than ever, forming a labor organization within a large multinational corporation has become next to impossible given the constraints of the NLRA. Of main concern, an employee wishing to bargain collectively must encourage a majority of coworkers to cast a vote in favor of forming a company-wide labor organization. How does this occur inside a company with 10,000 workers spread all over the United States? It doesn't.

A seismic shift occurred in work conditions after passage of the NLRA despite the Act's many deficiencies. Union membership steadily rose until the country entered World War II, at which time wartime constraints were placed on compensation. At the end of the war, unions began to strike *en masse* across various industries as the federal government released wartime wage caps. The rise of union strength after WWII activated resistance efforts from corporate interest groups.

Union membership increased to 30% of the workforce[53] in the 1950s and '60s before declining to roughly 20% when Ronald Reagan took office in 1981.[54] Fast forward 30 years and that number has dropped to almost 10%, not to mention how half of current union members work for a government institution such as a school district or police department.[55] Union membership among private firms has fallen dramatically over the past 50 years, and this number continues to decline each year as political leaders attack union membership with right-to-work and payroll protection bills. Sabotaging union dues is not meant to support worker rights. It reflects an ambitious effort on the part of business elites to undermine employee bargaining strength.

Republicans, who gained a congressional majority after WWII ended, moved to restrain union power starting with passage in 1947 of the Taft-Hartley Act, known formally as the Labor-Management Relations Act. The Taft-Hartley Act banned secondary boycotts, which targeted the supply chain of the main "primary" company sitting at the heart of a union's labor dispute.[56] This Act also enabled states to pass their own laws limiting a union's ability to require membership, i.e., the payment of dues. Referred to as "Right-to-Work" laws, political elites began using this provision of the Taft-Hartley Act to undermine unions financially.[56,57]

Conservatives like to market right-to-work laws as fair because workers should not be forced to pay compulsory union dues. Would it be fair to have these same workers decline fair wages, labor protections, and retirement benefits that the union helped secure? On average, a union worker earns approximately 28% more than a nonunion worker according to the Bureau of Labor Statistics, translating to over $200 per week more in pay.[58] Workers may not want to pay union dues but the lack of collective bargaining strength tends to translate into lower compensation and weak labor protections.

In the past two decades, attacks against unions have centered increasingly on limiting political activity under the guise of protecting paychecks. A "payroll protection law" seeks to limit a union's ability to use member fees for political activities, which tend to lean more liberal. Starting in 1992, voters in Washington State passed Initiative 134 with an overwhelming 72% in favor of forbidding union dues from being used for political purposes.[59] House Speaker Newt Gingrich and Americans for Tax Reform President Grover Norquist, along with many Republican state leaders and conservative groups, jumped on board this movement that started in Washington, but payroll protection bills have largely failed across the country apart from arbitrary successes in six states.[60]

Conservative groups organize misinformation campaigns surrounding payroll protection and right-to-work legislation to foster an aversion toward private union membership. In Washington State, a conservative group called The Freedom Foundation brought lawsuits and funded election campaigns starting in 2014 in an attempt to circumnavigate worker privacy and obtain contact information. The group sought to mail out antiunion marketing literature and go directly to union member homes.[61,62] These pro-corporate groups deploy carefully crafted rhetoric to paint union dues in a negative light. In the same vein, right-to-work legislation permits workers to opt out of paying union dues, bleeding unions of the financial resources needed to fight these attacks.

The National Labor Relations Board (NLRB) is the agency in charge of overseeing union issues. Under the Obama Administration, the NLRB made the process of unionization easier for employees working at a corporate franchise. Later, the Republican-controlled Congress and the Trump Administration conspired to put big-business sycophants in leadership positions at the NLRB. The new appointees included two corporate lawyers.[63] Initially, the NLRB overturned the Obama-era ruling but the case was litigated in the courts. As of December 2018, the U.S. Court of Appeals ruled in favor of the NLRB, barring the Obama-era ruling, thus making it harder to unionize.[64] The NLRB has the duty to oversee collective bargaining efforts in the United States but this example shows how the NLRB can be undermined from within its own leadership.

Even with the full power of the National Labor Relations Act, workers in the United States still fall short of the collective bargaining rights available to other workers around the globe. Ideally, a labor law would allow formation of an internal employee alliance capable of maintaining the collective power of the entire workforce on an ongoing basis. The workforce needs a formal method to communicate problems with union leaders, employers, and government officials. Collective bargaining rights must put workers in the driver's seat when it comes to finding innovative solutions.

Since 1994, significantly large multinational firms operating within the European Union must establish European Work Councils tasked with meeting at least once annually, serving as a mechanism to guarantee firm management negotiates with employees.[65] The United Kingdom enacted the Information and Consultation of Employees Regulations 2004, requiring management at large firms hold open communication and release financial data about critical matters with employees.[66]

Nordic countries, which are mislabeled as socialist, actually have flexible, democratic labor laws giving each industry the power to arrange suitable pay and workplace standards. Social media memes claim minimum wages in Denmark are extremely high but Denmark does not have a nationwide, fixed minimum wage as the United States does—most Northern European countries maintain industry-specific wages. In Denmark, a consortium of union interests called the Danish Confederation of Trade Unions bargains collectively with companies. Organized into the Confederation of Danish Employers, these companies organize into a parallel industry consortium and then work with the labor union consortium to set a minimum wage level appropriate for the given circumstances of the respective industry. This framework also leaves room for individual companies to further negotiate outside of the union consortium.[67]

These flexible labor laws ensure wage levels are reasonable for a particular industry, work schedules are an appropriate fit, and workers have more power to problem-solve with industry leaders. It becomes easier to address socioeconomic injustice with industry-level negotiations between workers and employers because women, immigrants, and minority groups face different situations based on the industry. In public accounting, a woman may be asked to work more than 100 hours per week during a tax season, making breastfeeding or a pregnancy very challenging. A high percentage of immigrants find work in the agricultural and tech industries. Women in the restaurant industry tend to endure a greater prevalence of sexual harassment from customers and coworkers.

The high wages seen among European countries often reflect collective bargaining efforts among unions, work councils, and companies. Germany, a country with higher manufacturing wages than the United States, did not institute a minimum wage until 2015 because of widespread collective bargaining powers.[68] The United States permits collective bargaining and unionization under the auspices of the NLRA, but this piece of legislation does not fuel industry-level bargaining powers. Passage of state bills allowing internal employee alliances would provide 100% of the workforce with a foundational layer of collective bargaining rights.

A blanket statewide or federal minimum wage may not respect the idiosyncrasies of an industry or geographic region. The lack of industry-level collective bargaining can cause discrepancies in the labor supply, creating unwanted inefficiencies in worker skills. Union confederations, as what exists in Denmark, encourage workers to migrate across industries as higher wages pull talent toward undersupplied areas.

Supply and demand forces do not drive wage increases, as many attempt to purport. Japan, Korea, and even the United States have undergone periods of low unemployment without seeing upward wage pressures. The microeconomic concept of supply and demand actually is meant to explain stability, meaning wages would return to an initial equilibrium point as supply and demand forces battle each other. Using supply and demand to explain macro-level wage growth represents an incorrect application of this microeconomic concept. Economic models correlate wage growth with productivity gains and money supply expansion.

The Mortensen economic model highlights how bouncing from one job to another in an attempt to negotiate higher compensation creates inefficiency for an economy. Nobel Prize winner Dale Mortensen showed that staying put with an employer and gaining assistance from a union to bargain collectively help drive the market for wages in a more efficient manner.[69] Global economic research also demonstrates that union workers are more productive. Unions set the standard for labor protections, safe work conditions, and living wages. Companies in which unions have set high wages draw workers away from nonunionized firms unless those firms also keep pace with union compensation.

Several studies examining unionization in China found that worker productivity at unionized firms, or amid a densely-unionized economic area, resulted in greater worker output.[70] An economic study involving 5,000 Japanese companies found that a union workforce galvanized higher wages, better output, and greater firm profitability.[71] Again, how can companies become more profitable when wage levels increase? Americans have been sold a lie that outsourcing and low wages are a necessary evil in order to preserve the financial health of corporate profits. The labor protections and bargaining rights seen across companies in China, Japan, Denmark, and many other industrialized economies demonstrate an opposite truth: The most profitable firms pay workers extremely well.

The most profitable areas of the United States consist of liberal tax laws, tight regulations, and high wages. Silicon Valley sits as the global epicenter for modern computer, software, and medical innovation because of the massive concentration of highly skilled workers. Union workers are better positioned to secure resources from management as opposed to allowing management to simply lower worker pay or outsource activity to a cheap labor nation as a way of boosting profit margins artificially. Overworking employees leads to disengagement, absenteeism, and errors. Companies attempt to boost profit with nonunionized workers who can be paid low wages without benefits; but despite longer hours and less personal leave, nonunion workers do not produce as much. The true path toward greater innovation has always required a financial investment in process improvements, logistics, automation, robotics, and skills development.

Inside the United States, areas that welcome low tax rates and unregulated industries have struggled economically over the past 150 years. The greatest driver of innovation is education, but a state with low tax rates cannot afford the resources needed for science, technology, engineering, and mathematics (STEM) training. Political leaders try to blame teacher unions and high teacher wages for problems with education, but technical classes require higher pay to attract highly skilled teachers. Many low-income areas cannot attract enough math teachers because of the inadequacy of financial resources, creating an ongoing divide in educational attainment.

A research report conducted through five leading universities highlights how unions ensure teacher quality is high,[72] yet in the current environment, underfunded school districts all across the United States struggle to find enough skilled teachers. How will lowering pay even further with a conservative push for teacher deunionization solve the funding problem in education when school districts lack the economic means to recruit skilled teachers in the first place? Teacher pay among low-income districts is already low, and attempts to destabilize income among these teachers through deunionization could greatly disenfranchise minority communities even further.

Teachers need resources to empower young minds. The turnover rate of math and science teachers is highest among all teachers, and new teacher recruitment efforts are even more challenging at disadvantaged schools.[73] The true shortage of math and science teachers in high-poverty areas is the direct result of how states fund school districts unequally. A wealthy school district has the resources to pay teachers double that of a low-income district; states must address the huge funding gap among local jurisdictions.

In many instances, teacher unions drive the political effort to develop classroom testing, enhance professional standards, and extend opportunities for teacher training.[74] Even the Cato Institute, a conservative think tank, affirms that that "empirical evidence" does not support the notion that collective bargaining is the cause of poor performance among students.[75] The ongoing attacks against teacher unions will only serve to reduce the education strength of the country.

Employees can now post anonymous wage data online through websites such as Glassdoor.com to help community members bargain during the recruitment process. In 2017, New York City passed a law prohibiting employers from asking about prior salary history.[76] In Colorado, the Equal Pay for Equal Work Act now requires employers to list salary expectations on job postings. This information helps to bridge the wage gap for women and minorities but it also gives more power to job candidates when they see the salary offerings among competing firms.

The Equal Employment Opportunity Commission (EEOC) attempted to gather wage data under the Obama Administration but the Trump Administration blocked its final release.[77] The data was meant to address wage disparity across various demographic factors. Expanding and protecting these activities help workers better negotiate wage and benefit packages when a union does not exist.

However, it's best to greatly expand the National Labor Relations Act to ensure collective bargaining rights extend to all workers. Why do Americans hail democratic processes then spin 180 degrees to accept a top-down, totalitarian style of workplace management? Unions parallel the democratic form of governance Americans embrace. The power to vote and organize collectively should extend beyond the political arena and permeate the workplace all across America. An open, team-based relationship with management ensures fairness in compensation and brings innovative ideas to the fore.

OUTSOURCING

On February 21, 1972, President Richard Nixon prepared a visit to the People's Republic of China to thaw the Cold War chills that blew amid the previous three decades of communist hostility.[78] The successful normalization of the Sino-American relationship signaled a new era of foreign trade. In 1980, the U.S. Congress conferred Most Favored Nation status on China, which effectively removed a litany of tariffs and allowed a better trade environment between the two nations.[79] As the 1980s rolled forward, a new buzzword emerged among corporate executives, business journals, and MBA programs: outsourcing.

U.S. businesses saw China as an ideal target for the burgeoning American outsourcing trend. Like a rocket, Chinese imports into the United States began to soar from a few million dollars until reaching $15 billion by 1990, $100 billion by 2000, and settling around $400 billion annually after 2010.[80] This newfound outsourcing craze meant U.S. corporations could ship jobs overseas, hire third-party manufacturers, and boost profit margins.

The U.S. business model that took root in the 1980s leaned upon tax loopholes, deunionization efforts, and deregulation. Outsourcing eliminated the need for U.S. business managers to think critically about productive investments in worker skills. In most cases, an entirely separate foreign company would manufacture on behalf of the U.S. company. Consumers bought products made in a foreign land, and U.S. dollars flooded out of the country at an ever-increasing pace. The cheap foreign products deflated the U.S. money supply, allowing the Federal Reserve to keep interests rates low historically. Large multinational corporations benefitted from both cheap interest rates and cheap exploited labor.

In 1993, the North American Free Trade Agreement (NAFTA) was signed into law by Canada, Mexico, and the United States. Pundits like to blame NAFTA for manufacturing job losses occurring throughout the 1990s, but the outsourcing trend had begun to heat up in the decade prior.[81] Of importance, 1993 signaled the end of a recession and imports increased as the economy recovered. Bill Clinton, a conservative Democrat, signed NAFTA into law, despite opposition from trade unions because economists affirmed that trade with Mexico was already poised to shift.[82] Factories were already migrating out of the United States into China without the presence of a formal trade agreement. Even if the United States never signed NAFTA, the European Union was already engaged in trade talks with Mexico, culminating in a trade agreement in 1997 that would open Mexico to trade anyway.

Anyone who bears a grudge against NAFTA for the loss of U.S. manufacturing jobs overlooks the fact that the United States does not maintain a formal trade agreement with China. A formal free trade agreement is not required for U.S. manufacturing firms to move facilities abroad. In fact, a trade agreement might benefit the United States, because as it stands, China provides unfair tax incentives to encourage firms to move abroad and set up operations in one of its free trade zones (FTZ).[83] Key FTZ exist in the areas of Shanghai, Guangdong, and Dalian. In the Dalian area of China outside Beijing, Intel built a $2.5 billion wafer manufacturing facility outside the purview of any U.S. government influence.[84] Chinese officials announced in 2016 the launch of seven new FTZ.[85]

It's important to note that the European Union did not outsource its manufacturing base to Mexico after entering into a free trade agreement. In fact, the European Union ran a €14 billion trade surplus with Mexico in 2015 while the United States experienced a $49 billion deficit that same year.[86,87] Why did the United States outsource two-thirds of its production capacity to China, Mexico, and other countries? How is it possible that the Europeans generate a trade surplus with cheap-labor nations? It cannot be distance because China sits 8,000 miles away from the United States. It cannot be cheap labor either because the Europeans continue to manufacture inside Europe where manufacturing wages are often higher than in the United States.

Outsourcing to faraway Asian countries has occurred because America lets multinational corporations do as they please.[88] Using a foreign third-party for manufacturing allows companies to dismantle union labor, upend employee compensation, and access cheap foreign labor.

Donald Trump popped into the reality show "Let's Be President" promising to kill the Trans Pacific Partnership (TPP) and renegotiate the North American Free Trade Agreement (NAFTA), babbling on about unfair trade agreements and bringing jobs back to America. Yes, the same jobs that U.S. business managers made the decision to outsource firstly.

TPP was an attempt to restrain the power of China's growing global reach as the country invests heavily in a Belt and Road Initiative, forming a massive trade network with Asia, Africa, and Europe. The Trump Administration opted instead to withdraw from the TPP and fight against China's dominance with a tariff-based trade war, damaging farmers and supply chains in the process. Meanwhile, in September 2021, China applied for membership in a new trade agreement set up by the former participatory countries to the TPP.[89] Instead of restraining China, the United States may end up isolated in the Asia-Pacific region.

The Trump Administration liked to blame NAFTA, the WTO, and China for America's lost jobs, but U.S. business managers are to blame. They are the ones who made the decision to shut down American factories and move production into cheap-labor nations. Frustrated and confused about job losses due to outsourcing, voters elected a fraudulent populist caught up in the same game of global manufacturing. The president's daughter, Ivanka Trump, manufactured her clothing line in China but now is looking toward Africa as a new source of cheap labor.[90,91] Donald Trump has done the patriotic thing and kept production of his legendary MAGA hats in the United States. However, most of the workers at the factory making Trump's MAGA hats are foreign-born Latinos, working inside the United States despite his effort to build a wall and keep out these same workers.[92]

In 2016, the kingdom of Saudi Arabia threatened to sell $750 billion of U.S. assets if Congress did not vote according to its wishes.[93,94] The most expensive home sold in the Washington, D.C., area was purchased in 2018 by the Saudi Arabian government for $43 million.[95] This home, dubbed Merrywood, was the childhood residence of Jacqueline Kennedy Onassis. The United States is selling its national treasures to the highest foreign bidder. Our penchant for cheap products, exploited labor, and investor profits primes the United States for not just a financial downfall, but a food shortage as well. Saudi Arabia continues to buy thousands of critical farmland acreage in California and Arizona, often with prime water rights, in an effort to export food back to its country.[96]

U.S. business managers in the inner world of multinational production wish to maintain their grasp on billions in overseas profit, and they engage in newspeak to confuse struggling working-class families about who is the real threat. Coordination with policy think tanks and corporate media networks redirect blame for the crumbling middle class onto China, NAFTA, immigrants, or so-called socialism. In the end, manufacturing jobs are shipped overseas based on an excuse for needing cheap labor despite record investor profits. Wages stagnate in the United States as money pours overseas, making the purchase of cheap imports a necessity for middle-class families.

The growing trade imbalance from imports puts the U.S. dollar at risk of swift depreciation, which could provoke hyperinflation and economic instability. For now, foreign business tycoons take those dollars made from manufacturing products and purchase U.S. assets, such as real estate, stocks, and bonds. America sells its long-term, income-producing financial assets to fund the continued importation of cheap products from abroad. Consider the massive divide in value. America receives cheap products that often end up in a garbage bin within six months and a foreign business now has the means to purchase our most coveted financial possessions. If foreign business tycoons sour on U.S. financial investments, then there will be nothing holding up the U.S. dollar anymore and a collapse will be guaranteed.

Outsourcing moves jobs overseas and strips away economic output. Congress attempts to stimulate the U.S. economy through budget deficits, which puts the country into greater debt. The Federal Reserve uses low interest rates to prop up the weakended labor market. The low interest rates hyperinflate U.S. asset prices, forming financial bubbles, and encourage corporations to borrow increasing amounts of debt as well. All told, outsourcing has serious long-term financial consequences of a completely unsustainable nature.

Even when companies outsource in an attempt to boost profit, there are plenty of case studies that demonstrate how low-cost production can backfire. In 2000, the United States Consumer Product Safety Commission issued a press release detailing Master Locks Company's recall of 752,000 gun locks made in China because the two sides of the locks could be separated without a key.[97] Formerly, production of these locks took place in Milwaukie, Wisconsin, until the company outsourced over half of the production to third-party Chinese firms. Quality-control issues and labor unrest forced Master Locks Company to reevaluate its outsourcing strategy and reshore production back to the United States and Mexico.[98]

This attempt to exploit cheap labor and lower costs can result in quality-control issues that significantly damage a company's brand image. Lululemon Athletica, a maker of yoga apparel, attempted to diversify the factories it hires in Vietnam. One of the factories churned out overly thin material that the company incorporated into its yoga pants. Customers exposed the problem after plunking into downward dog in yoga classes. The sheer scope of the backlash led to a significant decline in the company's revenue and unforeseen costs to rectify the situation. In total, Lululemon Athletica's attempts to exploit outsourcing backfired and the company faced a $60 million recall effort.[99]

In 2007, the U.S. Consumer Product Safety Commission announced the recall of 967,000 Fisher-Price toys made in China because they contained lead.[100] Even minor levels of lead can provoke neural dysfunction in children, leading to mental disorders and poor memory. Even today, the general public undergoes chronic exposure to lead from painted ceramic dinnerware such as plates and bowls made in China and other unregulated countries. In 2016, Democrats proposed a $70 billion spending bill called the True LEADership Act that would repair lead waterpipes all across the nation, but Republicans did not push the bill forward.[101] The $70 billion investment pales in comparison to treating the mental health disorders caused by lead exposure, not to mention the loss of lifetime productivity as afflicted children endure learning impairments.

In 2014, fifty Boeing 787 planes were grounded after a battery manufactured by an external Japanese company caught fire.[102] Legal disputes were settled after a mix of inquiries were made by company attorneys and government inspectors, highlighting the need for government inspections and courts to protect consumers and hold companies accountable. An economic system cannot function without these social institutions in place. Several years later, Boeing outsourced the software development of its 737 Max airplanes to temporary workers making $9 per hour. The software glitch resulted in two airplane crashes, the loss of passenger life, and lost revenue.[103]

To raise the production volume of the United States and boost profit margins sustainably, this country must start investing in robotics, logistics systems, and worker skills here at home. Reebok, which faces ongoing protests amid low wages in its Asian supply chain, established a production facility in Michigan, leveraging software and 3D printing to offer low-cost footware.[104] Use of technology in this manner leads to high-paying U.S. jobs, a reduction in the trade imbalance, and the distribution of money around the domestic economy. As a way of retaining production in the United States, the individual states need to invest in skills that drive innovation such as engineering, computer science, and operations management. In turn, setting up U.S. facilities promotes support fields such as legal, accounting, finance, construction, and city planning.

People often voice concerns about jobs being lost because of robotics and automation but societies were once heavily agrarian and the tractor did not cause a century of joblessness. Farm workers shifted to other industries as the tractor supplanted agriculture jobs. All areas of the United States need more people educated in science, engineering, and vocational trades in order to support high-tech manufacturing.

Conservative thinkers for many centuries have fixated on lowering costs in order to boost profit. They went as far as enslaving millions of people and employing child labor as a method of generating wealth. History shows that economies willing to invest in modern skills thrive whereas conservative areas that cling to dead industries and low taxes have a hard time forming high-profit industries. As profits plummet in an environment of low pay and weak job skills, managers seek to disenfranchise the workforce even more as a means of maintaining profit.

Modern economic labor models connect high worker compensation to productivity gains and money supply growth. Pay levels should move upward alongside productive gains as high-quality output brings more revenue in from financially-sound consumers. A modern perspective on profit maximization involves looking at how costs *support* revenue growth as opposed to the conservative perspective that falsely examines how costs *drain* profit.

As management shares the company's wealth with the workforce, a lower turnover rate of workers preserves the intellectual capital that accumulates internally over time. Workers need collective bargaining rights to ensure they have a safe platform to communicate innovative ideas to management and negotiate a living wage. The overall quantity of intellectual capital can be bolstered through social investments in vocational training and public education. As productivity gains advance via workforce skills and motivated employees, the entire society enjoys a higher standard of living from improved access to high-quality production.

INFLATION

In the wake of World War II, the global powers met at Bretton Woods in New Hampshire to stabilize European economies as their war-torn infrastructure needed to be rebuilt. The Bretton Woods Accord resulted in a new currency framework that fixed the exchange rates of 44 countries to the U.S. dollar. In turn, the U.S. dollar was pegged to $35 per ounce of gold. This framework proved worthwhile for the first few years as Europe made progress rebuilding in a stable currency environment, but the global powers held fast to the Bretton Woods Accord for more than two decades beyond what was necessary, creating serious currency imbalances.

As these imbalances continued to grow in the 1960s, strong inflation pressures emerged in part because the unemployment rate fell to historical lows. Just as it seemed the inflationary pressures would subside under the weight of a recession, Richard Nixon surprised the global community and abruptly ended the Bretton Woods system of exchange rates, disconnecting the U.S. dollar from this set $35-per-ounce gold price. Known as the Nixon Shock, this 1971 decision to unlock the dollar-to-gold peg brought serious inflation pressures to the fore.[105] Combined with the oil crises of 1973-74 and 1979, the stage was set for hyperinflation.

Now that the dollar was unlocked from the Bretton Woods constraints and the U.S. economy struggled from the Middle East oil restrictions, the Federal Reserve, America's central bank, felt empowered to start printing dollars and fueling hyperinflation. The Bureau of Labor Statistics (BLS), at the height of this extravagant period of inflation in the 1980s, argued that replacing home values with an artificial owners-equivalent rent (OER) would represent inflation better.[106] Some economists argue that homes are partly an investment and OER clarifies how much of a home's price represents accommodation as opposed to an investment return. However, treating homes as an investment is a privilege that applies uniquely to the wealthy who may own more than one house or who have a buffer of assets in case home prices decline in value. Personally, I do not perceive my home as an investment but rather an essential place of residency.

Instead of looking directly at home prices, including the underlying land value, the BLS started to only track an artificially constructed number to represent what you would charge, hypothetically speaking, if you rented your home. But you haven't rented out your home because you are living in it. Assuming that home price inflation is much greater than what the government numbers have captured, *real* household income might actually be much lower when adjusted for unadulterated, true inflation. Plus, making this switch to an artificial OER in the middle of this period of hyperinflation in 1983 was suspect because it let the Federal Reserve stop tracking home price inflation directly,[107] leading to the potential for underreporting inflation data and maintaining excessively low interest rates.

Imagine a scenario where a young couple making a combined $60,000 qualify for a $275,000 loan to begin looking for a first home. That couple wields the power of $275,000 when negotiating the price of a house. Now, fast forward in time and assume that this same couple is still making $60,000—wages are flat—but underreported inflation leads to low mortgage rates and a bank qualifies this couple for a $400,000 loan. What do you expect will happen to home prices now that this same couple has $400,000 in purchasing power to use in their negotiations instead of the former $275,000? You begin to see how home prices bubble upward as banks offer bigger loan packages to borrowers, not because of better wages, but rather as a result of excessively low mortgage standards. You also begin to see how homeowners go further into debt. Would it be better for a young couple to pay down a $275,000 loan or a $400,000 mountain of financial risk?

People often think that growth in home prices is the result of supply and demand forces, but the microeconomic concept of supply and demand actually explains why prices return to an equilibrium point. Supply and demand factors stabilize price levels, the opposite of price inflation. If the price of an item increases without a commensurate change in value, that increased price is called inflation by definition. If a three-bedroom home appears unchanged because the homeowners perform zero renovations, then the price of that home should not change one bit. But as the price of that unaltered home doubles, then triples, and ultimately skyrockets higher among a frenzy of high-risk mortgages, you are witnessing the effects of inflation and excess bank lending—not overdemand. Watching home prices balloon 12-15% in one year has little to do with an undersupply in the market and more to do with inflation created by unregulated mortgage standards and loose monetary policies.

I've heard people argue that land is limited and prices will rise because real estate developers cannot meet demand levels in urban centers, but Japan provides a prime example of how false this argument is. Land in Japan is highly limited and the country does not automatically experience excessive home price appreciation. Japan also experienced one of the worst asset price bubbles that burst in the early 90s and caused property values to decline as much as 90% in dense urban areas like Tokyo. If limited access to land really does cause price appreciation, then prices in Japan should have remained elevated. Instead, prices bubbled and popped.

According to the microeconomic principle of supply and demand, you would expect real estate developers to awaken and build more homes if home prices inflate from $275,000 to $400,000. The onslaught of new homes would bring home prices back down to the prior equilibrium point of $275,000, in theory. If home prices rise quickly despite the best efforts of real estate developers to meet increased housing demand, then you could conclude that the market has an excess amount of money (inflation) driving up prices. Too much money caused home prices to bubble in the mid 2000s—not an undersupply of land or home units.

The vast majority of Americans need home and land prices to remain stable, and stability is created through a regulated mortgage market, along with a stable interest rate environment. The early 1980s bore witness to a host of deregulation efforts in the mortgage and banking industries, culminating in the savings and loan crisis—the first of several boom-bust economic cycles. In 1982, Congress passed the Alternative Mortgage Transaction Parity Act to reauthorize the lending of interest-only and adjustable-rate mortgages,[108] setting the stage for the housing bubble two decades later. Housing needs to remain affordable for the middle class but the market for homes has become susceptible to speculative frenzies because the BLS treats housing as partly an investment asset.

A low rate of inflation, around 2% annually, is perceived as a critical part of maintaining an economic expansion. According to economists, this small amount of inflation helps drive consumption and it signals to the Federal Reserve that economic growth is occurring. Wall Street investors love a low interest rate environment because financial assets, such as stocks and bonds, perform better. However, artificially low interest rates can encourage excess borrowing on the part of the middle class. Distorted inflation numbers allow the Federal Reserve to keep interest rates too low with the potential for asset bubbles, which, when they pop, smack directly into an overleveraged consumer.

Forty years of outsourcing to cheap labor nations has created a strong deflationary downdraft. The price of textiles, consumer staples, electronic equipment has steadily declined in price, which by definition is considered deflation. Fearing these deflationary pressures, the Federal Reserve has lowered interest rates in an attempt to bring inflation up to its 2% target. In other words, the deflation sparked by outsourcing has been offset by hyperinflation in other parts of the economy. The cost of domestic essentials, such as rent, healthcare, food, and education have risen dramatically over the past 40 years.[109] Nowadays, low-wage workers face extreme costs for essential products and services despite the deflated costs for clothes and smartphones.

The Senate Finance Committee commissioned a panel of economists in 1996 to study the methodology behind calculating inflation. Referred to as the Boskin Commission, these economists concluded that inflation rates should have been 1.1% lower annually.[110] Around this same time, the BLS made administrative changes to the calculation methodology, which resulted in a 0.2% reduction in the reported inflation level.[111]

Investors cheer with joy when inflation is low because that helps drive up investment returns, but shuffling numbers around does not change the actual cost of living the general public experiences. It only changes the inflation number presented on paper, and revising the inflation numbers downward using an improper methodology translates into working-class Americans having a harder time surviving financially. Today, economists claim that shifts in inflation methodology have caused the reported numbers to be anywhere from 0.5% to 1% lower than what would be calculated using previous approaches.[112] In other words, fiddling with inflation methodologies can dramatically impact the inflation number used to make investment, mortgage, and lending decisions.

The government reported level of inflation has been mired in methodology challenges and heuristic adjustments over the past 100 years, and yet the inflation statistics have very real consequences to the financial health of every American. Retirees, especially former military personnel who risked their lives for this country, see an attenuation of benefits when inflation is underreported. Retirement benefits for military personnel and the Social Security program are adjusted each year according to numbers calculated by the BLS. Tax items adjust per inflation, causing working class Americans to pay more in taxes if inflation is artificially underreported.[113] Workers often negotiate wages and benefits bearing in mind BLS inflation rates. If statistics are reported as artificially lower than actual, wages and benefits will not keep pace with the cost of living. Truth be told, wages have been stagnating since the 1970s.[114]

How does the Federal Reserve reach its 2% target when the BLS consistently underreports actual inflation rates and outsourcing promotes deflation among nonessential goods? The Federal Reserve must overcompensate by hyperinflating rent, healthcare, food, and education costs above this arbitrary 2% target. All the potential benefits of lower consumer prices from outsourcing jobs for the last 40 years has been completely erased by the Federal Reserve keeping interest rates low, meaning there was no long-term benefit. The Federal Reserve inflated prices nonetheless and good-paying, union jobs left abroad. Meanwhile, excessively low interest rates spawned dangerous asset bubbles, such as the dot-com meltdown and 2008 housing bust.

Inflation tracks the price level of a fixed basket of consumer goods and services across urban geographic areas. This model of price tracking uses heuristic adjustments to capture rapid shifts in product features. It's easy to introduce errors and incorrect assumptions when artificially tweaking inflation data in this manner. Masking housing inflation with help from the OER caused economists and government officials to lose sight of the housing bubble forming in the 2000s. A new metric for tracking actual home price inflation emerged in 2006 toward the peak of the housing bubble. Professors Karl Case and Robert Shiller devised the Case-Shiller Index to track home prices nationally and among the top 10 and 20 cities. This index reported sharp increases to home prices despite what government statistics portrayed.[115]

Inflation statistics ignore how much people actually earn in relation to the cost living. The Boskin Commission offered an important recommendation to capture the true cost of living that people experience. Even if inflation were to be underreported, government statistics could calculate a metric meant to look at everyday expenditures directly. A cost of living index starts with wage levels and backs into an evaluation of what consumers can afford. Can the median worker afford a standard two-bedroom apartment and live comfortably? If prices rise and wages are flat, then that median worker will eventually find it impossible to afford rent, and perhaps other daily necessities such as food and healthcare. A cost of living index ensures that consumer prices and wage levels remain connected to an affordable middle-class life.

To reach its 2% inflation target, the Federal Reserve has showered the banking system with $8 trillion in reserves since the housing collapse that started in 2008. As the pandemic unraveled in early 2020, the Federal Reserve pumped $3 trillion in two months alone, sparking high rates of producer and consumer inflation not seen since the 1980s. Of course, the $8 trillion goes directly to Wall Street firms and not American families.

Political leaders and the Federal Reserve over the past 40 years have largely ignored the use of wages to stoke inflation, defaulting instead to lowering interest rates and running budget deficits to grow the economy. This approach assumes people will borrow more from banks and bid up prices using *borrowed* funds—not using higher wages to bid up prices. Higher wages give the middle class power to inflate prices, which would allow the Federal Reserve to achieve its inflation target. However, big banks and Wall Street investors thrive when the middle class is forced to borrow money to make purchases, and the Federal Reserve has dumped trillions of dollars on financial firms to ensure there will always be money to lend consumers.

The middle class operates inside an environment of stagnate wages, rising prices, and increasing debt loads. All of this begs the question, who should the economic system benefit? If an economic system is meant to ensure the general public has a strong standard of living, we undermine this objective as soon as income levels stagnate in the face of rising prices. An economic system cannot be considered *strong* when the elderly cannot pay for medications, hard-working Americans are priced out of housing, and schools cannot afford learning materials.

EDUCATION

The progressive reforms of the late-1800s encouraged children to attend primary school, causing business tycoons to fear the loss of child labor in their factories.[116] It took until 1938 to end child labor in the United States with passage of the Fair Labor Standards Act (FLSA), but the prior education reforms helped to boost productivity and move work away from manual processes. Education allowed high-wage workers to employ new innovations and produce a higher volume and quality of output, raising living standards for all consumers.[117,118,119]

California has grown into a global hotbed for modern technical industries. The roots were gathering water at Stanford University, shortly before the start of World War II. Two graduates, William Hewlett and David Packard, formed a co-owned business in 1939: Hewlett-Packard. A Stanford professor who mentored the two students, Fred Terman, was selected to head the military's Radio Research Laboratory at Harvard during the war. Originally educated at the Massachusetts Institute of Technology (MIT), Professor Terman sat as the president of the Institute of Radio Engineers, giving him the ideal background to staff a secret research group armed with the task of innovating radar countermeasures to protect allied planes.

Professor Terman left Stanford after the war but eventually returned to witness the school struggling financially. He realized the need to form stronger relationships with surrounding businesses. A plan to form an industrial park on Stanford's land caught his attention as he participated on the university's Committee on Land and Building Development. Terman used his influence to attract burgeoning companies with names such as

Lockheed, General Electric, and Hewlett-Packard to the Stanford Industrial Park.[120]

Professor Terman encouraged another pivotal entrepreneur, William Shockley, to innovate in the San Francisco Bay Area. A graduate of California Institute of Technology, Shockley initially headed east to study at MIT and work at Bell Telephone Laboratories. In 1955, Shockley returned to California to form Shockley Semiconductors Laboratories inside the Stanford Industrial Park, paving the way for development of transistors constructed using silicon. Employees of Shockley, blaming his poor management skills, soon fled the company to launch new silicon transistor upstarts. Shockley dubbed these men "the traitorous eight," but the rest is history as these eight men helped spawn a fast-evolving technology in an area known today as Silicon Valley.[121]

In 1968, two entrepreneurs started Intel Corporation, which would become a leading silicon-based company less than 15 miles from Stanford University. Co-founder Gordon Moore, observed what came to be known as Moore's Law, which predicted that silicon transistor density would double every year. Dr. Moore received a bachelor's degree from the University of California at Berkeley and a doctoral degree in physical chemistry from the California Institute of Technology.[122] Fellow cofounder Robert Noyce received a doctoral degree in physics from MIT.[123] The New England Board of Higher Education calculates that MIT graduates generate the highest rate of return among all northeastern universities.[124] Silicon Valley and America's high-profit technology industry would not have flourished without critical investments in universities and advanced degrees.

Ronald Reagan announced his candidacy for the California governorship in a 30-minute film, befitting of an actor, on January 4, 1966, just two years before Intel Corporation was launched. He spoke about unemployment and used the example of Palo Alto job losses "when an aircraft plant moved to the East Coast." The blame, he claimed, rested on the shoulders of increasing regulations, budget deficits, and welfare programs.

> "Where the need is temporary, the help should be temporary, aimed at restoring self-sufficiency. Working men and women should not be asked to carry the additional burden of providing for a segment of society capable of caring for itself, but which prefers making welfare a way of life, freeloading at the expense of these more conscientious citizens."[125]

Reagan advocated for unbound police enforcement in his speech and later gave praise to the incredible talent in California, while in between, rambling about the need for decency at universities. Sworn in as governor one year later, Reagan moved swiftly to push for budget cuts within the university system. Until this point in time, the University of California system did not charge tuition, only assessing a minimal amount in fees. Taxpayers incurred the tab to educate students; as much as people may loath taxes, it's impossible to have all the benefits of a well-functioning, modern society without a robust investment in education. Reagan was ignorant of the relationship between crime, welfare, and lack of education. He wanted to address crime rates and decrease reliance on welfare, but at the same time, ease funding for education—that's all incongruent.

The San Francisco Bay area had become the epicenter of the modern tech economy, and now Reagan sought to undermine it. We all benefit when a student learns about science, technology, engineering, or math (STEM) if that student later innovates products that we consume. Consider the progression of personal computer speed and functionality over the past half century. The tax dollars spent to fully fund STEM education can easily translate into a higher standard of living for all members of society.

A country brings a higher quality and quantity of products to the doorsteps of consumers (now with one-day home delivery) when companies retool processes, automate manufacturing, design complex product features, and improve transportation logistics—but all of these innovative practices require an investment in technical education.

The Stanford Industrial Park in California demonstrates the significant benefit derived from merging universities and businesses together. Cities such as Austin, Nashville, and Denver have been supporting relationships between companies and local universities to achieve above-average economic growth over the past several decades, showcasing a growing divide between cities that invest in research universities and cities that focus on low wages.[126] Advancing research connections between businesses and universities could add novel layers of production across the entire United States, but all of these notions of financial success and innovation will fail if cities and states ignore the need to modernize the education system.

The U.S. Department of Commerce projects a growing need for STEM-educated workers, and the agency notes how wages average 12% to 60% higher among STEM occupations depending on the level of education.[127]

The Bureau of Labor Statistics reported that job growth among STEM occupations has occurred twice as fast since 2009 compared to non-STEM occupations, with computer and engineering related fields leading the pack.[128]

Jurisdictions that embrace a low tax environment have struggled to properly educate workers, causing them to fall behind the economic curve. States that use low wages as a mechanism to attract companies end up with low-profit ventures. The types of products low-skilled workers make tend to result in thin profit margins, and these companies depend on social programs to fill the wage gap that forms between low worker pay and the high cost of living.

Sophisticated investment banks, venture capital firms, and private equity firms want to pour money into high-profit ventures in which you find highly-skilled, expensive workers. A marketplace that invests in highly educated talent, such as Seattle, where median incomes topped $80,349 in 2016,[129] will not unravel because a smattering of workers go from earning a minimum wage of $10.50 one year to $13 the next.[130] Investment firms do not care what the minimum wage is because they are looking at hiring highly-skilled workers who make far more than the minimum. As a result, investment money pours into key U.S. cities, such as Seattle, New York City, Los Angeles, Boston, Denver, and San Francisco, where high-paid workers reside, no matter what the minimum wage is.

A Harvard study calculated that U.S. GDP would grow 0.9% to 1.3% faster each year if students achieved similar proficiency in mathematics as their Canadian and South Korean counterparts,[131] but government support of U.S. colleges is dwindling. In 2016, the United States spent more on higher education relative to its GDP at 2.6% compared to all major economies, but the amount coming from public sources totaled only 0.9% of GDP, placing it in 23rd place.[132]

One study conducted through the Boston branch of the Federal Reserve System estimated that a four-year college education can cost roughly $75,000. That number may cause taxpayers to gasp for air. That seems so expensive, but factor in how an educated person pays back an estimated $470,000 in lifetime taxes and liberates $85,000 of government funds due to fewer demands for social assistance.[133] Now, taxpayers need to wake up and realize how much more they will spend if they do not make this investment in education. Putting forth $75,000 upfront on a young person's future generates a significant return on taxes calculated at over 700%; this one study did not include the additional production gains for the economic system—it only looked at the tax effect.

Virginia provides an important perspective on education funding as a result of duplicating a study in 2007 and 2011. The 2007 study found that for every $1 invested in education by taxpayers, the state received $1.31 back in extra tax revenue from expansions in business profits and wage gains, atop a further $13.31 in overall economic growth.[134] Over the next few years, the U.S. economy underwent a deep recession, the result of investment industry deregulation and irresponsible lending standards. Enrollment in higher education grew another 17% in Virginia by 2011 at which time the economic study was redone. The second results showed that every $1 spent on education produced an estimated $17.40 in increased production despite the extreme recession.[135] Amounts spent on higher education produce an exponential rate of return, which benefits everyone in the country.

U.S. business elites have sold the American public on this notion that outsourcing is the only path to profitability. America simply cannot compete globally if manufacturing firms are forced to pay workers a living wage, especially in the face of union pressures, or so we've been told. Yet, European countries who pay manufacturing workers 30% to 80% more than the United States operate inside high tax environments, offer better labor benefits, and face strict regulations.[136] Employment rates, wage levels, and productivity gains all correlate to educational attainment.

American companies say they must outsource to remain competitive, but European countries have found ways to keep their manufacturing domestic. Germany, Sweden, Switzerland, and many other top manufacturing countries have access to cheap labor abroad and they have signed trade agreements that could easily lead to outsourcing, but the engineering and science environment in these countries ensures production remains local.

Professor of Economics Ludger Woessmann from the Ludwig Maximillian University of Munich crossexamined the accumulation of skills from the Programme for International Student Assessment (PISA) test against Gross Domestic Production (GDP) and found that countries could add 1% more to GDP growth for every 50-point increase in average test scores.[137] Out of 72 countries where the PISA exam took place in 2015, Singapore topped the list with a mean score of 564 in math and 556 in science,[138] and the World Bank reports that Singapore had the fourth highest GDP per capita in 2015, roughly $30,000 more than America's GDP per capita.[139]

U.S. high school students score remarkably low on the math and science sections of the international PISA exam. The United States ranked 35th in math, a full 61 points below China and 36 points below Germany. In terms of science, the United States placed 25th among the 72 countries participating on the 2015 PISA exam.[140] The mean science score was 22 points behind China and 13 below Germany. Exceptionally troubling, the World Economic Forum, a nonprofit institution headquartered in Geneva, Switzerland, ranked the quality of science and math education in the United States as 33rd in the world.[141]

The Centre for Economics and Business Research (CEBR) in the United Kingdom recently examined engineering quality among 99 countries and tested it against the comparative strength of production. The CEBR Engineering Index merged together nine key elements of a country's full engineering system, including important support mechanisms and research concentrations. Northern European countries, along with Japan and South Korea, achieved top scores on the index with Sweden attaining the top spot. The United States sat in 17th place,[142] and it is little wonder why the country continues to drop in global production rankings and struggles to maintain a manufacturing base.

Out of the top 40 strongest global economies, the percentage of U.S. students earning degrees in natural sciences and engineering ranked 38th. The countries with the highest percentage of students earning natural science and engineering degrees have consistently been South Korea and Germany, with India rising up the ranks recently.[143] Engineering is a critical field for the modern manufacturing environment, and a significant portion of U.S. engineering degrees go to foreign students. A study examining the 2012-13 school year found that more than half of U.S. doctoral degrees in engineering, mathematics, statistics, and computer science were awarded to foreign citizens holding a temporary student visa.[144]

The U.S. does not hand a high percentage of STEM degrees to domestic students compared to other countries. Over 1 million foreign students entered the United States for the 2015-16 school year, and the foremost degree they chose was engineering.[145] Most of these students came from China; advancements in Chinese manufacturing concurrent to U.S.

disinvestment in its manufacturing base will further exacerbate the already massive trade imbalance between the two countries.

As soon as the seventh grade, the U.S. education system should begin to mimic subject-matter tracks seen amid community colleges or university programs. American universities and community colleges allow students to focus on a distinct major, but high schools adhere to a factory education model in which only one generic program is emphasized. Not enough U.S. states provide a bridge period between early foundational elementary studies and late-stage occupational preparation. The standard American high-school model saturates students with an intensive math and literature curriculum, and then all students take an identical test to assess abilities. It's little wonder why a high percentage of American students become disconnected and drop out prematurely.[146] Vocational and pre-professional programs can teach kids marketable job skills and create a more engaging school environment centered on favored career interests.

In many European nations, vocational tracks are highly developed and lead into organized apprenticeships. Over half of German students select this approach to education.[147] School districts across the United States align students for college matriculation, letting vocational trades wither on the vine. Most American high schools toss one or two vocational classes at a student but that does not provide enough training. High schools and community colleges must provide robust vocational educations and coordinate paid apprenticeships to develop marketable skills.

Some argue against specialized training during high school years worried that it might pigeonhole kids into a career early in life or cause low-income children to not enter college. But letting kids graduate high school without marketable skills presents a dangerous risk to lifelong success. The United States has a path to four-year universities through the community college system, and in reality, the high school system should offer programming in line with what's seen at a community college. Young Americans have unique opportunities to redesign their careers because of community colleges, lessening the worry that kids will end up stuck in an unsatisfactory career.

Several states have realized the significance of vocational training and apprenticeships, with North Dakota as a key leader in the high-tech manufacturing space. North Dakota's Education Technology Council promotes opportunities at the middle- and high-school levels, and the Registered Apprenticeships system then connects these technical studies with on-the-job training. The Centers for Excellence & Research Excellence champions the state's university system as a hub for research and development, which is similar to the Stanford Industrial Park model. Finally, the State Board of Career and Technical Education supports the development of technical skills among all North Dakota adult residents. All told, these social investments in technical education and workplace training have enabled North Dakota to grow employment in its high-tech manufacturing industry 14.3% faster than other industries from 2003 to 2013, compared to the national average of only 2.5%.[148]

Pennsylvania has developed a robust statewide network of vocational training programs accessible to high school students starting at the ninth grade. Known nationally as Career and Technical Centers (CTC), the state has formed more than 80 CTC schools providing training across dozens of programs, such as plumbing, heavy equipment operations, accounting, and electronics technology, among many other in-demand career fields.[149] The largest Pennsylvania CTC, the LeHigh Career & Technical Institute, serves several school districts in the eastern region of the state.[150] Students request to study at a CTC linked to their regular school, and if accepted, take both vocational classes and general studies full time. To graduate high school, students take a trade-specific assessment test administered by the National Occupational Competency Testing Institute (NOCTI), which 12 states treat as a suitable proxy for the standard exit examination mandated by the No Child Left Behind Act of 2001.[151]

No Child Left Behind, followed by the Every Student Succeeds Act of 2015, mandate that American children all take the same test to assess educational progress. We shove all students into one standardized box, thinking we are somehow mimicking the testing environment in other industrialized nations, but these countries offer a diversity of tests based on learning priorities. The American education model embraces a generic formula of math and literature, ignoring how diverse and specialized workplace skills have become, not to mention student interests.

European countries may offer more than 100 different assessment tests based on unique academic tracks. France, for example, offers three different general baccalaureate, one technical baccalaureate, and roughly 70 professional baccalaureate, which all serve as high school exit exams for university studies. Students concentrating on science will not take the same exact test as another cohort focused on economics or literature. In terms of vocational trades, French students have the option to select among more than 274 specializations. Approximately 200 certificates of professional aptitude serve as exit exams to assess skills,[152] allowing students to focus on an area of interest; vocational expertise prepares kids for the job market directly.

Exit exams to leave secondary schooling in Europe involve written essays, live verbal interviews, and short-answer questions, all of which align with classroom exams teachers would normally offer. In this environment, the exit exam parallels everyday classroom instruction. Students are not forced into learning random skills just to pass an industrialized, fill-in-the-bubble standardized test. Separate exit exams are formulated for each individual learning track, giving students the ability to embrace a unique talent and be assessed accordingly.

The United States tends to spend a high amount on average for primary and secondary schooling, but school districts rarely receive this "average" amount. Low-income districts scramble to find resources, making it challenging to teach STEM subjects and prepare for an industrialized exit exam. Wealthier school districts have the economic means to offer nearly double the teacher pay of low-income districts, helping students better prepare for exit exams and postsecondary education.[153,154] Inequities in school funding per a district model must be equalized with statewide and federal offsets.

State and local funding of high-research universities has dwindled over the last two decades, leading to growing inequality in higher education access as well. Taxpayer funding reached a peak of $14,221 per student in 2001 before sliding annually to a low of $9,216 by 2015. Students self-fund an increasing portion of higher education through tuition, which has doubled since 2001.[155]

Past generations have this fancy notion about getting a high-paying job with only a high-school education or working to pay for college. High schools used to offer robust vocational training, equipping students with marketable skills for the workforce. Today's cookie-cutter high school education means students must learn marketable job skills at a university, community college, or trade school, often with sizeable student loan debt. Online trolls spew the same nonsensical talking point, asserting that students should not take on student loan debt to cover tuition costs, but it's rare for high schools to equip students with in-demand jobs skills. Failure to educate these students after high school means a lifetime of job market friction. Plus, GDP declines and every member of society sees a reduction in living standards when kids are undereducated.

The one element that differs vastly in the United States compared to other countries is the overall amount of student loans, which stood at $481 billion in 2006 before the Great Recession hit. More than a decade later, in the first quarter of 2021, student loans swelled to $1.8 trillion. Every second of every day, another $2,726 gets added to this total.[156] New graduates begin careers with significant student loan payments that weigh on their ability to finance cars, homes, and weddings.[157] Student loan balances are worse among low-income households and college drop-outs who never complete a degree.[158]

But what happens when the economy sours because of a financial crisis and new college graduates face a high unemployment rate? The housing bubble caused unemployment among recent male college graduates to hit 26.6% in 2009.[159] No one plans to study hard for four years, graduate college, and face high unemployment with a mountain of debt. Society is irresponsible to put young people in this position, especially when considering how employers profit from an educated workforce and wages have stagnated because of pro-corporate policies.

As students receive financial aid, the disbursement goes directly to the school, which removes an amount for tuition. Any leftover is then handed to the student for personal expenses such as food and housing. This process allows schools to boost tuition rates unrestrained, pocketing as much of the financial aid disbursement as they see fit. The financial aid system must change to disburse money per separate categories: one for tuition and one for living costs. Schools would have less ability to spike tuition rates and grab the total disbursement.

The federal loan interview process used to determine how much financial support a family needs takes into account sources of income first and presents an amount for unmet need. Among low-income families, the amount for unmet financial need has doubled since 1990,[160] requiring low-income persons, many of who hold subprime credit ratings, to take on elevated levels of student loan debt to obtain an education, leaving many of these low-income borrowers in a highly fragile financial situation.

Women tend to earn less compared to men but they shoulder much more of the student loan indebtedness at a time when the United States needs to encourage a higher portion of women to study STEM fields. The overall nationwide balance of student loans now stands at more than $1.8 trillion, and 42% of women carry balances over $30,000 compared to 27% for men.[161]

Students report a high degree of stress from student loan debt with nearly two-thirds citing sleep disturbances and 70% complaining of headaches.[162] Personal finance company SoFi conducted a member survey of more than 1,200 borrowers, confirming that student loan debt prevents young individuals from traveling and hanging out with friends. Half of the people surveyed said the debt triggered depression.[163] A University of South Carolina study revealed how individuals with student loan balances experienced worse mental health complaints than their peers.[164]

The United States creates an unfair system when over 25% of student borrowers are delinquent or in default.[165] Student loan delinquencies have surged to $166 billion per quarter as of 2019.[166] A business can default on its debt after making a bad investment decision, but students rarely get released from their debt burden. Instead, Federal Student Aid, an office of the Department of Education, hires private firms to collect on unpaid amounts, including via wage garnishments that totaled $664 million in 2016 alone.[167] These collection agencies can earn anywhere from 6.5% to 17.5% depending on the action taken against borrowers.[168] The Department of Education estimated these collection agencies earned more than $2 billion in fees in 2016.[169] All the while, higher ed institutions, including for-profit universities, experience few consequences for high student default rates.[170]

The Department of Education maintains income-driven repayment (IDR) programs that lower monthly payments based on income levels. That sounds like a great way to reduce the burden of student loans until understanding how exactly unpaid interest is added to the loan balance. An IDR plan can provide short-term relief but the overall balance grows even faster under these plans, making it impossible to pay off the principal. The dream of homeownership evaporates after considering how a high student loan balance ruins a borrower's debt-to-income ratio and reduces this person's credit score, making it extremely difficult to procure a mortgage or other type of financing. In a Federal Reserve study, an estimated 400,000 workers with student loan debt could not afford a home, causing homeownership to fall from 45% to 36% among persons aged 24 to 32.[171]

A strong education will always entail a high financial cost but the benefits of an education do not just accrue to the individual student. All consumers gain access to better products and services, and taxpayers face fewer public assistance costs. It would be short-sided to reduce state expenditures for education without considering how standards of living would decline alongside wages; plus, more government expenditures would be needed for supplemental food, housing, and healthcare programs. The unemployment rate is chronically high for those Americans who never make it out of high school; recessions hit this group much harder.[172] The undereducated also represent two-thirds of the prison population.[173] The American public appears keen on tossing money into the criminal justice system despite the fact that an investment in education offers an incredibly high rate of return.

Other countries spend less on education but get better results for several reasons. A massive degree of inequality exists in how U.S. school districts receive funding, leaving low-income areas out in the cold with inadequate resources. Most important, the United States still adheres to an outdated, factory education model centered on standardized math and literature studies. The modern economy requires a diversity of skills, and the secondary education system, encompassing those years between seventh and twelfth grade, needs to incorporate more learning tracks with testing features unique to each individual track. America would equip more students with marketable job skills if it emphasized vocational training during these secondary years. Finally, higher education must be affordable without the grueling burden of student loan debt.

SOCIAL ASSISTANCE

A massive loophole in the Fair Labor Standards Act (FLSA) of 1938 permits states to implement a reduced federal minimum wage on tipped workers, with the last increase to $2.13 per hour occurring far back in 1991. Eighteen states, along with Puerto Rico, adhere to the $2.13 base minimum wage on tipped workers;[174] it is little wonder why the majority of these same states experience above-average rates of poverty. Of the 15 states with the highest rates of poverty, 14 of them pay tipped workers less than $3 per hour.[175] Tipped restaurant workers are a unique constituency because even though they work around food, a half-million still require government assistance to feed their families as a result of low wages.[176] Across gender lines, roughly two-thirds of tipped workers are women, and needing to live on tips can force women to endure sexual harassment. The restaurant industry bears witness to the highest rate of sexual harassment claims.[177]

In theory, tips are added to a base minimum wage, and the full wage should at least equal the regular federal minimum wage, now $7.25 per hour. However, compliance sweeps conducted by the Department of Labor have exposed a high degree of wage violations. In the 2010-2012 compliance sweep, for example, an audit of 9,000 restaurants revealed $5.5 million in unpaid wages from tip violations alone.[178]

A special minimum wage on tipped workers did not happen accidentally. In the wake of the Civil War, in lieu of paying wages, railroad porters and restaurant servers, many of whom happened to be former slaves, were expected to earn tips. America extended slavery by virtue of unpaid, but tipped, work.[179] Not until 1966 was a base tipped wage required, but it was set at only 50% of the standard federal minimum wage. Modern research notes that persons of color receive fewer tips on average, causing even greater income disparity across ethnic lines.[180,181]

The minimum wage set by the FLSA does not apply to agricultural workers, leading to exploitation of immigrant labor. Also, the FLSA includes a minimum salary for office workers set at $35,568 in 2020, or $684 per week.[182] A salary below this minimum will trigger overtime and statutory minimum wage. The FLSA provides no limitation on maximum work hours, so companies can impose work schedules in excess of 80 hours per week. The equivalent hourly wage for someone working 80 hours per week and earning $35,568 is $8.55. A more common 60-hour work schedule equates to $11.40 per hour.

President John F. Kennedy popularized the aphorism "a rising tide lifts all boats" in a Canton, Ohio, speech on September 27, 1960—remarks he gave concerning unemployment and how infrastructure was required to promote the economic well-being of all Americans.[183] In this same speech, President Kennedy mentioned how government assistance should be short-lived as people search for work. In theory, social assistance should only be used to help people through an emergency, but businesses increasingly compel workers to access government programs as a way to supplement low wages.

The U.S. Census Bureau calculates that household income among the bottom 10% of earners has remained stagnate since the 1960s.[184] Meanwhile, the cost of living for food, education, healthcare, and housing has skyrocketed. Anytime wages and benefits fail to cover the cost of living, public assistance programs step in to fill the gap. Even worse, the Bureau of Labor Statistics (BLS) reports that compensation since 2007 has fallen for workers amid the bottom 60% of overall income earners—now the majority of working Americans have slipped behind the cost of living. In juxtaposition, only the top 20% of wage earners have seen any significant increase to compensation levels.[185]

Since the 1960s, the flattening of wages in relation to inflated living costs has caused hard-working Americans to increase reliance on social assistance programs. The economic models that used to demonstrate a correlation between worker income and productivity gains have broken down. Over the past 40 years, productivity created through American innovation has skyrocketed but the ultrawealthy have pocketed much of the economic profit.

Initiated in 1939 as the Food Stamp Program, participants obtained colored stamps to buy produce. The Food Stamp Act of 1964, and later amendments, expanded the initial program and clarified benefits and eligibility requirements. As of October 1, 2008, the naming convention was updated to the less-conspicuous Supplemental Nutrition Assistance Program (SNAP).[186] Adult recipients of SNAP benefits often work full or part time, but low wages place them at risk of food insecurity, forcing taxpayers to supplement their low wages. In fact, 74% of households receiving SNAP benefits had a member working in the year before or after receiving benefits, demonstrating how the program serves hard-working Americans.

In 2015, 55% of SNAP recipients were senior citizens and children,[187] and unless conservatives wish to bring back child labor and force 80-year-olds into factories, these specific program beneficiaries will remain jobless. Most parents of child beneficiaries are either disabled or working. Only a small fraction of SNAP participants receives benefits because they are between jobs; many within this small unemployed pool still enroll in qualified employment training programs and they discontinue the SNAP program after regaining employment.[188] As a fail-safe to ensure people indeed work, nondisabled adults without children face a three-month limit on SNAP benefits unless they meet work requirements.[189]

Even students who receive SNAP benefits cannot participate in the program unless they work part time.[190] SNAP participation encompasses far more than students at educational institutions. As many as 25% of adjunct faculty members need public assistance.[191] Conduct a quick search on YouTube and you will find numerous stories of hard-working teachers living on the edge of poverty because of low wages and no workplace benefits.

In a speech given to the AFL-CIO in 2015, Senator Elizabeth Warren declared: "We believe that no one—no one—should work full time and still live in poverty."[192] A report compiled by Restaurant Opportunities Center United found almost half of restaurant workers require social assistance, and the estimated cost to taxpayers totaled $9.4 billion per year from 2009 to 2013.[193] A joint study between the University of California, Berkeley and the University of Illinois at Urbana-Champaign estimated that fast food workers alone cost taxpayers $7 billion per year due to wage supplementation.[194] Restaurant work can be physically demanding, and despite the obvious fact these people work extremely hard for a living, taxpayers must heavily subsidize poverty wages.

A single Olive Garden reportedly costs taxpayers almost $200,000 because of dependence on social assistance.[195] At one point, McDonald's Corporation supplied workers with a McResources phone line and website to learn how to access government assistance programs but this was quickly shut down after receiving media scrutiny.[196] In 2011, the *Argus Leader*, a newspaper in Sioux Falls, South Dakota, sued the U.S. Department of Agriculture to force disclosure of the SNAP dollars spent at retail stores. But at the last minute, the Food Marketing Institute, a powerful business advocacy group, filed a motion to halt compliance. In June 2019, the Supreme Court ruled against *Argus Leader*, which means companies can keep undisclosed the amount of SNAP dollars they earn on the revenue side.[197]

In 2004, the Democratic staff of the House Committee on Education and the Workforce used Wisconsin State Medicaid data to estimate that a standard 300-member Walmart Superstore cost taxpayers $900,000 in wage subsidies.[198] Jack Sinclair, an executive manager at Walmart Stores Inc., told investors that the company captures 18% of the food stamp market,[199] which equals roughly $13 billion.[200] Here is a scenario in which taxpayers subsidize the low wages of Walmart workers while SNAP recipients spend billions of taxpayer dollars at Walmart stores, and the exact amount spent is undisclosed to the public because the Food Marketing Institute filed suit.

The Ohio Tax Credit Authority offered Amazon property tax abatements to build warehouses throughout the state and create job opportunity, but the Ohio Department of Job and Family Services reported that 1,430 Amazon employees or family members were receiving SNAP benefits in August 2017.[201,202]

A high percentage of working families qualify for SNAP benefits, healthcare coverage, the earned income credit, and housing assistance, among other social assistance programs. A full 61% of Medicaid and Children's Health Insurance Program (CHIP) benefits accrue to working families.[203] Conservative leaders decry public assistance programs as free handouts, oftentimes fighting for spending cuts; at the same time, conservative leaders actively fight against strong labor protections and wage hikes, ensuring that an increasing number of hard-working Americans take reliance on government benefits to fill their pay gap. Across the board, conservative ideologues embrace this notion of individual self-reliance—that talking point sounds logical—but hard-working Americans have come to rely on public assistance because of low wages.

Large companies gladly pay workers low wages, forcing taxpayers to fill in the pay gap via programs such as TANF, EIC, SNAP, Medicaid, and CHIP, among other acronyms. The estimated cost to taxpayers of subsidizing wages in this manner equaled $153 billion per year during the Great Recession from 2009 to 2011.[204] These large corporations promise jobs, but the reality of low pay means that communities must allocate tax dollars to wage assistance programs. Meanwhile, companies receive tax abatements and favorable tax loopholes to pay less into the system.

Maybe you feel that no one should receive social assistance, but how do you justify low pay amid inflated living costs? All along the pay spectrum, from military personnel to paramedics and retail workers, compensation offered to the middle class, especially in a nonunion setting, simply has not kept pace with the cost of education, housing, healthcare, and food. Of note, the Congressional Budget Office reports that for every $1 increase in the minimum wage, the federal budget receives a net $.32 benefit from increased tax revenue and less reliance on social assistance.[205]

More progressive states have stepped in to pass higher minimum wage rates. Washington State enacted a $13.50 statewide minimum wage because of Initiative 1433 that will be phased in over time.[206] The city of Seattle itself passed a $15 minimum wage with a phase-in schedule that depends on the number of employees a company has. Smaller companies will not reach the $15 minimum wage until 2021.[207] Yet, despite these boosts to the minimum wages, Seattle still boasts an unemployment rate below the national average.[208]

Most of the states with fast-growing economies maintain minimum wage rates higher than the federally mandated rates. California, a state that conservative pundits lambast because of its progressive policies, experienced the highest growth rate in food service employment among the 50 states in 2019 despite a $12 minimum wage. Both Washington and California led the nation in retail job growth even though these two states have enacted some of the highest state and city-level minimum wage rates. Many other metropolitan centers in the United States are moving to a $15 minimum wage, and that should bode well for their economies.

This claim that higher wages lead to widespread unemployment could not be further from the truth. In fact, states with high minimum wages experience more robust economic growth than the low-paid areas of the country.[209] Large-scale investment firms could care less about a $15 minimum wage when evaluating the merits of a multimillion-dollar project in which they intend to use highly skilled, and equally, highly expensive labor. Seattle remains a highly attractive marketplace for investment money, and the infusion of cash into the area keeps employment strong.

Congress should shield American taxpayers with legislation aimed at forcing companies to repay wage subsidies. I dub this the UNPAID Act, or Unfair Need for Public Assistance Income Dependency Act. In 2018, Senator Bernie Sanders (D-VT) introduced the Stop Bad Employers from Zeroing Out Subsidies or Stop BEZOS Act, nicknamed after Amazon founder Jeff Bezos. The Stop BEZOS Act would levy a tax on corporations equal to the amount of social assistance, such as healthcare and SNAP benefits, consumed by workers.[210] Similarly, Sanders also introduced in 2018 the Stop WALMART Act, or Stop Welfare for Any Large Monopoly Amassing Revenue from Taxpayers Act, which sought to close the gap between CEO pay and median worker wages by disallowing corporate stock buybacks if thresholds were not met. In his press release, Sanders claimed that low pay at Walmart cost taxpayers $6.2 billion as a result of social assistance.[211,212]

Conservative ideologues enjoy asserting that a low-paid worker needs to accumulate skills if higher pay is desired. The American secondary education system does not furnish marketable skills to the majority of students, which forces them to continue onto community college, university, or trade school, often taking on crushing student loan debt in the process. In the end, workers who are trying to rise out of poverty increasingly end up squeezed between student loan payments and low wages. Gathering more skills serves little benefit if students graduate inside a recession or hold no collective bargaining power.

My time in the investment industry brought clarity to who exactly freeloads off the government. The ultrawealthy use their influence to procure government contracts and favorable tax policies. They knead political leaders into sabotaging labor reforms and regulations. As a struggling family asks for $200 in supplemental food assistance, conservatives promote a feeling of shame for use of public funds. But these same conservatives hypocritically ignore the unfair and undemocratic playing field created to retain wealth in the hands of a few families for generations to come.

The real problem, and one not being communicated sufficiently, is the need for an organized labor movement to promote living wages and employee benefits. The union effort in America has fallen asleep. Workers must exert a unionized voice to lobby their employers, bearing in mind that the majority of social assistance goes to people who work.

They have jobs, so stop demonizing them!

TAXATION

A rise of American exceptionalism accompanied the victories of World War II. This war was won through the sacrifice and combat strength of Americans, but equally in importance, the war turned in America's favor because of a massive buildup of military weapons such as tanks, planes, and warships. Hard-working Americans built 17 aircraft carriers in the time Japanese laborers built six. In one year of the war, the United States assembled more planes than the Japanese turned out during the entire Second World War,[213] but all of this production came at a huge cost. Accounting for inflation, the United States spent an equivalent to $4 trillion defending this nation and the world against imperialism.[214]

In 1944, to pay for the war effort and secure victory, the American Congress pushed the top marginal income tax rate up to 94% at the federal level.[215] The minimum tax bracket rose to 23%.[216] The average American paid an effective tax rate in between these two percentage rates. By 1980, the massive federal debt accumulated during WWII was nearly resolved because of high tax rates over the prior 35 years. The highest income tax rate then stood at 70% and the lowest tax bracket imposed a 14% tax rate on the first rung of a person's income. Ronald Reagan stepped into the presidency vowing to lower taxes, and he was able to push down the top marginal income rate to 28% by 1988. However, the lowest tax bracket, which impacted lower-income persons more heavily, actually went up to 15%.[217] At the same time, Federal Insurance Contributions Act (FICA) payroll taxes grew almost 7%. Under Reagan, the wealthy saw their top tax rate fall 42% while the middle class faced 8% more of newly-raised income and payroll taxes.[218] Meanwhile, U.S. government debt levels began to grow precipitously.

The United States maintained high corporate tax rates on the heels of World War II until the end of the Vietnam War, and then in 1975 began a decade-long process of expanding the number of corporate tax brackets and lowering tax rates per each bracket.[219] The share of tax revenue coming from corporations has been cut in half since WWII whereas the amount of government revenue from individual and payroll taxes has nearly doubled, pushing more of the tax burden onto hard-working Americans. The percent of taxes levied on high-net-worth estates also fell by more than half to allow the ultrawealthy a means to pass along intergenerational wealth.[220]

Ever since WWII ended, an increasing percentage of the federal tax burden has been slowly shifted onto working-class Americans. In 1958, Congress began allowing corporations to elect Subchapter S status, meaning business taxes could be assessed at the individual level, and not the corporate level. An S corporation does not face payroll taxes on dividends, setting up a lucrative tax loophole.[221] Hard-working Americans endure payroll taxes on all earnings, but an S corporation owner has the power to sidestep these payroll taxes through dividend distributions.

During the height of the Vietnam conflict, President Lyndon Johnson had to negotiate with a Republican Congress for a tax surcharge to pay for the wartime costs. The Republicans asked for a slew of concessions before permitting the surcharge.[222,223] Decades later, President George W. Bush broke from the 140-year patriotic tradition of raising taxes to fund war efforts and cut amounts wealthy Americans paid for income, capital gains, and estate taxes while giving the middle class a pittance of tax savings.[224,225]

George W. Bush launched an extensive promotional campaign to convince the American public to send troops overseas after the September 11 attacks. As soon as the war got underway, intelligence officials knew that documents President Bush used to substantiate the war were in fact falsified.[226] The president threw the military into an unfunded war based on phony claims and recycled troops through multiple tours to avoid the political backlash a draft would provoke; yet the American public was rewarded with tax savings.

Parents had to ship their children in military service donated bulletproof vests to protect poorly fortified vehicles against roadside explosions.[227,228]

Families who had loved ones being sent into battle had to scrounge together money to purchase and ship expensive military equipment overseas.[229]

The same people who hug the American flag and toss around the word patriotism did not dip into their pockets to fund these contemporary wars. Conservatives have become vehemently opposed to raising taxes, and plutocrat think tanks and corporate media networks have supported this fight against higher taxes over the past few decades. However, Republicans engage in the old switcheroo by shifting the tax burden onto the middle class and reinforcing this notion that taxes seem high. Taxpayers call for lowering taxes, and the Republicans make good on their promise to lower taxes, but only for the rich.

The Republicans flouted their latest creature—the Tax Cuts and Jobs Act (TCJA) of 2017—as a tax cut for the middle class. But the TCJA placed restrictions on itemized deductions, which benefit the middle class, because the Republicans in Congress wanted to lower the corporate tax rate to 21%. In the 2018 tax season, middle-class Americans faced surprise tax bills because they could no longer itemize deductions just as corporations received a massive tax reduction. A survey of CEOs revealed that corporations will use tax savings to primarily pay down debt, but also purchase more company stock to bid up prices artificially. Few CEOs are expected to use the corporate tax savings from the TCJA to pay their workers more.[230]

In 2009, liberal filmmaker Michael Moore went on conservative talk-show host Sean Hannity's program. Hannity complained about paying a tax rate of 60% on his income.[231] Of importance, I would not disagree with Hannity's assessment that he experiences a high tax rate, but he should blame the same Republicans he spends his nights defending and promoting. Sean Hannity, who makes millions as a conservative pundit in the heavily taxed jurisdiction of New York City, has every right to complain about high taxes, but he falls for the Republican's ploy. Hannity pays a lot in taxes because multinational corporations pay few if any taxes. Plus, he could have lowered his tax obligation using itemized deductions, such as from the purchase of an elite NYC condo, but the TCJA places significant limits now on those deductions, rendering homeownership a useless tax strategy in many cases.

The middle-class life is slowly slipping away as a result of mediocre wages, high living costs, and increased taxation through a mix of income, sales, excise, property, and payroll taxes. The tax burden is foisted on hard-working Americans to create room to lower taxes on the ultrawealthy.

Over time, the ultrawealthy have collected ways to minimize taxes owed using special corporate deductions, legal trusts, private foundations, and S corporation status. Only the ultrawealthy benefit from a QTIP trust, GRAT, generation-skipping trust, marital trust, or bypass trust. A wealthy business owner can gift stock to a family member and hand down intergenerational wealth. A high-net individual can make a sizeable charitable contribution to a private foundation and apply that amount as an itemized deduction against taxable income. Of note, the TCJA of 2017 did not limit the charitable contribution itemized deduction.

The largess of having made a sizeable donation to a private foundation sounds praiseworthy, thinking that rich people are concerned about a community's philanthropic needs, but the ultrawealthy have increasingly used private foundations to undertake a political agenda—and charitable contributions serve as a tax deduction, lowering taxable income in the process. In 2013, foundations held assets of $800 billion, and there is nothing stopping this money from going to nonprofit groups doing biased policy research or holding so-called "educational" summits in which topics revolve around advancing political ideals.[232]

The 1960s and early 1970s witnessed a boon to the progressive movement with passage of the Clean Air Act, Clean Water Act, Occupational Health and Safety Act, and a suite of President Lyndon Johnson's Great Society legislation, including the Food Stamp Act of 1964. The program's name was later changed to Supplemental Nutrition Assistance Program (SNAP) in 2008 to better reflect how households receive food support as a supplement to current earnings as opposed to full coverage of a household's entire food bill. By the mid-1970s, a select group of nonprofits supported with private foundation money reignited the conservative movement against this progressive agenda.

One of the more prominent donors, the Scaife Family Charitable Trust, donated $195,000 to the Heritage Foundation in 1975, helping to catapult this nonprofit into the national spotlight.[233] The Scaife family derived their fortune from Andrew Mellon whose daughter married Alan Scaife. Andrew's grandson, Richard Mellon Scaife, would use the family's wealth to fund conservative institutions throughout the 1980s and 1990s.[234] Since this time, large private foundations and multinational corporations have continued to pour money into the Heritage Foundation, American Enterprise Institute,

Manhattan Institute, and many similar organizations, all tax-free and all aimed to promote a business-friendly, conservative ideology.[235]

Fred Koch, a chemical engineer, built a fortune through the mid-twentieth century, mainly through construction of cutting-edge oil refineries. In 1977, Charles Koch, one of Fred's four sons, spearheaded the effort to launch a libertarian think tank, the Cato Institute. Seven years later, in 1984, another one of Fred's sons, David Koch, founded Citizens for a Sound Economy (CSE) with the intention to fight against any type of tax at the state and federal level. In 2004, CSE was rebranded Americans for Prosperity (AFP), and the newly-reorganized institution's focus expanded.[236] Using state offshoots, the Wisconsin branch of AFP went to work dismantling the the state's public employee union with help from Governor Scott Walker. As a result of their attacks, union membership among public employees in Wisconsin fell from 50% in 2011 to 19% by 2017.

At the same time AFP was infiltrating states to undermine unions, the organization was escalating its anti-tax campaigns with help from a fringe movement among conservative voters—the so-called Tea Party.[237] AFP's nationwide infrastructure has been successful in halting tax increases and union efforts, but AFP's greatest impact may very well be its effort to sow doubt about climate change through anti-science propaganda in concert with the Cato Institute. Greenpeace reports that the Koch brothers have spent over $168 million since the mid-1980s to fund 90 groups involved with climate change denialism.[238] Of note, all this money that flows into these organizations serves as a charitable tax deduction for the Koch family, allowing them to escape taxation. Even worse, a 2014 lawsuit filed by the State of California against Americans for Prosperity Foundation, a 501(c)(3) charitable organization, affirmed that nonprofits cannot be forced to disclose their donors.[239]

This network of conservative nonprofit policy "think tanks" have led the charge to lower taxes for America's ultrawealthy, and wealthy families receive a tax deduction on money contributed to these think tanks. U.S. courts ruled in favor of this money flowing toward political agendas, in particular during the 1970s, but culminating in the landmark 2010 Supreme Court case *Citizens United v. Federal Elections Commission*, which allows corporations, nonprofit organizations, and labor unions to engage in political advertisement without any financial limit. This money has been used to lead the American public to believe that a low tax environment is required to drive the economy forward despite evidence that states with low tax revenue per capita have created widespread deficiencies in healthcare, education, infrastructure, and middle-class stability.[240]

The American public is now met with a torrent of inaccurate newspeak to confuse voters about how companies need low taxes to pay strong wages. Corporate taxes are levied on taxable profit after consideration of expenses; therefore, employee compensation, along with investments in technology, modern equipment, and factories, reduce taxable income. In fact, a company can reduce its corporate income tax bill to zero if it spends all its money on worker compensation. High taxes do not kill jobs as the pro-business elites advertise. Any company worried about a high tax bill should actually hire more workers, pay them an appropriate wage, and fund benefits—these actions reduce taxes!

As corporate tax rates fall, more of America's tax burden falls onto employees, and investors receive more cash dividends subject to lower tax rates. Multinational firms claim that low taxes are needed to remain competitive and preserve jobs domestically, but profit is a function of revenue minus expenses. Taxes are not factored in this equation, and companies do not calculate their tax liability until after paying workers. An increase in payroll expenses will lower taxable income for these multinational firms.

Low tax rates encourage business executives to hand investors a cash dividend. Initiating my career in public accounting enabled me to interact with U.S. business managers as they discussed tax rates and corporate investments. I heard managers say firsthand that they favor distributing cash dividends to owners, many of whom are institutional investment firms, when tax rates are low. As tax rates climb, these same managers discuss ways to invest money in the company's cost structure or pay higher wages to obtain a tax deduction. Simply put, employee compensation is a tax deduction and business owners seek out tax deductions when tax rates are high.

The Congressional Research Service found that both consumer savings and corporate investment decline when tax rates are lowered. Gross domestic production (GDP) also declines when the federal government runs large budget deficits. Today, growth in the economy is a full percentage point below what it was when top marginal income tax rates were 70% (or higher). As an example, growth in GDP rebounded in the 1990s at the same time Democrats sought to raise taxes on the wealthy.[241]

In 2013, Apple CEO Tim Cook went before a congressional committee to discuss tax havens, specifically the many loopholes Apple uses to sidestep paying taxes. Republican Senators loudly condemned the investigation, going on long rants about how Apple creates jobs—albeit many of the jobs are created in China. Cook sat in front of this congressional committee and stated, "My understanding is there is not a tax residence for either—for any of the three subsidiaries that you just named" when asked about Apple Operational International, Apple Sales International, and Apple Operations Europe. Cook was discussing how Apple's three subsidiaries do not establish a legal presence in any tax jurisdiction.[242]

In the United States, filing incorporation documents with a state triggers tax jurisdiction in that state, but the same event in Ireland does not. Only when a company is managed and controlled in Ireland will a taxable presence be established. Multinational firms have incorporated *en masse* in Ireland, but they keep management and control outside of Ireland, in order to exploit this tax loophole. Managing and controlling a company inside the United States does not constitute a taxable event, allowing Tim Cook to run a multinational company out of California without fear of a massive tax bill. Even though Apple triggered a tax juridiction in Ireland, the company negotiated with the Irish government a tax rate of less than 2%.[243]

Now comes the task of pushing revenue into Ireland to fully enjoy this sub-2% tax rate. The company's intellectual property was placed into a subsidiary called Apple Operations International that maintained zero employees. Then, the main company leased the use of this intellectual property for roughly $10 billion per year, transferring huge sums of money into this puppet subsidiary that had no employees. Another subsidiary called Apple Sales International captured much of the company's revenue from foreign sales, ensuring the United States could not tax that revenue. This process moves a cluster of revenue into Ireland where it receives favorable tax rates. Costs can remain in the United States because companies do not pay taxes on costs; in contrast, these costs, such as payroll expense, serve as a tax deduction.

To illustrate how well the company dodges taxes, Apple Inc. in 2011 paid—not the 2% negotiated with Ireland—but a tax rate of 0.045%.[244] That would be equivalent to an American who earns $60,000 paying only $27 in taxes for the entire year, but we all know working-class Americans pay much more. To make matters worse, Apple experienced a stellar tax avoidance year in 2014, paying an effective tax rate of only 0.005%.[245] That's equivalent to this same person making $60,000 only paying $3 in annual taxes.

In 2012, Apple Inc. avoided as much as $9 billion in U.S. taxes through loopholes constructed using Irish subsidiaries.[246] Each of Apple's 47,000 U.S. workers in 2012 would need to pay $191,489 in taxes, hypothetically speaking, to offset the lost corporate taxes of which Ireland's tax haven system deprives the U.S. Treasury.[247] Now we get a example of how much the tax burden has shifted onto the middle class.

Apple Inc. outsources production to Foxconn Technology Group, Jabil Green Point, and Pegatron Corporation, among others, never establishing a tax presence in China. As a result, Chinese tax authorities cannot levy corporate taxes against Apple because the company never sets up a direct tax residence. This is true for all multinational corporations that outsource production to a third-party manufacutring firm. Back home, Apple rents an office in Nevada, a state with no corporate income taxes, to avoid California state tax residency.[248] Apple, the most profitable multinational corporation in the United States, has learned how to escape taxes by outsourcing production to third-party facilities in China, setting up foreign subsidiaries in Ireland, and renting an office in Nevada.

The tax haven game only starts with the beautiful Irish countryside. Referred to as the Double Irish with a Dutch Sandwich, multinational corporations start the tax game in Ireland before transferring earnings into a Dutch holding company. Normally, companies cannot hold a large pool of investments long term, so they use Dutch law to move money into a so-called holding company. Finally, these corporations transfer their investment holdings into Caribbean holding companies for long-term storage.

In 2014, Google Inc. moved $12 billion through Google Netherlands Holdings BV onward into its resting place in a Bermuda subsidiary, generating a $2.4 billion tax savings.[249,250] The company repeated this process in 2015 and saved $3.6 billion.[251] Under pressure from the European Union, the Irish parliament voted to close the Double Irish tax loophole to new participants but it will keep the loophole open to existing participants until 2020.[252]

Foreign tax havens do not exist without the blessing of U.S. tax code. Initially, Subpart F, enacted in 1962 by President John F. Kennedy, sought to tax passive income of foreign subsidiaries. Subpart F in its former glory would have considered many of the transfers to Apple Operations International and Apple Sales International as taxable events, giving rise to a large U.S. tax bill. However, the Treasury Department revised Subpart F tax forms in 1996, opening the floodgate for multinational firms to treat foreign subsidiaries as untaxed entities simply by marking one checkbox on Form 8832.

Known as the "check-the-box" loophole, Subpart F tax avoidance was expanded upon in 2006 with a "look-through" rule, which allowed untaxed foreign subsidiaries to transfer money to one another.[253] The Congressional Joint Committee on Taxation estimates that these loopholes permitted multinational firms to avoid paying $83.5 billion in U.S. taxes in 2014[254]—that's just one year.

Republicans have refused to modify Subpart F despite numerous bills sponsored by Democrats to close the tax haven loopholes.[255] Their argument asserts that multinational firms create jobs, but they are not creating jobs in the United States and employee expenses lower taxable income. The lack of corporate tax liability means working-class Americans must fund government programs, and low wages force reliance on these government programs.

Even when a large U.S. company keeps production domestic, the tax code allows half the income to go untaxed according to the "passage-of-title" rule; a multinational company needs to simply find a buyer able to transfer products in international waters.[256] Smaller companies struggle to transfer products in this manner to apply this tax avoidance scheme, giving larger firms a significant advantage in the global economy.[257,258]

The Guardian, a British newspaper, found that 340 multinational companies with names we all know such as Pepsi, Heinz, and FedEx dodge taxes in Luxembourg.[259] Perhaps one of the worst offenders, Walmart Stores Incorporated, was found to have funneled $64.2 billion through at least 20 Luxembourg subsidiaries despite operating zero stores in the country.[260,261] In fact, the closest site of a Walmart store is located 5,100 kilometers away in Moncton, Canada.

Luxembourg is a small country of 1,000 square miles and a population of 576,000 denizens[262] nestled between the powerful economies of France and Germany. I lived next to Luxembourg in 1998 where it was a quick bike ride along the Mosel River to cross over the border. Without having this proximity to Luxembourg, I might have skipped over it completely, yet that would be a tragedy for this conversation on tax havens because Luxembourg stands as a world leader for tax schemes. Luxembourg maintains the third-highest gross domestic production (GDP) in the world when computed on a per person basis. In 2015, the GDP per capita of Luxembourg was $103,838 compared to $56,116 for the United States.[263] What fuels this country's massive economy?

Foreign subsidiaries of U.S. firms reported profit of 0.6% in France and 0.4% in Germany relative to the GDP levels of these countries. That's a very small amount of profit exposed to taxation in these two countries. However, when it came to Luxembourg, U.S. subsidiaries reported profit equal to 127% of GDP, meaning U.S. companies are pushing revenue into this tiny country at an alarming rate.

The tax scheme in Luxembourg is threefold. Companies combine a low tax rate with an 80% tax exemption on royalties. Then, a 1% tax rate is levied on interest income assessed on internal loans.[264] Suddenly, multinational companies can move passive income into Luxembourg for massive tax savings as Subpart F of the U.S. tax code looks the other way. Finally, Luxembourg grants special tax exemptions on cash dividends to foreign corporations.[265]

The European Union is working to shut down the tax haven schemes in Ireland and Luxembourg. As of 2017, Luxembourg will begin complying with European standards on intercompany loans, and this may very well end the country's reign as a central tax haven in Europe.[266] To the dismay of Apple's CEO Tim Cook, the European Union ordered Ireland to assess $14.5 billion in taxes on the company,[267] an amount significantly more than the $10 million assessed in 2011. However, the EU's general court overturned this order in July 2020, letting Apple to escape this tax bill.[268]

Even if the European Union flexes its might and succeeds at cleaning out the loopholes in the European tax system, U.S. companies still have access to many other tax havens throughout the world. Almost three-quarters of the largest U.S. companies store profit inside Caribbean subsidiaries to the tune of $2.5 trillion.[269] Another report calculates that just 50 U.S. companies hold $1.4 trillion in offshore holdings. Ranked as #1 in the world as of 2016 is Apple with overseas holdings of $215 billion followed by Microsoft with $102 billion.[270]

Why would these companies stash $2.5 trillion overseas only to watch it sit idle in foreign subsidiaries? This massive wealth would start to dilute over time because of inflation. Moving money into an Irish, Dutch, Luxembourgish, or Caribbean subsidiary is just an accounting feat. A transaction is recorded as a bookkeeping activity, meaning the $2.5 trillion exists overseas merely on paper.

In terms of investing this cash, these companies have moved the actual money into U.S. and other global assets. An estimated 66% of Microsoft Corporation's cash "reported" overseas is held in U.S. bonds.[271] Apple holds $41.7 billion of its overseas-listed funds in U.S. Treasury bonds, meaning U.S. taxpayers give $800 million per year in interest payments to Apple despite the company dodging U.S. taxes. Since 2010, U.S. taxpayers paid an estimated $1.2 billion to just 10 U.S. companies holding U.S. Treasury bonds. The holdings earn interest paid by U.S. taxpayers despite being reported in foreign tax havens.[272]

Ultrawealthy executives can obtain a Visa, MasterCard, or American Express credit card with a potential credit limit up to $1,000,000 per month, make undisclosed purchases in the United States, and use foreign cash to satisfy the credit card bill. Many of the Caribbean tax havens refuse to report these transactions to the Internal Revenue Service (IRS), allowing the ultrawealthy to evade billions in tax dollars.[273]

The sneakiest of U.S. corporations will loan overseas cash back to a U.S. parent company, and even though the foreign subsidiary must report the corresponding interest income, the overseas tax rate tends to be close to zero. Major public accounting firms even provide guidance on how multinational companies can arrange intercompany loans to "repatriate cash and achieve tax efficiency."[274]

Over a three-year period from 1997 to 2000, Tyco Electronics Corporate Holdings Inc. entered into intercompany loans, which allowed the U.S.-based parent to deduct $2.86 billion in interest expense for tax purposes.[275] The IRS objected to these intercompany loans, leading to a 15-year court dispute that finally resulted in a tentative agreement in 2016 for Tyco International to pay between $475 and $525 million in back taxes.[276] The IRS continues to battle other companies that have undertaken sizeable intercompany loans as a way of moving offshore cash back into the United States.

In 2004, President George W. Bush encouraged passage of the American Jobs Creation Act of 2004, which allowed a one-year tax holiday so multinational firms could repatriate funds at a low tax rate of 5.25%.[277]

But why would companies need to repatriate money that already sits in U.S. assets, especially when taxpayers pay the interest income on any Treasury bond holdings? Multinational firms shuffle "paper" profits into foreign subsidiaries—not cash. The reason being, these companies cannot pay dividends to investors if these earnings are reported on the books of foreign subsidiaries. Earnings must be shuffled around on paper back to U.S. tax forms in order to enrich investors with a dividend distribution.

The American Jobs Creation Act of 2004 gave multinational firms the option to show these earnings on U.S. tax forms subject to a 5.25% tax. Over $300 billion of overseas earnings were reported in the United States during this repatriation tax holiday, but instead of creating 500,000 new jobs as congressional leaders claimed it would, 79% of the funds were used for stock buybacks and 15% were distributed as cash dividends to investors. In the end, these firms cut 21,000 jobs and escaped paying billions in U.S. taxes.[278,279,280]

More recently, President Donald Trump signed into law the Tax Cuts and Jobs Act of 2017, which required further repatriation of earnings, but CEOs already said they will use these earnings to pay down loans, buy back company stock, fuel new merger activity, and hand investors dividends.[281] It's even theorized that Trump has escaped corporate taxes for years using loss carryforwards, which permit the negative profit in one period to offset taxable profit in future years.

Multinational firms are organized to decrease state taxes as well. Most states assess corporate taxes according to apportionment factors that identify where a company holds property, hires workers, and conducts selling activity.[282] It's an easy one-two punch to escape state taxes if a manufacturing firm outsources both workers and property to a foreign country—very little activity gets apportioned to the state. Multinational firms can exploit a number of U.S. tax code loopholes including check-the-box and look-through rules, the foreign tax credit, income tax deferral, manufacturing apportionment, and incorporation jurisdiction.

Kansas pursued a low-tax agenda as an economic strategy, but instead of seeing financial gains, the state generated a projected $1.1 billion revenue shortfall as of 2019.[283] In normal situations, a state would need to issue bonds to fill this revenue shortfall, but Kansas faces higher interest charges because the budget deficits triggered the bond rating agencies to lower the state's credit rating twice within two years.[284] Now, instead of money going toward education and infrastructure, Kansas taxpayers must come up with more money to pay the higher interest charges on its bonds, and that money just flows to investors outside Kansas.

Tax remittance to a local, state, or federal revenue department does not cause money to disappear into a financial abyss. The money is invested into public works, education, and national defense projects before reentering the general economy. Anyone that complains about paying taxes may want to travel around an underdeveloped country where citizens pay low taxes but live without running water, stable electricity, a sewage system, and paved roads.

The vast majority of people who receive government assistance are either working, disabled, retired, or enrolled in an educational institution. Taxpayers opposed to welfare and social handouts must object to corporate managers who freeload off the tax system and force taxpayers to subsidize low wages.[285] Living wages give businesses a tax deduction to eliminate taxes (no matter the tax rate), and hard-working Americans are less likely to need social assistance when paid appropriately.

In today's world of global commerce, multinational corporations place a heavy reliance on airports, seaports, and roadways, all of which cost money. Saying that these companies create jobs and should not pay taxes is akin to a homeowner getting free trash collection, free water, free electricity, and free WiFi just for renovating the driveway. Wouldn't that be nice? Corporate America gets free government assistance right now, and as conservatives love to point out how nothing is free, then by all means, pay attention to how hard-working Americans get stuck with low wages and a massive tax bill.

Conservatives claim to respect individual responsibility and hard work, so why do they tolerate lazy corporate executives who outsource jobs and exploit tax havens?

TRANSPORTATION

After the end of World War I in 1919, the United States sought to test domestic road conditions to determine America's war capabilities. A convoy of 81 vehicles under the control of the U.S. War Department set course from mile 0, the origin point for all interstate highways marked in Washington, D.C., destined for California some 3,251 miles away. The Transcontinental Motor Convoy, as it was called, took more than two months to traverse the country. Road conditions were abysmal, hampering vehicles in mud, ditches, and even quicksand. One 200-yard stretch took seven hours to cross.[286]

In tow with this convoy was then Lieutenant Colonel Dwight D. Eisenhower, a road trip enthusiast and the future Supreme Commander of Allied Forces in World War II. During the Second World War, General Eisenhower witnessed how the *Reichsautobahnen* roadway permitted the German military to swiftly move troops and supplies from one warfront to the other. Eisenhower applied these insights after being elected the 34th President of the United States as he pushed for a new interstate freeway system.[287]

As early as 1921, the federal government passed legislation to encourage interstate road construction but with the caveat that states would pay nearly the entire cost. State governments to this point emphasized a network of turnpikes, meaning interstate roads that would assess tolls collected by private companies. Not until the Great Depression did federal appropriations increase by any substantial measure.

The Federal Highway Act of 1938 commissioned a study on the merits of toll-free roads, concluding that an interstate system could not raise a sufficient amount from toll fees. Of concern, short-distance travel would make toll assessment difficult unless the interstate system invested heavily in toll facilities, but added facility costs would require high tolls fees, which would encourage drivers to simply remain on local access roads.[288]

Eisenhower's landmark Federal Highway Act of 1956 differed from its predecessors because of the quantity of freeway miles called for, along with the funding mechanism. The federal government would bear 90% of the costs estimated at $24.8 billion over a 12-year period in order to build 41,000 miles of interstate freeways. The 1956 Act also established robust construction standards to permit higher speeds and greater safety. As seen today, interstate roads offer rest stops, wide shoulders, and ample signage.[289] Legislation since 1956 has brought the total U.S. freeway mileage to 46,726.[290]

The United States Postal Services (USPS), long before 1956, began lobbying for road development to expedite mail delivery. People had to travel on foot or via horse to pick up mail from a central post office.[291] Today, the same people who don't want to subsidize the USPS receive products shipped in from all over the world, passing through seaports and freeways, to be dropped right at their doorstep. The USPS supports the business world, expanding logistics across the global economic system.

The entire span of transportation infrastructure required significant investment over time, but imagine life without freeways or at-home delivery. The added cost on each product shipment from a business to a customer without this organized transportation network would make consumption very expensive, leaving rural dwellers, many who protest taxes, with a significantly lower standard of living.

American political leaders began to embrace the idea of a taxpayer-funded freeway system, void of any tolls, as a way of reducing the amount spent adjudicating auto accidents, which had placed a heavy burden on the court system before 1956. Vacation travel, work commutes, emergency transport, and product shipment all rely heavily on what Eisenhower created 60 years ago. Taxpayers may gripe about a gas tax levied to maintain the interstate freeway system, but car owners faced high vehicle maintenance and fuel costs from the poor road conditions in existence before 1956. A safer freeway system also reduced deaths and injuries. All told, the American public experiences fewer driving costs, safer commutes, and increased access to consumer goods as a result of toll-free transportation.

Corporate CEOs place access to interstate roads as a top priority far above low tax rates. Every single day, 55 million tons of products are moved around the country with a value of almost $50 billion.[292] The transportation industry represents 10% of the entire economic system.[293] Every single person benefits when products can be quickly and inexpensively delivered. Just look at the growing trend toward one-day delivery from Amazon and Target, among other large retail chains. As companies transport more goods overall, an increased need for workers arises, along with higher worker pay.

A primary goal of an economic system must include moving raw materials into the hands of manufacturing firms and then getting final products shipped to consumers in an efficient manner. Moreover, workers must be productive at work, but a long, stress-filled commute drains energy before the workday even begins. Research into traffic congestion illustrates how working-class Americans bear a terrible burden when a nation underinvests in transportation infrastructure. Long commutes compromise family time, increase fuel usage, toxify the environment, and wear down vehicles faster. Vacation plans may be scraped to avoid peak holiday congestion. Instead of going shopping, consumers may stay at home. Retail stores get hit the hardest when cities experience worsening traffic jams.

A study in Oregon found that delivery congestion forces businesses to hold 5% to 8% more inventory, encumbering facility space with idle merchandise.[294] Commercial drivers are still paid even when sitting in traffic congestion. Bottlenecks are not a productive endeavor and only contribute to economic inefficiency. This problem with traffic is nothing new, but the United States has ignored the need to fund suitable solutions. The American Society of Civil Engineers (ASCE) gave America's infrastructure a grade of D+ on its 2017 report card.[295]

To achieve economic gains, commercial transportation must be free-flowing away from the traffic congestion caused by passenger vehicles. The goal is to get commuters and random drivers off the road to provide unfettered movement for business travel, freight shipments, and local product deliveries. Taxpayers may consider toll systems a better mode of payment to target vehicles using roads, but two problems exist with this mindset. Products delivered to retail stores or directly to a home are carried along the roadway, causing consumers to pay for tolls indirectly via higher product prices. The noncommercial users of the road, such as travelers, shoppers, and commuters, may refrain from accessing local businesses when a toll is imposed. Another problem seen in areas with toll roads is that drivers reroute to a nearby roadway outside of the toll network, increasing traffic jams along parallel access roads.

Administration of toll facilities and user accounts drains resources needlessly and creates an impediment to the free flow of products. I have encountered passenger tolls in the Denver, Tampa, and Seattle areas, and setting up an account and paying the tolls has been a nightmare. Florida sent me a bill for someone else's toll once and I had to call and email several times before the fee was removed. Toll administration needlessly increases the size of overall government bureaucracy. Why do the same people who decry big government bureaucracy call for tolls?

Anyone who has lived in the Seattle area can speak to the fruitless policy of adding more freeway lanes. The roadway system remains at a chronic point of saturation that could have been alleviated in a cost-effective manner if proper investments in alternative transportation options were made when first advocated for in the 1950s. A phenomenon called *induced demand* keeps road congestion high no matter the number of lanes available.[296] As more lanes are added, drivers shift behavior in a way that maintains congestion pressures in what American economist Anthony Downs referred to as the Fundamental Law of Traffic Congestion, back in 1962.[297]

A four-lane freeway struggles to hold anything more than 7,600 cars per hour during rush hour traffic in a major city corridor,[298] with bumper-to-bumper gridlock. Yet light rail can transport the same amount of people, if not more with added train cars.[299] The number of passengers carried via public transportation varies considerably with some light rail and subway lines jammed to capacity and others needing further ridership to cover costs. To encourage subway and light rail use, taxpayers should subsidize these forms of transportation. Why should passenger vehicles get free access to subsidized roadway infrastructure but anyone taking a subway or light rail must pay a fare? An individual car breaks down a paved road with each use, costing taxpayers through road maintenance, but these costs are subsidized through the tax system.

U.S. cities have spent anywhere from a low in Sacramento, California, of $19 million to a high of $174 million in Buffalo, New York, per track-mile for light rail.[300] Pundits often claim that a two-lane segment of freeway only costs an estimated $2 to $3 million per mile in a rural setting and upwards of $10 million per mile in an urban area based on a study that looked only at Arkansas.[301] Naysayers of public transportation regurgitate these findings as an obvious indication that roadway transportation costs far less than light rail, but a closer look at costs in other cities—not just Arkansas—reveals a different reality on light rail costs.

Light rail and highway projects at the turn of the 21st century around Denver, Colorado, both involved costs of roughly $21 million per mile.[302,303] Later, a 2016 transportation project in Denver involving light rail and freeway construction involved $46 million per track mile for new light rail capacity to the airport and the separate freeway expansion also cost roughly $46 million per mile.[304] I lived in Denver just as the light-rail line opened and it made airport travel much more convenient.

In Portland, Oregon, the initial cost for 32 miles of light rail cost roughly $1.8 billion when adjusted for inflation, representing $46 million per mile for brand new tracks.[305] However, adding one lane to the pre-existing I-205 freeway in the Portland area will cost $450 million over a six-mile stretch, representing $75 million per mile, and that is not brand-new road construction.[306]

The cost of connecting the Seattle-Tacoma airport to the University of Washington via light rail went beyond $200 million per mile,[307] and advocates against light rail seem justified in their fight because of this astronomical cost until realizing that freeway construction around the same area faced costs in excess of $200 million per mile.[308] Despite similar construction costs, the key differences between transportation forms are that light rail lasts longer, takes up less urban space, and can move more people than a freeway system,[309] whereas road traffic encumbers commercial transportation, and auto accidents entail huge social and healthcare costs.

In addition to direct expenditures, light rail comes with added health benefits. For starters, light rail use requires walking at a time when America faces growing health issues from sedentary lifestyles. Light rail can link into cycling infrastructure, which saves taxpayers overall due to lower road maintenance costs, not to mention lower healthcare costs. Most important, cleaner city air reduces cases of asthma and other pulmonary complaints.

Failing to invest in all realms of public transportation stifles economic activity on a grand scale, and light rail continues to be flouted as overly expensive. Analysis on the topic must take into account the density of an area, along with the costs of nearby roadways. It would make little sense to plug a light-rail line into Cheyenne, Wyoming, because the relative cost is too high compared with freeway lanes. In areas like Seattle, Boston, New York, Los Angeles, and other high-density population zones, studies show that adding more freeway lanes does not alleviate gridlock per Downs' Law of Traffic Congestion. Moreover, light rail costs relatively the same as freeway infrastructure in major cities but affords many additional benefits.

Light rail offers an indirect economic benefit to everyone in the country, even people living in Cheyenne, Wyoming, or some other rural city, through lower consumer prices. The city of Houston processes over 150 billion pounds of imported goods annually,[310] making it the primary U.S. seaport. The Texas A&M University Transportation Institute calculated that traffic congestion added $1.1 billion to the cost of goods moving through Houston in 2014.[311] Data put together by the American Transportation Research Institute determined that traffic gridlock in metropolitan areas added $47 billion in added freight costs to products throughout the country in 2014.[312] Everyone living in a rural area can gripe about taxes and argue against light rail due to high costs, but traffic logjams in key population zones end up driving costs upward for all American consumers, and it makes U.S. exports less competitive.

INRIX, a global leader in traffic research based in Seattle, Washington, puts the annual cost of roadway congestion at nearly $300 billion per year, with Los Angeles leading the pack. INRIX also included the loss impact of commercial goods moving through the bogged-down Los Angeles roadways. This car-loving city wastes more resources due to traffic than any other in the world, estimated at $9.6 billion or $2,408 per driver in 2016.[313] U.S. cities only spent $7.1 billion on subway and light rail networks in 2014,[314] a far cry from the economic waste traffic jams create.

In key metropolitan areas where significant gridlock occurs, state planners need to start designating lanes as commercial-only use.[315] Currently, most cities have only experimented with high-occupancy lanes for passenger vehicles. Concentrating more passengers into a single vehicle sounds logical but it rarely breaks from Downs' Law of Traffic Congestion, meaning high-occupancy lanes negligibly reduce logjams.

If roadways are split between noncommercial and commercial lanes, behavior in the community will shift to where light passenger vehicles will maintain the same level of congestion, but this congestion will no longer interfere with product shipments. It costs the economic system dearly to run semi-trucks, local delivery vans, and sales agents into traffic alongside passenger vehicles. The upfront investment of restricting lanes to only commercial use and pushing commuters, tourists, and shoppers onto public transportation options, such as light rail, would result in billions of dollars' worth of net savings.

Taxpayer subsidization of infrastructure, including roadways, airports, and seaports, may seem unfair at first glance, but a proper economic assessment must account for the cost savings to businesses of having free-flowing shipment. The economic system that takes root organically without much government oversight or taxpayer support is too often disorganized and underdeveloped, resulting in negative drag on commercial activity. Third-world, underdeveloped countries tend to operate without much governance or tax revenue. While the thought of low taxes may sound appealing, living in third-world conditions does not. Economic forecasts find that the United States must make roughly $200 billion in railway investments to keep pace with freight demand over the next two decades.[316]

Every five years, the Chinese government institutes a development plan, which is common among communist nations. As of 2018, the country's thirteenth plan reported that urban railway reached 5,760 kilometers.[317] China boasted 60% of the world's fast trains back in 2016, but it keeps adding track miles at a rapid clip, including a multicity train network connecting commercial freight shipments directly into Europe.[318]

Studies on commuter light rail costs in the United States miss a major mark in their assessment: They overlook how American light-rail systems are still in their infancy, and costs will remain higher than average as tracks are first laid in some of the most populated areas. Europe built rail lines through high-density zones years ago at roughly the point where the United States disinvested in rail transportation. The Europeans demonstrate a much lower rail cost at roughly €28 million per mile,[319] which seems appropriate for later-stage development. In 2017, the Government Accountability Office was selected to study reasons for why U.S. construction costs are much higher than European ones, but Congress killed the study before it got underway.[320]

Investments in transportation infrastructure create jobs directly through construction efforts, but the indirect consequence of robust transportation infrastructure is something taxpayers often overlook. If a company can reach a larger customer base, including in rural areas, then the company will produce more, hire more, and enjoy greater profitability. Job creation occurs throughout the entire economic system, not just in construction and commercial driving, when investments in transportation are made. Failure to assess the taxes to afford modern infrastructure means product delivery will be more expensive to all consumers, resulting in a lower standard of living.

What price tag can you place on a parent making it safely home after work because of the higher safety standards set forth in the 1956 Federal Highway Act? How much higher is your standard of living because of an organized transportation network involving seaports, airports, and freeways? How much more do you earn annually as a result of productivity gains achieved as firms ship products more easily? To this aim, any encumbrance on commericial transportation must be removed.

HEALTHCARE

Healthcare benefits expanded rapidly during WWII as the War Labor Board froze wages. Employers used benefits to sweeten the pot when attracting job seekers. Slightly under 10% of Americans had a health insurance plan before WWII. A decade later, half of the public was enrolled in health insurance with the largest concentration being employer plans.[321] Right after the war ended in 1946, Congress passed the Hospital Survey and Construction Act, also known as Hill-Burton, which rapidly expanded nonprofit hospitals, nursing homes, and public health centers, extending healthcare infrastructure into as much as 40% of the rural areas where no hospitals existed prior.[322] Institutions funded with Hill-Burton construction grants needed to provide a portion of care at a reduced-cost or free of charge to the community.[323]

Nonprofit hospitals operate as tax-exempt organizations, and charitable donations to these institutions provide a tax deduction. Just as Hill-Burton helped the construction of new nonprofit hospitals, corporations began to infuse donation money into them as a means to avoid taxes. Per the tax code, a taxpayer cannot influence how a small, individual donation is used; however, large corporate donations permit control over how the money shall be used. All told, corporations began to impact nonprofit hospital administration, "lowering utilization within each facility, reducing the quality of care, and generating unwarranted operating costs."[324]

Up until 1966, the healthcare system in the United States resembled the Canadian system wherein a similar mix of government, nonprofit, and corporate contributions provided the bulk of funds. Canada passed the Medical Care Act of 1966 to publicly fund services and pay for hospital care on a prepaid basis.[325] Back then, the cost to administer healthcare in both countries was roughly the same, or approximately $300 per person.[326] In this same decade, America's healthcare system experienced a privatization push of its nonprofit hospitals, along with subsequent merger activity of the newly privatized corporate hospitals, all of which would ultimately change the course of healthcare costs for America. Anti-trust laws, which could have reduced this merger frenzy, simply did not exert sufficient pushback. As the 1970s rolled on, hospital merger activity increased roughly ten-fold as compared to the prior decade.[327]

The National Health Planning and Resources Development Act of 1974 effectively ended the Hill-Burton era, but it provided some of the same construction grants to communities. However, corporate philanthropy and government grants were not enough to feed the growing healthcare costs. Nonprofit hospitals increasingly turned to the bond market for funding. Now, hospitals had to maintain strict accounting standards and operate more like businesses to appease bond investors.[328] The days of serving the local community had waned, and now hospitals would serve Wall Street.

In 1973, under the Nixon Administration, the federal government wanted to formalize managed health programs with passage of the Health Maintenance Organization (HMO) Act. This healthcare model, rooted in the Kaiser Foundation health plan in California, operated differently by paying a pre-selected group of physicians a fixed salary. Henry Kaiser served an instrumental role in shipbuilding during the Second World War and used health plans to compensate workers. Kaiser's health program encompassed primary care services, testing, procedures, wellness care, and hospital emergencies, amid a portfolio of healthcare practitioners, including osteopathic doctors, dentists, and optometrists. Of main importance, the HMO Act called for health education to be given to patients.[329] However, patients showed an overall dislike for HMO plans due to the lack of power to select a physician.

In response to HMO plans, insurance companies began to embed managed program features into their own plans. Dubbed PPO and IPA, for preferred provider organization and independent practice association, these plans grew in prominence starting in the early 1980s because they allowed patients to select their own doctor, albeit limited to who was credentialed with each specific insurance company. In many cases, patients could go see a specialist without prior referral from a primary care doctor.[330]

The United States seemed poised to embrace managed care models that focused on reducing costs and paying out healthcare dollars according to preset amounts—that was, until Ronald Reagan stepped foot in the Oval Office. The Tax Equity and Fiscal Responsibility Act of 1982 (TEFRA) changed the Medicare reimbursement model. President Reagan introduced a conservative-style revenue approach in which hospitals would begin to bill according to the precise nature of each itemized service and insurance companies began to adopt this new approach for paying health services as well. Instead of a bundled payment to cover estimated healthcare costs, hospitals could now function as a business and obtain their revenue through a fee-for-service (FFS) billing requisition.[331]

At the same time, President Reagan took a hacksaw to the Women, Infants, and Children (WIC) program, which gives low-income nursing mothers and pregnant women, along with their young children, access to food, baby formula, and dietary supplements. WIC helps to ensure proper birth weight of children, noting that low birth weight corresponds to high child-mortality rates.[332] The United States ranked 56th in the world for infant mortality in 2017.[333]

In the 1990s, the health system underwent a significant phase of consolidation. Providers formed integrated clinics, and hospitals merged under corporate umbrellas. Many institutions during this period converted from nonprofit to for-profit status. Instead of insurance companies negotiating prices with small, individual providers and treatment facilities, the newly formed hospital conglomerations wielded greater pricing power to force insurance plans to cover a wider scope of expensive specialists. Laboratory tests that could be performed externally were directed to in-hospital sites where the costs tended to be much higher.[334] Unlike a purely HMO system that seeks to lower utilization rates, hospital conglomerations generated more income with high usage rates from providers paid per visit or procedure, e.g., fee-for-service billing.

Congress passed the Health Insurance Portability and Accountability Act (HIPAA) in 1996 with provisions aimed at pushing back against unscrupulous insurance practices. Insurance companies could not deny coverage to enrollees who had another plan within the prior 18 months and who had health conditions existing at time of plan initiation. The Affordable Care Act (ACA) passed in 2010, otherwise known as Obamacare, moved the goalpost on these two items. Insurance companies must now cover all preexisting conditions and plans cannot not be denied to new enrollees if application occurs during open enrollment. Republicans successfully fought to remove the tax penalty levied on uninsured Americans, claiming citizens should not be forced to carry insurance,[335] although what is rarely discussed are the numerous exceptions to this penalty that already existed on Internal Revenue Service Form 8965.

In 1995, the United States spent 13% of its gross domestic production on healthcare. This amount steadily rose to 17% by 2010, the year Obama signed the ACA, when this percentage rate immediately flatlined.[336] After passage of the ACA, the rate of medical care inflation reported by the Bureau of Labor Statistics had not registered such low numbers since the early 1960s.[337] The ACA's overall cost containment worked.

Why did healthcare spending stabilize but insurance premiums balloon after the ACA passed? America's electorate turned against the Democratic Party in the 2016 election in which a key complaint was higher insurance premiums. Voters appeared justified in their anger, until you examine one devilish detail: The Congressional Budget Office estimates that premiums would be even higher without the ACA.[338,339] Even though people complain about the recent surge in premiums, the rate of increase was one-third slower from 2011 to 2016 compared to the 63% surge in premiums from 2001 to 2006 under the Bush Administration. The Democratic Party squandered an opportunity in the 2016 election cycle to highlight how the ACA calmed the rise in both insurance premiums and medical debt.

The Affordable Care Act has saved families from the nightmare scenario of outrageous medical bills. Before the ACA, both insured and uninsured patients would be hit with hospital bills well over $100,000, especially given that insurance companies employed loopholes to deny coverage or imposed coverage limits. Some conditions can lead to lifetime costs well over $1 million.

The ACA put in place out-of-pocket spending limits, and even though these plans require high deductibles and patients with large medical bills may still undergo financial hardship, burdensome medical debt has declined. A survey of bankruptcies in 2007, before the ACA came along, revealed 35% of filers had medical debt over $5,000, and those with insurance coverage who confirmed having an illness incurred average medical expenses of $17,943, an amount well above ACA out-of-pocket spending limits—and these people had health insurance! Without insurance, that medical debt rose to an unbelievable $26,971, which would devastate the median household financially.[340]

Bankruptcy data also fail to tease out medical payments from all financial sources. A family with significant medical bills may leverage a house, run up credit cards, or sell assets to pay down medical bills before entering into bankruptcy, which would underreport the healthcare burden and related financial distress.

Unpaid medical bills are the number-one reason for debt collection calls, but since passage of the ACA, the number of families struggling to pay medical debt has declined over 40%.[341,342] The percentage of Americans contacted by collection agencies because of medical debt declined from 18% to 15%.[343] That may not sound like a big shift, but a 2015 Federal Reserve report discovered that the median out-of-pocket medical debt load fell to $1,200.[344] Lower-income persons now face an average of $1,000 in Medicaid debt, down from $1,600 in 2014 when the ACA took full effect.[345] Conservatives seek to demonize the higher costs that arose post implementation of the ACA. However, total out-of-pocket medical expenses rose only 1.3% in 2014, one of the smallest increases in modern history.[346]

As families faced annual premiums averaging over $19,000 in 2018,[347] it's obvious that the overall cost of healthcare must still decline. At 17% of gross domestic production (GDP), the United States still spends the highest percentage of its economic capital on healthcare compared to all other countries on the planet. Among the developed world, Sweden spends the second most on healthcare at 11.9% of GDP. Many of the European powers spend between 9% and 11% of GDP on healthcare.[348] A major issue with the U.S. healthcare system is that these dollars do not even go toward healthcare, rather administration. In other countries, amounts allocated to administration tend to be much less—in many cases, half as much.

Studies from the prior two decades continue to unearth how the medical establishment spends way too much on bureaucracy, much of which is the result of FFS billing. Hospitals over time show a consistent pattern of spending roughly 25% of revenue on administration.[349,350] Corporate, for-profit healthcare institutions experience admin costs roughly 6% higher than nonprofit-run institutions.[351] The ACA barred insurance companies from spending more than 20% of premiums on administrative tasks. High administrative costs lead to lower healthcare quality, and patient care equally erodes.[352]

In theory, administrative personnel can help contain costs through protocol restraints and utilization reviews, but these constraints may not outweigh the incentive to bill for excess services under a FFS model, along with the time physicians waste wading through a paperwork maze. Studies show that as much as a quarter to one-third of hospital care is unnecessary with FFS billing, demonstrating that HMO plans remove the incentive for excess care.[353] Many studies have shown that hospital services are much lower amid an HMO network, especially when physician remuneration is fixed. Among hospital workers, administrators made $237,000 on average in 2013, whereas primary care physicians made an average of $185,000.[354]

The insurance gamut is a cumbersome affair for primary care clinics. An administrative employee must confirm insurance benefits before a new patient's appointment. If laboratory testing or advanced imaging is needed, more phone calls go out to verify coverage benefits. A referral to a specialist can involve both administrative and physician time exploring who has available appointments within the patient's insurance network. Unfair to patients, an in-network hospital can house an out-of-network physician, leading to a surprise medical bill. The United States has a different paperwork bureaucracy for insurance claims, automobile accidents, workplace injuries, Medicaid, Medicare, and the list goes on. At the end of the day, these payors can deny payment if forms are not completed properly.

TEFRA of 1982 began the process of moving insurance companies away from cost reimbursement over to a revenue-based model of payment per diagnostic codes, greatly increasing the time and overhead costs physicians spend on dealing with billing activity. A 2012 study found that the United States spent $471 billion in billing costs that year alone.[355] Clinics and hospitals send paperwork off to payors, and then these public and private payors shuffle this billing paperwork around—perhaps finding a way to deny payment—before finally remitting a discounted amount. Two 2009 reports estimated that the average physician spends over $70,000 in total costs dealing with insurance matters annually.[356,357] Another study demonstrated how physicians spend over one full workday on administrative tasks each week.[358] Throw into the mix exorbitant costs of malpractice insurance, alongside student loan debt from medical school, and physicians bleed income.

An increasing number of healthcare students are women, and medical residency timing reflects a common age when women start a family. The

Trump Administration reversed 16-hour workday limitations on medical residents, permitting 28-hour shifts. It's detrimental to the health of a fetus and newborn child when a female medical resident is forced to work 28 hours straight.[359] Studies show that exhausted residents make serious mistakes, which prompted this change to 16 hours in the first place. The residency programs, paid for with taxpayer dollars through Medicare, force medical residents to spend 40% of their time on paperwork.[360] Hospitals seem like administrative paperwork factories full of burnt-out residents as opposed to healthcare facilities.

Since passage of the ACA, the budding senior population—the Baby Boomer generation—does not seem to be driving costs higher. Consolidation among hospitals and clinics has led to inefficiencies, especially when a hospital monopolizes diagnostic testing. Reducing hospital bureaucracy and requiring the use of external laboratory and imaging centers could greatly reduce healthcare expenditures. However, a major tie-in to this conversation and a significant area of excess healthcare spending alongside paperwork is overtreatment within the healthcare system. Too many prescriptions for unnecessary laboratory tests, diagnostic images, pharmaceutical drugs, and follow-up visits occur in America's system for several reasons. Healthcare providers get paid per service, they overtreat to defend against the possibility of a lawsuit, hospital administrators define standards of care, and patients want short visits in which lifestyle interventions cannot be sufficiently discussed.

The Dartmouth Atlas Project has tracked medical interventions in the United States for more than two decades. They calculate that 30% of healthcare spending entails unnecessary care, and researchers at Dartmouth say that number may be conservative.[361] The Institute of Medicine reiterated this finding that 30% of healthcare spending—$750 billion back in 2009—which would equate to nearly $1 trillion in 2018-dollar terms, was the result of unnecessary care. In cases of chronic illness or end-of-life care, a greater use of medical interventions actually decreases a person's lifespan.[362]

Overall, medical errors are the third-leading cause of death in America, roughly 250,000 cases per year, behind heart disease and cancer. The needless overtreatment of patients results in more deaths than motor vehicle accidents.[363] The largest share of the medical errors involves medication mismanagement or overmedicating, followed by undertrained or burned-out healthcare providers.[364,365] Almost one-third of the American public uses prescription painkillers in a given year and the death toll from all-cause drug overdose now exceeds 50,000 people per year—again, an amount more than motor vehicle accidents.[366] An excess of opioid prescriptions has fueled an addiction crisis in which patients later turn toward heroin or illegally-obtained opioids, such as Fentanyl.

The blame for unnecessary care must be spread among all stakeholders, including hospital administration, healthcare providers, and patients. Hospitals look for ways to boost revenue, defining treatment protocols or recommending expensive in-house procedures, imaging, or therapies. For example, the United States maintains one of the highest rates of Cesarean sections among industrialized countries, or roughly 32% of all births end with surgery[367]. The World Health Organization had told the United States to reduce the proportion of Cesarean sections. Much of Europe experiences half this rate, but all too often, hospital administration defines the care doctors provide in America. In a fee-for-service system, a standard of care that involves surgery provides hospitals with more revenue; the incentives encourage overtreating patients.

To seemingly address patient concerns and sidestep legal problems from insufficient care, healthcare providers often overprescribe drugs or offer referrals to expensive specialists. Equally so, patients push back against treating disease with lifestyle or dietary interventions. Medication and surgery have become the primary treatment approaches, even when a lifestyle change or healthier diet would act as a long-term, inexpensive solution.

Patients rarely ask: "Do I really need this procedure or drug? What are my alternatives?" In theory, doctors should communicate all treatment alternatives per state law, but lifestyle or dietary options are not regularly discussed. I spoke to a cardiologist once about his advocation for dietary changes. He mentioned how patients would get released from the hospital after major heart surgery and go right back to old habits. He liked to give dietary advice, often recommended it, but he expressed disillusionment over the low rate of commitment.

Doctors really want to help patients, and a little pill is a straightforward way to tackle a health concern. However, drugs rarely cure a health problem completely. The patient remains in a state of managed disease, which can be very expensive over a person's lifetime. Certain conditions like schizophrenia, type 1 diabetes, genetic disorders, and other *incurable* diseases require ongoing drug management, without question, but the modern human seems to face an increasing number of *curable* inflammatory diseases related to dietary habits and poor lifestyle choices.

Conservatives rail against the "nanny" state and toss insults at anyone trying to tax unhealthy food and drink, but society bears a significant economic cost when someone drinks soda, smokes, devours fast food, or chugs beer. Conservatives preach individual responsibility, but very irresponsible behaviors drive up healthcare costs for everyone. As much as 20% of healthcare expenditures can be traced back to smoking, drinking alcohol, inactivity, and excess body weight.[368,369] So-called sin taxes must be considered. The upfront cost of a junk food tax, anti-smoking initiative, or wellness program can lower society's healthcare expenditures overall, fueling a fair environment for Americans already making healthy choices.

The Affordable Care Act (a.k.a Obamacare) signed into law in 2010 made strides toward compensating doctors for longer visits so lifestyle counseling could take place. Section 2713 of the ACA requires coverage of immunizations, health screenings, and well-woman visits. That sounds great, but over 70% of medical schools do not meet the minimum course hours for nutrition; at 25 hours, this minimum is already paltry.[370] The medical establishment can refer to other licensed practitioners such as osteopaths, naturopaths, chiropractors, or registered dieticians, who study nutrition to a greater extent, but medical doctors often overlook or refuse to make these referrals.

Switzerland, a country with a strong embrace of private capitalism similar to the United States, enjoys a low-cost healthcare system dominated by private insurance. In fact, the United States incorporated a larger portion of its healthcare system into government agencies since passage of Medicare and Medicaid in 1965. How can the Swiss keep costs low despite allowing free-market health insurance to dominate the system? The Swiss model mixes nonprofit basic insurance with profit-based plan supplements. To contain costs, patients incur higher copayments for a brand-name drug when a generic alternative exists. The insurance industry in Switzerland monitors for overtreatment and can force repayment of unnecessary care.[371] As an example, and one that may sound absurd by American standards, the Swiss Medical Board advocates against annual and biannual mammograms, citing high cost, harm, and the potential for incorrect diagnoses.[372]

Similar to the insurance mandate seen in Switzerland and the one initiated with the Obama-era Affordable Care Act in the United States, Japanese citizens are also required to obtain health insurance. Unlike the United States, both Switzerland and Japan erect a base of nonprofit payors into their systems. In Japan, unused revenue gets carried forward to the next year instead of being distributed to investors. Patients see doctors more often, they undergo more diagnostic imaging, and they boast the longest average hospital stays in the developed world. Yet despite the higher utilization rates, costs remain low in Japan, even in the face of a surging senior population with a long lifespan.[373] Doctors make less in Japan, and that may sound disadvantageous, but American physicians lose money to clinic administration, student loans, and malpractice insurance.

Mortality rates of mothers giving birth are almost three times higher in the United States than both Switzerland and Japan; child mortality is roughly twice as much.[374] Even with its insurance-based system, Switzerland ranked third among 195 nations for healthcare access and quality, as noted in a 2015 report funded by the Bill and Melinda Gates Foundation—Japan ranked 11th. The United States, with the highest costs per person of any country, ranked 35th.[375] The chance of an American dying from a health condition between the ages of 30 and 70 is 13%, according to the World Health Organization. For the Swiss and Japanese, it's 8.8% and 8.7%, respectively.[376]

Since 2008, Japan has imposed mandatory screening for metabolic issues related to obesity on anyone between age 40 to 74. Test results above a certain threshold require referral for lifestyle counseling.[377] Japan regiments aggressive prevention measures that many Americans might consider authoritarian, but as obesity rates rise above 30% in the United States, only 3% of Japan's population is considered excessively overweight.[378]

In case you haven't noticed, America is not a bastion of health despite leading the world in healthcare spending. A person experiencing a heart attack gets placed in a costly ambulance, undergoes an expensive surgery, and stays in a $1,800-per-night hospital, but America has not mastered preventing this heart attack altogether. The same goes for type 2 diabetes, atrial fibrillation, thyroid disease, depression, anxiety, back pain, and so many other conditions kept in a chronic state of management without a curative resolution.

A major cause of modern curable disease, and a driver of metabolic syndrome, obesity, and type 2 diabetes, is fructose. It sweetens beverages and processed foods but it also fattens the liver, forms unwanted lipids, overstimulates hunger, and converts into uric acid. After successfully turning corn sugars into high-fructose corn syrup in the 1970s, consumption of fructose steadily reached 150 pounds per year for the average American, especially because the U.S. government has spent over $100 billion on corn subsidies since 1995.[379] Assuming a typical apple contains 10 grams of fructose, 150 pounds of sugar is equivalent to eating 3,400 apples per year or roughly nine apples every day. Because most people consume potatoes as their main source of vegetable, you would need to eat approximately 370 potatoes every day to consume the same volume of fructose as what food producers shove into processed foods and soda.[380] It's simply not possible to overconsume fructose on a healthy diet.

A University of Cambridge review study estimated that sugar-sweetened beverages account for 18% of diabetic cases,[381] costing America's healthcare system an estimated $44 billion. That figure only looks at diabetes from sweetened beverages. Concentrated fructose is found in processed foods apart from soda and a high-fructose diet fuels other health conditions beyond type 2 diabetes.

It can be expensive to buy fruits and vegetables, therefore all too often, people seek low-cost calories, loading up on an excess of unhealthy foods. Research demonstrates that Americans can save money when they focus on cost per nutrient or price per adequate portion size.[382] Low-cost food that lacks nutrients ends up being overconsumed, and families spend just as much overeating cheap calories than if they purchased nutrient-dense food in the first place.

As society shifts to producing higher-nutrient fruits and vegetables, an economy of scale can be achieved; that should bring down costs for high-quality food. In addition, the U.S. Department of Agriculture estimates that 30-40% of food simply goes to waste, which drives up costs for everyone.[383] Food lays in the fields and orchards, rotting because of anti-immigration policies; for example, anti-immigration policies that led to labor shortages cost Santa Barbara County $13 million in unpicked crops in 2016.[384] Americans want large portion sizes at restaurants, causing uneaten food to be thrown away; meanwhile, Americans struggle to afford produce.

The Centers for Disease Control and Prevention (CDC) reports that health problems result in $225 billion of lost productivity each year, and the obesity epidemic largely drives this number.[385,386] Productivity levels decline when employees report to work encumbered by back pain, headaches, fatigue, depression, and so on. In many cases, a person struggling with physical and mental health issues could heal if granted a short medical leave, but often employers choose to fire ill workers instead, resulting in a mix of increased stress, financial difficulties, and lost medical benefits.

Employers that adopt wellness programs can witness a dramatic turnaround in absenteeism and experience productivity gains, but work overload must be equally addressed. An overload of stress can drive anxiety, bipolar episodes, and depression, along with fuel a desire to eat junk food. Mental and physical health concerns that go undiagnosed and untreated all too often lead to lower incomes.

To be honest, America is not really a place for health. Stress-inducing workloads and car-oriented infrastructure promote unhealthy lifestyles while American culture underappreciates nutrition. Finland ranks high in global education but spends 30% less per student than the United States. The country links its success, boasting the highest college matriculation rate in Europe, to outdoor play and specialized programs.[387] The U.S. Department of Agriculture made great strides under the Obama Administration to fund school gardens and farm-to-school programs, offering a mix of outdoor activity and nutritious foods. Experts in this arena note that kids who are exposed to vegetables quickly pick up the habit of eating them. The medical community knows that the brain functions better with physical activity, such as outdoor play and gardening.[388]

School garden programs teach young kids about healthy eating and help to form lifelong relationships with nutrient-dense vegetables. Greater implementation of bike infrastructure in a community reduces harmful vehicle emissions and car accidents while providing physical activity. Healthcare solutions must go beyond the halls of medical institutions and look at the broader determinants of health.

The Centers for Medicare and Medicaid Services (CMS) and regional health plans are trying to encourage accountable care matched with bundled payments, moving the federal system away from President Reagan's 1982 fee-for-service approach. Cost bundling means an integrated team is paid according to a target amount per health condition. This payment system reduces the incentive to recommend unnecessary services while it motivates successful health outcomes.[389]

Accountable care refers to using an integrated model of specialists who coordinate a patient's healthcare right from the start as opposed to making random referrals to other healthcare providers and asking patients to jump through burdensome scheduling hoops over a long timeframe. In Seattle, patients reporting back pain at the Virginia Mason Spine Clinic first meet with a team of specialists. The upfront cost of an integrated appointment cuts the average patient's missed workdays in half, the clinic can see 60% more patients, and the overall costs are lower.[390]

In 2011, Medicare began a new initiative to expand the "bundled payment" concept, linking payments for the various services received during an episode of care. The Centers for Medicare & Medicaid Services (CMS) Innovation Center tests payment and healthcare delivery models in order to reduce costs and improve health outcomes. CMS has rolled out this bundled payment model nationally through the Bundled Payment for Care Improvement (BPCI) initiative, Comprehensive Care for Joint Replacement (CJR) program, and Oncology Care Model.[391] A bundled payment acts like a capitation system in which hospitals or clinics receive a fixed amount of money for each patient's care episode, but CMS is attempting to include quality of services and outcomes into the mix.

Value-based models resemble accountable care plans in which both apply cost bundling to pay for services. A value-based approach goes one step further to address key determinants of health such as housing security, food access, and patient education. Outreach to other community services may form part of a patient's health plan, similar to working with a social service aid at a hospital now. Section 3001 of the Affordable Care Act kickstarts an experimentation phase of value-based models starting with five programs.

» End Stage Renal Disease Quality Incentive Program (ESRD QIP)
» Hospital Value-Based Purchasing (VBP) Program
» Hospital Readmission Reduction Program (HRRP)
» Hospital Acquired Conditions (HAC) Reduction Program
» Value Modifier (VM) Program

In addition, the Medicare Access and CHIP Reauthorization Act of 2015 (MACRA) promotes this shift toward value-based reimbursement with a new payment approach called the Quality Payment Program. Hospitals and clinics earn rewards for the long-term health of patients and face penalties for hospital readmissions or unresolved health complaints.

A care cycle starts with preventative measures before a person even sees a doctor. As patients come in for treatment at a hospital or clinic, a value-based model uses a collaborative, team-based approach to addressing the disease itself, along with potential comorbidities. For example, a person with type 2 diabetes should be reviewed for kidney, eye, and foot issues. The goal is to reward healthcare providers for outcome *quality* as opposed to service *quantity*.

Utah Alliance for the Determinants of Health provides an example of how community organizations can work together to reduce healthcare costs and prevent disease. The Alliance works to raise health levels through programs that address "housing instability, utility needs, food insecurity, interpersonal violence, and transportation needs."[392] The future of healthcare involves a truly value-based system that looks at the full-care cycle, not just one appointment with a doctor.

Increasing access to education and paying sufficient wages help people afford food, obtain stable housing, and enjoy positive mental health. More focus must be placed on food access, physical movement, and environmental toxins to prevent diseases of modern living. Community investments in social institutions apart from healthcare may very well have the greatest impact on disease prevention. Consider how 90% of type 2 diabetes and 70% of colon cancer could be prevented with dietary changes, smoking cessation, decreased alcohol use, and physical activity.[393]

Europeans have mastered the "built" society, designing infrastructure around physical movement with parks, walkways, pedestrian zones, and bike trails. Continued small investments in communities and workplaces can lead to significant long-term healthcare savings. As the saying goes, a local, pesticide-free apple per day keeps the doctor away. That's coming from a native Washingtonian. To maximize health, eat real food, drink water, meditate before bed, engage in moderate exercise, and balance work commitments.

OVERWORKED

Not long ago, young children worked in dangerous factory conditions for the benefit of corporate profit, an act that would be largely decried today. Yet the movement to ban child labor in the United States faced opposition. Two early laws, passed at the start of the 20th century, were overturned by the Supreme Court, prompting Franklin Delano Roosevelt to threaten stacking the Court with new justices in the 1930s beyond the standard nine members.[394,395] The largely pro-business Supreme Court became more favorable to upholding social legislation as a result, finally allowing passage of the Fair Labor Standards Act (FLSA) in 1938 to end child labor and implement a minimum wage. However, the initial FLSA passed in 1938 did not extend to all industries and it set a low minimum wage rate.[396]

Even back in the early twentieth century, proponents of child labor and low wages voiced the same talking point about needing cheap labor so companies could remain competitive. Antilabor elites used slurs like "communist" and "socialist" against President Roosevelt.[397] The cabal of multinational firms sought to convince the American electorate that a vote for higher wages and labor protections would somehow unravel the entire economic system. The Great Depression helped change public sentiment toward child labor, wishing that children enroll in primary school to save jobs for the adults.

The United States has an archaic set of labor laws, mostly put in place because of the dire economic conditions during the Great Depression, but these labor laws ignore the reality of a modern, high-tech economy. Of importance, there are still no maximum work hour limits in the United States. There is an economic myth that suggests high work hours lead to greater output. In truth, the growth of high-quality output is mainly the result of modern technologies integrated into the workflow. Scores of research papers came out as far back as 100 years ago highlighting the merits of shorter workweeks despite skepticism from factory owners.[398] We must move away from thinking that long hours translate into greater output and understand instead how investments in technology, process improvement, and incentive pay drive higher output per hour. As we achieve productivity gains through innovative practices, we have more room to boost wages and provide for personal life balance.

Countries that clock high work hours often experience low economic output and rank low in global gross domestic production (GDP) per capita. In 2018, Mexico led the industrialized world with the highest average work hours at 2,148 hours per year (41 hours per week) but ranked 74th in global output, according to the World Bank.[399,400] In Japan, where work hours surpass those of the United States, the economy has remained stagnate for decades and its society battles with an epidemic of death caused by overwork, a term the Japanese call *karoshi*.[401]

American business culture overlooks how long hours start to become counterproductive. Excessively long work schedules begin to compromise a worker's ability to rethink job duties and innovate processes. Only through innovation will an economy achieve greater output per hour and offer consumers access to a higher standard of living. If all U.S. workers drive up their level of production, consumers enjoy a broader volume of quality products and services. Every economic model that explains wage levels links an increased ability to pay high wages with investment or innovation, not microeconomic demand and supply factors. If companies exploit cheap labor in lieu of investing in innovative practices, a low output environment is guaranteed and companies will struggle to remain competitive.

People think that innovation, especially manufacturing automation, leads to widespread job losses, but economic models point to how investment money, much of which is used to afford new technologies and equipment, encourages employment. Robotics, computerization, and so forth result in greater output per worker as opposed to a replacement of jobs altogether. Farm equipment moved society away from agrarian work onto other tasks as opposed to causing permanent unemployment.

In 2014, a one-year experiment got underway at a retirement home in the town of Gothenburg, Sweden, to test the theory that workers can achieve similar levels of output at 30 hours per week compared to the standard 40-hour workweek.[402] Gothenburg's City Council pushed for this experiment, and preliminary findings suggest there are key reasons why a 40-hour workweek may not optimize output. Many of the study participants asserted that they waste less time at work and feel more refreshed due to the shorter workweek. Long-standing employees with a significant accumulation of skills and intellectual capital seek to remain in the workforce longer when faced with a shorter workweek schedule.[403] For example, employees who feel overworked may call in sick more often as a method of boosting personal leave. What's the point of a 40-hour workweek if employees waste time on social media or retire early?

A 2014 Gallup Poll reports that a staggering 40% of the American workforce submits to working 50 hours or more per week, with as many as 18% working an extreme 60+ hours.[404] In contrast, only one percent of the workforce in Sweden works 50 hours or more in an average week.[405] Almost no one there is forced to sacrifice time with family or personal events for the benefit of corporate profit.

In 2018, New Zealand financial firm Perpetual Guardian ran an eight-week experiment to study the impact working only four days per week would have on productivity. The company's entire staff of 240 employees participated in the trial and compensation levels remained the same. Test results highlighted how worker productivity, job engagement, and customer service improved. The number of employees reporting less stress grew by 7%, and 24% more confirmed having a better work-life balance.[406]

Since 2000, France has set in place a 35-hour workweek across the country. Many pundits misunderstand the nature of this law. An employee who goes beyond 35 hours simply accrues more vacation time or receives overtime pay. The law even applies to professional workers such as lawyers. Often, more than half the workforce receives overtime pay in a given week, clocking an average of 40 hours—five hours above the target work limit.[407] A shortened workweek may not be ideal for certain industries or lead to better economic outcomes in every situation, but France solves this dilemma by simply providing workers with more vacation time or overtime pay if they go beyond the work hour limit.

At the turn of the 19th century, organized labor in the United States fought to minimize work hours to 40 per week. An amount of work above this threshold would trigger overtime pay, creating a disincentive for employers to compel more worktime. However, the FLSA has several categories of work considered ineligible for overtime pay. Job roles that trigger overtime rules mainly involve physical labor, but as modern society migrates to computer work, a greater percentage of the workforce falls outside the scope of FLSA overtime rules. Combined with a lack of maximum hour limits, employers have an incentive to keep piling on the work, ignoring the need for personal time.[408]

In a political atmosphere where conservative leaders espouse rhetoric about family values, these same politicians do nothing to address the consequences on the family from excess work. Compared to other developed nations, the United States clocked average workweek hours of 1,790 in 2015. Yet in Germany, where workers earn more per hour and enjoy a greater range of benefits, their 2015 average workweek was only 1,371 hours[409]—that equates to one full day less every week of the year, and Germany still outproduces the United States.

The United States has the largest trade deficit in manufactured goods ever seen on the planet, registered as –$891 billion in 2018, outsourcing much of its factory jobs to Mexico, China, and Southeast Asia.[410] Germany ran the largest trade surplus in the world that same year, amounting to +$294 billion.[411] Countries with annual work hours similar to Germany, roughly 1,400 per year, can produce upwards of 50% more per hour, which translates to around 30% more output than the United States after adjusting for the shorter workweeks.[412] Innovation leads to greater output per hour, and European countries use the productivity gains to work fewer hours. Why work 60 hours per week in a constant state of burnout only to watch as American manufacturing crumbles under the weight of outsourcing and disinvestment?

A high percentage of American workers toil for 50 or more hours per week and long hours increase stress and burnout rates with dire consequences. The National Highway Traffic Safety Administration reports that more than 800 traffic deaths each year are the result of drowsy drivers.[413] A *Harvard Business Review* article states, "We now know that 24 hours without sleep or a week of sleeping four or five hours a night induces an impairment equivalent to a blood alcohol level of 0.1%"[414] Commercial truck drivers must limit road time to 70 hours per week. While that is an improvement over the prior 82-hour limit, it is still a truckload of time.[415]

A safe work environment is essential, especially among truck drivers, airline pilots, and chemical producers. Someone working 60 or more hours per week will face compromised brain function. In turn, the person may not offer an employer peak mental performance—the type of thoughtfulness required to rework processes, insert new technologies into the workflow, and simply keep a workplace safe. America has decided that burnout proves a person's self-worth in a workaholic, consumption-driven culture, but long workhours result in a chronic state of underperformance, fatigue, emotional declines, and sleep disturbances.[416] We have this scenario in which workers feel obliged to clock long hours, but chronic burnout diminishes innovation; meanwhile, health issues surface as a result of being overworked. Many employers offer no sick or personal leave to allow employees sufficient rest to hit the reset button.

The independent nonprofit China Labor Watch (CLW) began investigating labor violations inside China in 2000. To meet demand, Chinese firms like to house a large workforce for surge production volume. An American firm will place an order with a Chinese supplier, and the supplier will immediately require long overtime schedules to meet the deadline given. Then, workers will rest idle until another order comes through the pipeline. Chinese law imposes a 36-hour limit on overtime hours on a monthly basis.[417,418] Chinese firms argue that between weeks with downtime and other weeks with long overtime schedules, the work-hour limit is respected within the monthly timeframe.

Apple, Inc. has been implicated in the controversy over long work hours due to labor reports put out against its suppliers. Apple does not manufacture its products directly in China but outsources production largely to Foxconn Technology Group, Jabil Green Point, and Pegatron Corporation. CLW found that Pegatron Corp. required workers to clock long hours above the maximum imposed by Chinese law.[419] Workers at Jabil Green Point earned $1.82 per hour in 2015, equal to what the average Chinese worker earned a decade earlier, and long work hours above the legal limit were discovered at one of their factories as well.[420]

News articles highlight long work hours at Foxconn with low commensurate pay and challenging living conditions. A report by the Chinese media drew attention to Foxconn's requirement that student interns work overnight in order to graduate school.[421] Foxconn promised to improve wages and work conditions but Apple shifted more production to other, lower-cost facilities. It appears that paying someone a living wage weighs too heavily on profit margins. Apple reported 2015 comprehensive profit of nearly $52 billion,[422] sufficient to give all 1.6 million workers[423] in its supply chain an annual bonus of $32,479.

These electronics suppliers also make parts for Sony, Microsoft, Nintendo, and other firms, but labor rights organizations like to scrutinize Apple. Labor watch groups protest Apple suppliers going beyond the national work-hour limit, turning situations into human rights exposé because a clear metric is overstepped. Yet the United States has no federal overtime maximum, and a large percentage of the U.S. population works at a rate that would violate Chinese law.

The *New York Times* printed an article in 2012 cataloguing numerous cases of death, suicide, and injury at facilities in China. In one such incident, aluminum powder used to polish iPads collected on the floor of a Foxconn facility in Chengdu. The dust, a highly hazardous compound, exploded on May 13, 2011, killing four and injuring 18 people.[424,425] As much as this story is alarming and newsworthy, work conditions inside U.S. firms are oftentimes worse.

The *New York Times* and labor watch groups can point a finger at Foxconn and Apple for deaths and explosions, but the U.S. Chemical Safety Board heads investigations over worse events at U.S. firms. A few months before the explosion at the Chengdu factory in China, five workers were killed in a dust explosion in Gallatin, Tennessee.[426] Chemical explosions occur every year inside the United States with limited media attention and zero human rights controversy.

Every seven seconds, a worker is injured in the United States, representing 4.6 million incidents per year. The loss of work or slowdown in function equates to 104 million days of lost production.[427] Men who missed workdays due to an injury were 72% more likely to die from suicide. In general, people who must rest at home because of a workplace injury have higher rates of depression and drug use, the latter fueling the growing opioid crisis.[428,429] Injury prevention is key to protecting the American public from serious long-term health issues.

A person made to work despite an injury can experience a worsening of complaints. As health deteriorates, the American public ends up with a more expensive healthcare bill down the road. If a worker cannot fully recover and enters disability, then the economic system pays a fortune through social assistance remuneration and the complete loss of output.

The Norwegian government offers partial compensation for workers with health problems.[430] The United States has very little middle ground—either a worker must submit to the long hours of a job or seek full disability. A partial disability keeps a person in the workforce paying taxes, offsetting the cost of disability assistance. Later, the person might return to a normal schedule after the health condition improves. The community spends less overall for healthcare and social assistance when people can recover from injuries or illness. These types of wage subsidies can be seen all over Europe, and they give injured workers a chance to add value to the economy.[431]

Instead, the United States allows firms to simply fire employees with health complaints, pushing people onto the social safety net or toward a life of homelessness or imprisonment. Only Montana allows employees a probationary period to make improvements; termination must be for "good cause" after probation ends.[432] All other states give companies the right to fire employees "at will" without any cause or forewarning.

The United States lacks solutions for workers with short-term health conditions, and this comes with consequences for everyone. Take, for example, a contagious infection such as influenza or Covid-19. More than 60% of private-sector employees receive zero sick leave benefits,[433] especially among lower skilled positions, and these workers often lose pay if they take sick leave. So, the sick worker stays at work and grinds along in a sluggish state, underperforming by as much as one-third normal productivity levels, and introduces the infection to the entire workforce. Coworkers take that illness home to their kids. A worker who is sick or overworked could trigger errors that negatively impact a customer, or the virus can spread to customers directly. More than half of restaurant workers present to work when sick.[434] Would you like some highly contagious virus with your pizza?

A research paper dubbed the American Productivity Audit calculated that sick workers who show up to work cost companies $150 billion annually. The American Medical Association found that arthritis, headaches, and back pain make up one-third of these costs. Companies attempt to save money on the front end by starving workers of benefits, but a small investment in sick time permits a worker to fully heal and later present to work better able to engage in productive activities.[435]

The number-one killer of Americans is heart disease, and prolonged sitting or standing at work without contrasting movement places a heavy burden on the cardiovascular system. One medical study found that immobility lasting three hours or more negatively impacts arterial function.[436] A medical review paper noted that sitting contributes to type 2 diabetes,[437] which carries myriad comorbidities and can exacerbate heart disease. Lack of movement can also provoke back pain. The medical community recommends changing positions frequently throughout the day intermixing standing and sitting with breaks in between to walk around.[438]

A company that wants to sit an employee down in a chair for 15 hours straight and squeeze as much work as humanly possible out of that person ignores all the economic benefits a "happy and healthy" worker can impart. After a certain point, spending an increasing number of hours at work starts to create burnout and lack of focus. The human body can only endure so many hours of sitting in one place or standing at a piece of equipment before the attention span wanes, and this loss of focus can result in errors, inefficiency, or injuries.

The Fair Labor Standards Act (FLSA) does not require meal or rest breaks, and a majority of states have not stepped in to require meal breaks either. Only eight states require rest breaks and 20 states offer meal breaks (usually 30 minutes) for working adults,[439] leaving 30 states with employees who must quickly shove down food in between serving customers. One survey revealed how 86% of workers feel that an increase in breaks would help boost productivity. Forty-one percent of respondents reported feeling exhausted, but the majority of the workers considered taking breaks too difficult, with 25% saying they do not even break for mealtime.[440] American business culture demands unnatural sacrifice from employees to where many barely have time to eat.

Another survey indicated that when workers do take a lunch break, half get 30 minutes or less.[441] This quick pause in work may be insufficient to rejuvenate the body. Instead of putting stock in quality of life and using innovative practices to work smarter, we sacrifice our health just to work longer hours. We attempt to impress our bosses through a commitment to being overworked only to walk in one day faced with a pink slip and a canned speech about how the company needs to outsource jobs to remain competitive.

We all enjoy access to more products and services than 100 years ago because of automation, process improvement, computerization, faster delivery speeds, and fabrication upgrades. The collective umbrella these topics fall under is referred to as innovation; subsequently, an underpaid, overworked, and disenfranchised employee does not innovate. High pay levels with strong benefits lead to loyal workers who remain fully engaged in their jobs. In turn, all consumers and companies benefit from an increased volume of high-quality output that loyal workers produce.

According to the Center for Economic and Policy Research, "The United States is the only advanced economy in the world that does not guarantee its workers paid vacation days and paid holidays."[442] Even when Americans receive two-weeks of paid vacation, 40% do not use it all, leaving on average three personal leave days unused each year.[443] Many workers use vacation time to simply clean their homes, run errands, or visit a doctor.

Europeans often receive four to six weeks of paid vacation each summer, and this time spent away from work ends up prompting greater levels of output overall as workers get a chance to reflect on their job roles and seek new avenues for innovation. European firms embrace modern manufacturing techniques, permitting higher pay and shorter workweeks. The European public profits from more personal time whereas their American counterparts slave away all week, only to watch as per capita output continues to decline in relation to the European economies. The American public works harder to achieve less output, and this leads to overall lower pay available to the middle class.

The Family and Medical Leave Act signed into law in 1993 offers 12 weeks of *unpaid* leave among larger companies with 50 or more employees, which means parents at smaller companies and the economically poor are unable to take leave for health or caretaking reasons. Nearly 40% of the workforce is not covered under the FMLA; among those covered, almost half say they cannot afford to take unpaid leave.[444]

The Fair Labor Standards Act, passed long ago in 1938, needs critical updates that reflect the modern workplace. An ever-growing number of well-educated women continue to pour into the workforce. Companies, in turn, benefit whenever female workers can undertake a long-term commitment to building a career. Women need genuine protections against sexual harassment and extended paid leave for childbirth or adoption. An increasing number of births involve complications or result in surgery, such as a Cesarean section.

A lack of childbirth leave ignores the needs of a developing child. A practice termed kangaroo care reveals that an infant's neural development depends on human contact with a parent or guardian.[445] Asking a new parent to immediately report back to work negatively impacts the long-term mental health and intelligence of a child.

Childbirth leave is a necessary price to pay in order to ensure the welfare of a newborn child. Moreover, it empowers parents to fully embrace family life. After Major League Baseball made childbirth leave available to male players, online trolls and radio pundits ridiculed the men attempting to take parental leave.[446] The United States can no longer afford to embrace toxic masculinity. Childbirth leave affords both men and women an important human experience. Why would people toil long hours at work in a state of unproductive burnout when they could be home with their newborn infant?

California already enacted paid family leave offering eligible employees up to six weeks of limited compensation. A smattering of companies offers longer periods of paid family leave.[447] The upper managers at Patagonia, based in Ventura, CA, explain that paid leave lowers costs overall. Women who receive paid childbirth leave almost all return to work, eliminating turnover costs. Parents have access to on-site daycare after the childbirth leave ends, and Patagonia finds that this resource increases worker engagement.[448] American managers fear compensation costs but a dissatisfied workforce can massacre customer revenue and drive inefficiency into the heart of job performance.

Sweden's paid childbirth leave seems overly expensive with 480 days but the country supplants other costs. As the European Union reports, countries reduce healthcare costs when parents can tend to a newborn for a sufficient length of time.[449] Parents who receive paid childbirth leave rely less on public assistance and unemployment benefits. A higher percentage return to work later, adding to the country's production volume and tax base.

The Swedish economy continues to move upward in global ranks despite these robust labor benefits. They had a weak episode in the 1970s but conservatives and liberals in the country banned together and began applying economic research to develop strong policy measures. Norway already far surpasses the United States in per capita production. Conservatives exclaim that these countries can undertake unique social policies because they are small and homogenous, but the United States is organized into 50 individual states and six territories, many of which are small and homogenous. States like Colorado, Ohio, and Minnesota—the list is really long—have small, homogenous populations comparable to northern Europe.

Conservatives rail against socialism in Scandinavian countries but few have ever stepped foot in the northern region and even fewer understand the political culture. Touted as one of the best medical-leave benefits in the world, Sweden's 480-day policy should not be blamed on socialism. Sweden faces a duality of political forces between liberal and conservative parties much like the United States, and history has given Sweden myriad conservative prime ministers. Sweden's robust childbirth leave comes from the fact that roughly 46% of parliamentary officials are women.[450] The United States falls short at only 24% as of the 116th Congress,[451] and it is little wonder why a majority-male Congress has not passed more laws that benefit women.

At later stages of pregnancy and once paternity leave ends, parents should receive condensed work schedules limited to 30 hours per week. New parents are often sleep compromised. The shorter workweek would permit more time with the child and greater opportunity to sleep. Pilot programs in Sweden demonstrate that working only 30 hours per week can lead to comparable output as a 40-hour workweek mainly because employees report feeling more rested and able to keenly focus for the full 30 hours as opposed to feeling sluggish and wasting time within a 40-hour schedule.[452]

The American public struggles to understand the relevance of shorter workweeks despite the rise of a modern, brain-based economy. Humans must refresh their minds and come to work each day with optimal mental clarity. In the meantime, the family unit benefits from a reduction in work hours, especially in the wake of adoption or childbirth. This incessant urge to push employees to the edge of their limits ignores the modern reality that output levels flourish when workers use their brains to innovate. We no longer toil alongside children in a factory or plow a field using a donkey. Times have changed and the primary goal of U.S. businesses must now be innovation—not long hours.[453]

As kids grow older and parents resume normal work schedules, households face an increased need for daycare services. The United States spends a negligible amount on childcare assistance compared to other industrialized nations, placing a heavy financial burden on working parents.

Over one in four families with young children spends more than 10% of gross income on childcare; among low-income families, that rate averages nearly 20%.[454] Childcare assistance is not available to many low-income parents, and when states do provide benefits, mandatory copayments often exceed 7.2% of income.[455]

The American dream has morphed into the process of waking early, dropping off kids at an expensive childcare center, clocking nine hours on a timecard, driving home through bumper-to-bumper traffic, rapidly eating processed food in front of the TV, and then spending one hour with the kids before saying goodnight. Why sacrifice time with family only to encounter suboptimal work performance?

Imagine an economic environment where companies remain profitable, pay workers more, and extend mandatory personal leave. Fortunately, that scenario exists among all industrialized countries apart from the United States—no need to theorize about the impact of better labor laws. Americans achieve less output when they forego sleep, sacrifice their health, and accept low wages. The attempt to grow an economy through long hours, outsourcing, and low taxes has ransacked America's manufacturing base and drained the middle class both financially and emotionally.

RETIREMENT CRISIS

Defined guaranteed retirement plans—ones offering long-term, set benefits in retirement years—came to life in limited scope during the late 1800s. Two key events inspired their use starting in 1921. The Metropolitan Life Insurance Company started to offer group contracts and the Internal Revenue Service confirmed that investment gains inside retirement accounts would receive tax exemption until such time as amounts were distributed to beneficiaries in retirement years.[456]

The Roaring '20s spawned a stock market bubble with help from interest-only mortgages. As the Great Depression struck the financial system, Congress passed the Home Owner's Loan Act in 1933, forming a government institution to take up failing interest-only mortgages and convert them into fixed 15-year amortized loans.[457] History books fail to shed light on how interest-only mortgages caused widespread bank failures 80 years before the 2008 housing collapse.

In 1935, Congress passed the Social Security Act, causing some companies to move away from providing retirement plans. Guaranteed retirement plans came roaring back a decade later during World War II. Wartime caps on wages forced companies to use employee benefits, such as pension plans and health insurance coverage, as a mechanism to recruit workers.[458]

This timeframe between WWII and the 1980s bore witness to a highly stable economic environment. No elaborate bubbles formed and actuarial tables could easily predict how much companies needed to set aside for guaranteed payouts years later. The number of private-sector workers participating in guaranteed pension plans grew steadily until, by the late

1980s, almost half of the nongovernmental workforce enjoyed employer-sponsored retirement benefits.[459] It appeared an increasing percentage of the workforce was poised to live out retirement years in a financially sound manner, especially after passage of the Employee Retirement Income Security Act (ERISA) of 1974, which bolstered the reliability of benefit guarantees. However, events starting in the 1980s foreshadowed the demise of stock market stability and a guaranteed retirement along with it.

The banking industry faced tight restrictions for 50 years after the Great Depression until Congress began a pattern of deregulation in the early days of the Reagan Administration. This deregulation spree from 1980 to 1982 opened the savings and loan industry to higher risk investment choices such as real estate, stock certificates, and junk bonds. Savings and loan institutions had mainly stuck to reliable fixed-rate mortgages as their core means of revenue. In 1980, mortgages represented 80% of the assets held by savings and loan institutions. That number dropped to 56% by 1986.[460]

President Ronald Reagan believed the savings and loans institutions should figure out their own solutions without government intervention, embracing a *laissez-faire*, conservative ideology. In a few short years, an industry already faced with mounting bankruptcies quickly doubled in size due to a relaxed regulatory environment.[461] The migration of savings and loans institutions away from stable mortgages, combined with deregulation and high growth, would set the stage for a slow-rolling, decade-long financial crisis—the first of the major boom-bust cycles.

In 1987, economist Alan Greenspan wrote a letter confirming that assets held at the Lincoln Savings and Loan company were safe. Shortly afterward, Greenspan became the chair of the Federal Reserve System, and two years later, Lincoln Savings and Loan went bankrupt, costing taxpayers $3.5 billion.[462] The overall government bailout of the entire savings and loan industry would cost taxpayers an estimated $160 billion.[463] Greenspan, a man who falsely touted the savings and loan system as safe, would control the nation's money supply for the next 20 years.

On October 19, 1987, two months after Greenspan took over as chairman of the Federal Reserve, the value of the New York Stock Exchange dropped 22.6% in one day. This crash entailed the new age of risk and rise of bubble-fed policy. The blame for this freefall in stock value was laid at the feet of novel derivative instruments combined with automated trading mechanisms. No matter the cause, Greenspan swept in like a superhero with

Federal Reserve System money to save the day. The Federal Reserve bought up Treasury bonds and the central bank target interest rate was lowered.[464] Greenspan's swift reaction helped stabilize the markets in the short term, but it created a shift in thinking inside the investment community—that the Federal Reserve would bail out Wall Street in the future.[465] The Federal Reserve's quick fix to stock market malaise also meant this one institution, headed by Greenspan, would hold too much power over the nation's economy, especially when disaster struck.

As much as $20 billion was removed from retirement plans in the 1980s.[466] Hedge funds were borrowing money to take over companies and then raiding pension assets to pay off the original loans—this process is referred to as a leveraged buyout. The largest reversion occurred in 1986 when Exxon withdrew $1.6 billion in assets. In 2003, Exxon would be faced with a $10 billion shortfall in its employee pension plan.[467] United Airlines, which reverted $254 million in pension assets in 1985, declared bankruptcy on its four pension plans in 2005, offloading the retirement obligations onto taxpayers.[468] Congress enacted a 50% excise tax on pension plan reversions in the Omnibus Reconciliation Act of 1990 to slow this practice.

The excise tax limited reversions after 1990, so large companies looked for a new path to raid pension plan assets. Roughly 11% of guaranteed retirement plans were converted into cash balance plans in the 1990s,[469] reflecting a hybrid plan type in which employers funded individual accounts and retirement funds grew according to a rate tied to U.S. government bonds.[470,471] International Business Machines Corporation (IBM) provides the most notable example of fund misallocation using these conversions. Their switch from a guaranteed benefit plan to a cash balance plan in 1999 allowed the company to pull $650 million from worker accounts of which $200 million was siphoned into top-hat plans for upper managers—tax loopholes always exist to benefit the ultrawealthy.[472,473]

Pundits claim that low current worker-to-retiree ratios were the cause of pension plan frailty during the 1990s. Conservatives like to use the example of General Motors' worker-to-retiree ratio to blame workers for issues with corporate pension plans. Logistically, this ratio should not matter because companies set aside money years in advance of a person's retirement. Consider a worker who started with General Motors in 1960 with hopes of retiring in 1990. The company would have set aside funds annually for three decades based on actuarial forecasts of investment growth and the retiree's estimated lifespan. Pension assets should, in theory, be sufficient to fund that worker's retirement—the funds should already exist no matter the worker-to-retiree ratio observed in 1990.

General Motors created a mess when it encouraged early retirement at age 55 in an attempt to downsize the workforce, suddenly driving a major change in actuarial assumptions.[474] The company was attempting to leverage NAFTA, which was signed into law in 1993, as a way to move jobs to Mexico. However, assets would be insufficient to fund greater pension benefits that came about after General Motors encouraged early retirement. The low worker-to-retiree ratio had nothing to do with the pension plan shortfalls at General Motors—wanting to rid itself of U.S. workers and outsource to Mexico was the cause.

In general, pension plans became frail in the early 1990s because obligations grew with declining interest rates, corporate raids in the decade prior drained assets, human lifespans increased, and market volatility kept investment values unpredictable. Retirement plans would not get relief until the mid-1990s when interest rates stabilized, keeping retirement obligations steady. The stock market began to steadily grow again, helping to elevate the value of pension plan assets. However, the dot-com bubble began to form in 1998 when the Federal Reserve, under the control of Alan Greenspan, lubricated the financial markets with low interest rates to protect the economy against the collapse of Long-Term Capital Management (LTCM), a hedge fund that caused widespread financial chaos after losing a massive bet on Russian bonds.

Long-Term Capital Management was founded in 1994 with $1.25 billion of funding. In a few short years, the firm grew to house $140 billion in assets, but the hedge fund entered massive leveraged positions against those assets to expand investment positions further. Approximately $1 trillion was placed at risk as LTCM made a fateful bet on Russian bonds. In August 1998, Russia's economy collapsed and the country defaulted on its sovereign debt.[475] Through negotiations with the Federal Reserve, a $3.25 billion bailout of LTCM was arranged,[476] and Greenspan instructed the Federal Reserve to pump money into the economy to shore up the country's financial system. The target interest rate was lowered from 5.5% to 4.8%. Greenspan saved Wall Street from its own bad behavior, but fueled the ensuing stock market bubble in the process.[477]

The rush of money into the system concurrent with the rise of internet firms drove the stock market to insane highs. My roommate at the time was glued to CNBC and quickly got me addicted to tracking the stock market's ascent. A few months later, I decided to return to school to study both finance and accounting.

As the dot-com boom took center stage, Congress was working hard behind the scenes to deregulate the financial industry. Completely ignoring the financial calamity after LTCM's failure in 1998, President Bill Clinton signed the Gramm-Leach-Bliley Act into law in 1999, which allowed investment banks, commercial banks, and insurance firms to merge once again, a feat outlawed during the depths of the Great Depression by the Glass-Steagall Act of 1933.[478] Instead of learning an important lesson from LTCM and taking risk out of the financial system, the Gramm-Leach-Bliley Act created the opposing reality in which financial institutions could merge until becoming "too big to fail."

The boom period of the dot-com market bubble led to a $242 billion pension plan surplus,[479] which encouraged many companies to withdraw excess gains from plan assets. True, reversions were subject to a 50% excise tax but loopholes exist—tax loopholes always exist for the ultrawealthy. Companies could channel pension assets into other employee benefit funds, such as ones for healthcare, without incurring the excise tax. This practice freed up corporate cash that would otherwise go to pay employee benefits in general.

The surge of stock prices in the final hours of the dot-com tech boom allowed companies to show some of the excess plan assets as corporate profit. Bell Atlantic's pension plan afforded the company an extra $627 million in reported earnings.[480] General Electric, a company that had not contributed to its pension fund since 1987, booked additional earnings of $331 million in 1997 and $1 billion in 1998.[481,482] By 2002, in the aftermath of the bubble bursting, 90% of corporate pension plans were underfunded to the tune of negative $222 billion.[483]

In the aftermath of the dot-com bubble, it was discovered that Arthur Andersen, the independent accounting firm hired to audit the financial position of publicly traded companies, was complicit in their fraud. One company in particular, Enron, provided an absurd example of the financial negligence that rattled retirement plans during this time period. In 1986, Enron received permission to withdraw $232 million from its pension plan.

Years later, near the peak of the dot-com boom, Enron's pension plan sat $82.5 million underfunded.[484] Enron instructed the already underfunded pension plan to invest retirement assets in the company's own stock. Then, the company's infamous and highly illegal practice of booking corporate liabilities into subsidiaries came to light, triggering Enron's stock price collapse and wiping out retiree benefits.

State and local pension plans fell victim to overzealous removal of asset surpluses as well. California saw the stock market bonanza as an infinite pool of wealth and showered state workers with generous retirement benefits. CalPERS, the state's pension fund, tripled in size throughout the 1990s,[485] prompting the California legislature to pass SB400 in 1999, altering the formula used to calculate retirement payouts. Now, certain state workers could retire at age 50 and receive up to 90% of current pay upon retiring. CalPERS based these lavish retirement benefits on sustained 8.25% growth in investment values.[486] However, 2001 rolled around and the Dow Jones Industrial Average fell 6%. Even worse, Nasdaq, the home to many technology companies behind the dot-com boom, plummeted 78% over the next two years.[487]

As the stock market meltdown unfolded in late 2000, the Commodity Futures Modernization Act was signed into law by President George Bush. This Act allowed "sophisticated parties" to trade derivatives without oversight, introducing the world to unfettered risk.[488] Investment firms used their "sophistication" to roll together bank mortgages into structured bond products then insure them with a derivative instrument called the credit default swap—all with little regulatory oversight. These packaged mortgages came to be known as MBS, which stands for mortgage-backed security.

The Federal Reserve stepped in to solve the nation's woes and dropped the target federal funds rate to 1% by June 2003.[489] These low interest rates put massive upward pressure on pension plan obligations right as plan assets collapsed from the dot-com bubble bursting. The federal funds rate remained at 1% for the next 10 months during which time a speculative mortgage frenzy took root. Per the Case-Shiller national home price index, prices grew at roughly 6.5% coming into 2000. By 2005, home prices were growing at a 14.5% annualized rate.[490] However, government inflation data, put out by the Bureau of Labor Statistics (BLS), captured none of this rapid home inflation because the BLS switched to using the artificial owner's equivalent rent (OER) back in 1983.[491] Artificial OER numbers, which have no existence in the real world, distort the true rate of inflation being reported. Overlooking true home inflation meant that the Federal Reserve could keep interest rates low, driving housing speculation further.

Years of financial deregulation, novel derivative instruments, and Federal Reserve stimulus set the stage for a massive run-up in home values. Investment banks began to package billions' worth of mortgages together into mortgage-backed security (MBS) and slap insurance contracts—the credit default swap—on them, and call it a day. Credit default swaps were viewed as easy money for financial firms because they only covered investment losses if a significant portion of homeowners defaulted on their mortgages; no one thought there would be widespread home defaults. All the deregulation from the prior two decades allowed these mortgage concoctions to exist, and the investment community believed they actually reduced systemic risk.

These new financial instruments, built using a package of mortgages and credit default insurance, were broken apart into separate tranches based on prioritization of cash inflows from mortgage borrowers. Investors who owned a high-quality tranche had priority over holders of lower-quality ones. As homeowners made their monthly mortgage payments, money would flow past the banks and proceed to investors in the order of tranche quality. Investors holding top-rated tranches had first dibs at money coming from homeowners, making this portion of the financial instrument highly secure, or so was thought. Lower-rated tranches were considered higher risk because they only received leftover cash flows, but that was okay because home prices were rising quickly and everything was insured by a derivative instrument that covered default: the credit default swap.

Mortgage lenders used this umbrella of safety to loosen lending standards. Because they were "sophisticated parties" per the Commodity Futures Modernization Act of 2000, regulatory oversight was limited. Much of the high-quality prime mortgage lending was dominated by government-sponsored enterprises, mainly Fannie Mae and Freddie Mac. Up-and-coming mortgage lenders focused more on the subprime market, but that was now considered low risk because investment banks were taking subprime loans and packaging them together into MBS, which the credit rating agencies were treating as safe investments.[492]

The credit rating agencies, such as Fitch Ratings, Moody's Investors Service, and Standard & Poor's, gave the top tranches on structured loan products high credit ratings despite all the underlying loans being subprime junk. Investors bought MBS tranches, perceived to be low risk, at an increasing clip, fueling the practice of advertising mortgages to hard-working Americans just to form more MBS.

Lending standards continued to slip to meet this frenzied mortgage demand until the point where the middle class could borrow huge sums of money without any documentation of income or net worth. Known as "no-doc" or "low-doc" loans, borrowers could self-report numbers on mortgage applications without verification by the banks. Alt-A mortgages were another permutation in which borrowers with prime credit scores applied for loans with low or no documentation. The term NINJA loan arose because borrowers could apply for and receive mortgages despite having "no income, no job, and no assets."

The build-up in systemic risk was not limited to the mortgage industry. Corporate junk bonds and high-risk foreign debt, along with mortgages, were packaged together into collateralized debt obligations (CDOs). Magically, high-risk assets received a stellar credit rating before being sold to unsuspecting investors. The firms packaging these loans did not stop there. These firms began experimenting with synthetic CDOs that took the risk level to all new heights. Unlike a CDO, which was composed of actual loans, a synthetic CDO was a bet based on a separate "reference" product. In 1997, synthetic CDOs emerged to help banks manage risk, and the amount created was too miniscule to track. A decade later, these artificial loan products became a $100+ billion, large-stakes gambling device.[493]

The seeds of the housing bubble were planted in the early years of the Reagan Administration with passage of Title VIII, Alternative Mortgage Transaction of the Garn St. Germain Depository Institutions Act of 1982.[494] Congress thought it would be safe to bring interest-only mortgages back from the dead despite their destructive legacy in the Great Depression. Mixed together with the Gramm-Leach-Bliley Act of 1999 and the Commodity Futures Modernization Act of 2000, investment firms finally had what they needed to rain interest-only mortgages down on the American public—a feat which had not happened since the 1920s.

In the Roaring '20s, homeowners could take out interest-only mortgages in which interest would be paid for seven to 10 years, and then the borrower would get smacked with a massive increase in the loan payment. Many of the interest-only mortgages reset in the 1930s when the jobless rate skyrocketed, leading to widespread home loan defaults and bank failures.[495] Needless to say, Congress banned interest-only mortgages in depths of the Great Depression.

Fast forward 80 years and roughly 25% of new mortgages between 2004 and 2006 were interest only.[496] To attract low-income borrowers to the debt party, mortgage lenders targeted this demographic with an introductory period, usually five, seven, or 10 years, in which only small payments were required to cover interest charges. The "blame game" propagated in the media made it seem like low-income, subprime borrowers were the cause of the housing crisis. Low-income persons worked hard to stay in their homes despite the financial collapse occurring all around in the economy. In fact, low-income persons as a group did not experience the highest rate of mortgage defaults. Investor-owned homes were the cause of most defaults as investors walked away from home they did not inhabit.[497]

Even if low-income, subprime borrowers took on too much debt, mortgage defaults should have spawned a slow-rolling, decade-long financial mess, similar to what the savings-and-loan crisis created back in the 1980s. However, hedge funds tied to investment banks, thanks to the Gramm-Leach-Bliley Act of 1999, used debt to leverage up and create large portfolios of MBS and CDO. The entire "house of cards" collapsed rapidly in little over a year due to hedge funds losing huge bets on these loan products. First of the major losses occurred at the French company BNP Paribas when it had to close two hedge funds on August 9, 2007, creating a mini shock to the stock market. In 2008, hedge fund implosions would cause Bear Stearns to fail in March and Lehman Brothers to file for bankruptcy in September,[498] leading to a meltdown in the economic system known today as the GFC, which stands for global financial crisis.

Most of the ensuing actions taken to bail out the economy favored large corporations. Congress passed the Troubled Asset Relief Program (TARP) in October 2008, offering a collection of stabilizing ventures aimed mainly at financial firms, but reaching into the mortgage and auto industries as well. A significant portion of bailout funds, mixed together with Federal Reserve support, propped up American International Group (AIG) to the tune of $182 billion.[499] AIG had taken the lead offering credit default swaps, and these products generated massive losses as mortgages failed. In contrast, two of the TARP programs, the Making Home Affordable Program and Hardest Hit Fund, directed only $46 billion toward homeowner relief.[500]

The U.S. government dove deeper into debt, accumulating over $12 trillion in Treasury bonds in the wake of the GFC. Tax revenue will need to eventually be raised to pay these debts lest the American government declares bankruptcy. Even a bankruptcy will not satisfy 100% of the debt, meaning tax revenue still needs to be raised over the long term. Running up government debts to rescue an economy is based on research from the venerated British economist, John Maynard Keynes. Of course, political leaders completely mutilate his theoretical framework to justify large-scale budget deficits. Keynes called for short-term and small budget deficits to reignite a floundering economy in the grips of a mild recession.[501] The current group of corporate politicians twisted this call for brief stimulus into a massive buildup of government debt.

The TARP program transformed rules surrounding the Federal Reserve as well. Up until this point, the Federal Reserve System, enacted in 1913, could only invest in U.S. Treasury bonds backed by the full faith and credit of U.S. taxpayers. This arrangement instilled confidence in the U.S. dollar worldwide, making it an important currency for global economic stability. The Term Asset-Backed Securities Loan Facility (TALF), a TARP program, authorized the Federal Reserve to buy MBS, the same mortgage-backed security instruments packaged full of junk mortgages that brought down the economy in the first place. TALF transitioned over $1.7 trillion in MBS off the balance sheet of banks and onto the Federal Reserve's balance sheet, which is backed by the full faith and credit of U.S. taxpayers.[502,503]

Ben Bernanke, the Federal Reserve Chairman at the time (known also as "Helicopter Ben" for an off-the-cuff remark he made about throwing money out a helicopter to rescue the economy), went on an MBS buying spree, transferring risk away from banks. This buying spree helped to lower the effective federal funds rate below 0.2%.[504]

Of utmost importance, a decline of interest rates increases actuarial estimates for retirement plan obligations. In the wake of a financial crisis, guaranteed retirement plans end up squeezed between a collapse of investment values on the asset side and increased projected obligations on the liability side. Simply put, retirement plans never evolved to account for chronic boom-bust cycles caused by an unregulated investment industry.

Conservatives like to blame unions and worker-to-retiree ratios. They clamor about pension contribution rules. In the end, the death of guaranteed retirement is really an issue about economic volatility grounded in unregulated lending practices, high-risk derivative products, and overzealous Federal Reserve stimulus.

Contribution retirement accounts, such as a 401(k), have grown in popularity as more companies terminate or bankrupt their guaranteed benefit pension plans, but these contributory accounts are mainly funded directly from workers. A full 30% of private-sector workers do not put money aside into their 401(k) or other contributory plan, and the percentage is lower among part-time or low-paid workers. Two-thirds of the lowest-paid Americans do not utilize their contribution plans at all.[505] If a recession occurs during retirement years, asset values in contributory plans may not be sufficient to keep retirees afloat financially.

Corporate America once offered a large portion of the workforce guaranteed retirement benefits as part of overall compensation. Currently, only 19% of the private-sector workforce has access to a guaranteed retirement plan.[506] Employers fund this type of retirement plan, and more important, benefits paid during retirement years are guaranteed for life. The amount an employer funds on behalf of a worker into a retirement plan can represent an additional $15,000 to $20,000 in compensation that the worker does not receive immediately, but is paid into the pension fund on the worker's behalf for retirement years.

In lieu of paying workers more or funding guaranteed pension plans, much of the corporate wealth generated since the GFC has gone toward dividends, stock buybacks, and mergers. More than $4 trillion worth of stock buybacks have occurred since 2008, helping lift stock market indices.[507] Companies used 60% of earnings from 2015 to 2017 for stock buybacks, artificially pumping up stock prices.[508] CEOs affirm that the Tax Cuts and Jobs Act (TCJA) of 2017 will only fuel these practices, which benefit investors—not workers. Buybacks in 2018 amounted to nearly $1 trillion with help from the TCJA.

To suspend the freefall in asset values during the GFC, the Federal Reserve and Congress undertook a massive bailout regimen, but companies have used this period of historically low interest rates to buy back stocks using $3 trillion of borrowed funds. Corporate America has loaded up on debt and used the proceeds not to invest in equipment, factories, or workers but to pump up stock prices artificially.

General Motors needed an $11 billion taxpayer bailout in 2008 in the midst of the GFC but the company a decade later decided to lay off

14,000 workers to save $6 billion. Over the same timeframe as these layoffs, the company bought back $10 billion in stock to benefit investors.[509] In similar fashion, another iconic American company, General Electric, faced a $30 billion shortfall in its pension plan, but the company repurchased more than $30 billion in stock at a time when it planned to lay off 12,000 workers.[510,511]

Congress passed Dodd-Frank in the wake of the GFC to reduce high-risk behavior on the part of "sophisticated parties" who claimed to not need much regulation but yet drove the American economy off a cliff. Fly-by-night lenders who dominated the high-risk mortgage industry until 2007 nearly vanished in the housing bubble's aftermath. Mainstream banks, such as Wells Fargo, Bank of America, and JPMorgan Chase, which finance mortgages using customer deposits, took back the mortgage industry with stronger underwriting standards. These three banks wrote 50% of the home loans in 2011. However, this period of responsible lending was short-lived seeing how these banks only wrote 21% of mortgages in 2016 as shadow nonbanks reemerged once again.[512]

Dodd-Frank, which came into law to address the sins of the GFC, does not directly apply to nonbank mortgage lenders unless a nonbank poses a major systemic risk. Regular commercial banks can extend lines of credit to nonbanks as a way of sidestepping Dodd-Frank regulations. In a way, Dodd-Frank has encouraged greater risk in the financial system because the large commercial banks now funnel money over to private equity firms and shadow nonbanks, which then extend the higher-risk loans that Dodd-Frank would otherwise prohibit.[513]

The nonbank lending community has crafted a new high-risk derivative product called a mortgage servicing right (MSR). An MSR ties its value to the service fees charged to manage a mortgage. Some of these nonbank mortgage lenders stockpile MSRs on their balance sheet, representing a significant portion of assets, upwards of 20% in many cases.[514] Unlike the high-risk investment products of 10 years prior, these MSRs are much more volatile.[515]

In the decade of suppressed interest rates since 2008, an explosion of lending has occurred among weaker companies with high debt-to-equity (leverage) ratios. Total leveraged loan volume has reached over $1 trillion, and more than 70% of the loans are considered covenant lite, meaning they maintain poor underwriting standards.[516] The covenant-lite loans now given to corporations resemble the no-doc or low-doc loans handed out to consumers like candy before 2008. Some of the country's largest private equity firms now issue leveraged loans as a method of allowing commercial banks to circumnavigate Dodd-Frank regulations. Many of these loans end up packaged into a collateralized loan obligation (CLO), once again raising concerns about triggering a financial crisis.

Even though leveraged loans are given to companies in poor financial standing, 60% of CLO tranches receive the highest credit rating possible.[517] Only a select few companies, along with the U.S. government, achieve this high credit rating, but through the magic of financial engineering, risky leveraged loans, many with covenant-lite standards, earn this highest credit rating as well.

Investment banks have helped high-risk companies issue bonds at an alarming rate since 2008. Nearly half of investment grade bonds teeter on the edge of junk credit status, and several of the top bond managers attest that many of these bonds deserve to be rated as junk already.[518] The market for junk bonds itself has nearly doubled since the GFC.[519]

The financial system appears to be walking into another unsustainable bubble. The overall volume of consumer debt across all areas—mortgages, auto loans, student loans, and credit cards—now exceeds the record set before the GFC.[520] The investment industry set a new record as well. Margin loans, the debt investors use to double-down on stock positions, reached $513 billion in 2017.[521] Margin debt allows investors to borrow against their stock portfolios and buy even more stock. This trick bodes well when stock prices rise, helping investors to capture even more gains. But if a stock market crashes, a high volume of margin loans exacerbates losses.

Subprime debt, which centered on the mortgage market before 2008, has migrated over to education and auto lending. Delinquency rates among student loan holders has grown to 11%, and many student loans are held among subprime credit borrowers. Subprime lending among auto loans has grown to $280 billion amid an overall $1.17 trillion auto loan market.[522] As an example of low documentation standards, Santander Consumer, a key subprime auto lender, only checked credit scores on 8% of borrowers.[523]

The investment community remarks that times are different because the average credit rating of borrowers is higher and default rates are low overall. In 2006, before the major housing crash occurred, the investment community made similar observations. The methodology used to calculate personal credit scores has changed since 2006, making comparison difficult.[524] Default rates tend to reach incredibly low levels before a downturn in the economy. Higher average credit ratings mean nothing if someone becomes unemployed with a sizeable portfolio of housing, automobile, student, and credit card debt.

Covid-19 economic lockdowns and the subsequent disruption to consumer behavior has dropped a major bomb on this pile of corporate and consumer debt. The Federal Reserve has reacted by loading up its balance sheet with trillions of dollars' worth of debt instruments. Despite record unemployment and widespread economic uncertainty for the middle class, the Federal Reserve has stepped in to protect financial firms from any stress. Again, they reduced interests to near 0%, which negatively affects pension plans. Stock market indices have reacted to these low interest rates by doubling in price at one of the fastest rates ever seen.

As the stock market continues to set new records highs, even during a pandemic, American companies face a pension shortfall estimated at $553 billion among large companies, per a study conducted through Boston College's Center for Retirement Research.[525] Few workers fully fund their own contribution plans or save enough overall to remain financially secure throughout retirement years. Consumer debt levels continue to mount across home mortgage, auto loan, student loan, and credit card borrowing. As opposed to building financial wealth for retirement, the middle class sinks further into an abyss of debt.

The Federal Reserve's pandemic response has simply fueled another stock market bubble in a manner similar to what occurred in 1998 in response to Long-Term Capital Management's demise. However, this time, the ensuing inflation created from the Federal Reserve rapidly pumping up the money supply may prove nontransitory and too excessive to control without significant countermeasures. Only time will tell how all the financial mismanagement over the past 40 years will play out but history says that dire financial consequences lie ahead.

CALL TO ACTION

In the early 1900s, a factory in New York City, the Triangle Shirtwaist Company, was producing a new garment that combined a button-down shirt with a skirt. Fashion was shifting away from the more conservative dresses of the time. A fire broke out on March 25, 1911, forcing 600 workers packed onto three floors to scramble toward the exits. Until this time, fire drills and sprinkler systems were recommended by the city but not mandated. An elevator operator hastened to shuttle dozens of workers down the one elevator in operation.[526] As the fire spread through the building, women began jumping to their deaths from 8th- and 9th-story windows. In the days that followed, it was revealed that the owners, Max Blanck and Isaac Harris, had kept an exit door locked to prevent theft.

In total, 147 workers lost their lives.[527] The youngest to perish were two 14-year-old girls, highlighting how child labor was still rampant in the United States.[528] The two owners eventually escaped prosecution. However, the national discourse around workplace safety, unionization, and labor laws began to shift dramatically. America was called to action.

The International Labour Organization (ILO), a special United Nations agency, asserts four fundamental rights for workers. Paramount is that child labor must be abolished. According to the 1900 U.S. Census, an estimated 1.75 million children aged 10 to 15 toiled in mills, coalmines, and factories.[529] Only a few states had passed laws protecting children by this time. Even then, child labor protections might only have meant children would be limited to a 10-hour workday instead of the normal 12- to 15-hour one. Child labor laws for much of U.S. history were watered down and did not levy an outright ban. Few good statistics were kept on the number of dead or injured children, but incidents of child abuse and illness were well known. The U.S. Supreme Court continued to strike down child labor laws as unconstitutional until President Franklin D. Roosevelt threatened to stack the Court with more justices.[530] The threat apparently worked because the Court upheld the Fair Labor Standards Act (FLSA) of 1938, which greatly enhanced child labor protections.

The second ILO declaration opposes discrimination and harassment in the workplace, an issue that the U.S. Congress would not tackle to any significant degree until the mid-1960s Civil Rights legislation. Still today, women and minorities face a strong current of discrimination and harassment. A *Cosmopolitan Magazine* survey found that one out of every three women face sexual harassment in the workplace.[531] In the investment industry, more than half of women report inappropriate sexual advances.[532] Today, a greater percentage of women graduate college than men, and their average economic output tends to be higher.[533] But female workers are paid less in most industries, especially the investment industry.[534]

Most men walk through life oblivious to the harassing behaviors they levy against women or the overall extent of sexual abuse women experience in a lifetime. Sit in a room full of women who are asked questions about abuse, harassment, and discrimination, and the majority will have personal experiences to report. This issue is not discussed with any sufficiency as a culture, and few employers conduct appropriate forms of antiharassment and antidiscrimination training. This failure to mitigate inappropriate behavior means that future generations of women will be subjected to the pain harassment and abuse causes. Men would never want their mom, sister, or daughter to experience this pain, but yet they often tolerate inappropriate behavior as if it does not circle back to their own families. In reality, women experience rape, assault, abuse, and harassment all the time but America's toxic masculine culture allows men to continue their behaviors.

To assess discrimination in hiring, researchers sent out resumé with both conventional names and ethnic-sounding names. A National Bureau of Economic Research investigation revealed that resumé with common European-sounding names received callbacks from employers 10% of the time while employers called back 7% of the resumé listing an African-sounding name.[535] Skills and other factors were kept consistent; the only difference was the sound of the person's name.

The ILO dedicates their third declaration to fighting against forced labor. At any given moment, as many as 400,000 people work under forced conditions, especially women and children.[536] More than 70% involved in America's forced labor system come to the United States legally on a visa, but employers pay an illegally low wage or subtract for food, housing, and other living expenses.[537] The issue of forced labor increasingly involves citizens of India, China, and Vietnam who do not cross along Mexico's border. It becomes nearly impossible to break the chains of oppression due to language barriers, financial hardship, threats of violence, and intimidation of family members.[538]

The United States knows too well the consequence of historical slavery and the racism it spurs. A bloody civil war sought to end this institution, but slave labor simply took on a new face in the United States. The FLSA allows for a tipped minimum wage, which stands today at only $2.13 per hour. Former slaves did not earn wages; they worked for tips, but now today this legacy tipped wage still applies to a large portion of restaurant workers.

A growing percentage of enslaved labor in the United States is perfectly legal because private companies carve a workforce out of the prison system. After the Civil War, America attempted to abolish slavery with the 13th Amendment but this constitutional amendment excluded protections for individuals found guilty of a felony. As the story goes, incarceration of former slaves after the Civil War allowed states to sidestep the new-found protections of the 13th Amendment to the point where 2.2 million people now call prison home.[539] Obviously, a high percentage of the prison population (37.5%) are of African descent.[540] One out of three black males is expected to flow through the prison system in their lifetime,[541] creating a *de facto* form of slavery, incentivizing arrests and strong police enforcement in black communities. In certain states, a felony conviction also precludes voting in elections.

Most of the labor laws aimed to protect workers against unfair wages and unsafe conditions only cover "employees," a term which asserts a specific legal definition and excludes prison workers; thus, corporations have jumped on the chance to manufacture products inside prisons.[542] Federal Prison Industries, Inc. was founded in 1934 to manage relationships between corporate America and the federal prison system. This program, also known as UNICOR, now oversees roughly $2 billion in manufacturing production. In their 2016 report, they noted that inmate-derived revenues slumped, prompting them to seek out more businesses willing to use prisoners for work.[543] Well-known brand names such as Starbucks, Walmart, AT&T, and McDonald's, to name just a few, have used prison workers along their supply chain, either directly or through an indirect supplier.[544,545]

Proponents of prison labor argue that felons acquire skills through corporate-sponsored work and it serves as a mechanism to give back to society. That may very well be true, but recent work strikes demonstrate how inmates feel enslaved by their prison tasks. On September 9, 2014, prisoners organized the largest strike seen in the United States against unfair labor practices. An estimated 24,000 inmates across 29 states participated on the strike, an act considered illegal and punishable by solitary confinement, loss of privileges, or denial of parole. The strike occurred because inmates do not have the right to strike legally without fear of punishment.

The right to walk away from a job allows workers to address wage concerns and unsafe conditions. Inmates have no power to control their work situation and wages, which range anywhere from $0.12 to $1.15 per hour, but which are often subject to deductions. Some states fail to pay inmates anything.[546] Using a felony charge to justify enslavement is an affront to the several hundred thousand who died fighting to remove slavery as an American institution.

Once released, a felon faces scrutiny when seeking employment. An ex-felon has served out a punishment and should not be denied a job because of a past conviction. Known as "ban the box" or fair chance laws, certain states block employers from asking about past felony convictions.[547] The debt to society has been paid, and a lack of employment can lead to recidivism. Noninvestment in an inmate's rehabilitation means more community members fall victim to future crime and the community must pay for yet another expensive investigation, trial, and prison term. As a person returns to jail on a new conviction, taxpayers must dig deeper into their pockets to support an ever-growing prison establishment.

Norway leads the world in rehabilitation efforts among its prison population and boasts one of the lowest recidivism rates among developed nations at 20%. The United States is motivated by a desire to strike back against criminals and inflict a sense of punishment, resulting in a high rate of solitary confinement and recidivism of 76%.[548] How much does this failed approach to incarceration cost United States taxpayers?

The maturity of a society to put vengeance aside and get to the root of a person's criminal behavior—many prisoners are poorly educated and/or suffered abuse as children—means that thoughtful rehabilitation efforts can reduce recidivism, saving taxpayers money. Americans may want to retaliate against criminals, but in the end, communities endure more incidents of crime and victimization without proper rehabilitation programs.

Norway follows a policy of restorative justice, personalizing crimes and placing context around victimhood to help reform behaviors. Norwegian prisons focus on teaching vocational skills, and job security after release is an important part of preventing repeat criminal offenses.[549] Life in a Norwegian prison mimics dorm life at a university. Several rooms open to a kitchen and a living room area,[550] allowing inmates to maintain positive daily routines. The human brain adopts behaviors based on environment, and unhealthy habits that form in prison can take years to undo. The United States shuffles prisoners into poorly furnished concrete rooms behind steel bars. This environment only serves to create antisocial behaviors and fragmented daily routines, which encumber attempts to reintegrate inmates into everyday life once the prison sentence ends.

True, it takes money to implement prison education and therapy programs. Would you rather iron out criminal behavior and equip ex-prisoners with in-demand skills or put resources toward long-term, repeat adjudication and incarceration with episodes of release that involve poverty, crime, and victimization? As the United States suffers to maintain its manufacturing base in part due to a lack of vocational skills, Norway's manufacturing companies pay upwards of $60 per hour.[551] Can the United States afford to dismantle its manufacturing base due to a weak investment in vocational skills, leaving millions in a state of poverty, and simply imprison out-of-work community members once they turn toward crime?

Finally, the ILO's fourth declaration speaks to the right to bargain collectively. In 1932, during the depths of the Great Depression, the Unemployed Councils and United Auto Workers staged a protest known as the Ford Hunger March outside the Ford Motor Factory in Dearborn, Michigan. Henry Ford, an opponent of organized labor, was the richest American at that time despite the Great Depression's impact on auto sales. Police used tear gas on the protesters, which caused the crowd to start throwing stones. Harry Bennett, a Ford Motor executive, along with the

Dearborn police, began shooting into the crowd. As the day came to a close, four of the protesters were killed and dozens more were injured.[552]

Three years later, in 1935, Congress passed the National Labor Relations Act (NLRA), also known as the Wagner Act, which allowed two or more employees at a company to engage in collective bargaining activities. The NLRA mandates that a majority of a "bargaining unit" come together as a "labor organization" to approve a union representative.[553] Several ambiguities exist in the law's language that companies exploit to block unionization.

Companies have some power to reject the selected representative. The "bargaining unit" needs to combine workers amid "similar" job roles, but the exact nature of what constitutes a bargaining unit or similar job role is open for debate among employees, the employer, and the National Labor Relations Board.[554] It's challenging to join together a majority of workers into a bargaining unit across a multinational organization or among part-time employees, such as restaurant servers, retail clerks, and adjunct faculty.

Conservatives dislike this notion of tax money going to poor, lazy people. It makes them so bitter. So why not give workers the power to negotiate fair compensation and labor protections, especially because research shows such rights drive economic output higher? It's a win-win for companies, taxpayers, and workers. This way, fairly compensated, hard-working Americans will greatly decrease their dependence on social programs and they will feel incentivized to innovate, increasing the country's economic output and corporate profit potential.

The country needs to update the National Labor Relations Act to empower workers with collective bargaining rights so they can negotiate proper labor protections and compensation levels with employers. The current legal environment makes collective bargaining incredibly difficult, especially as companies merge or retain facilities across multiple states or countries. In the end, U.S. companies can simply outsource operations to a foreign country if a union successfully forms. U.S. business executives have undertaken a 40-year campaign to dismantle unions and undercut the workforce through outsourcing efforts.

In April 2013, the Rana Plaza, a building in Bangladesh that housed five garment factories supplying western retail vendors, collapsed, killing 1,131 workers.[555] Additional people were injured. The building had originally been constructed to bear the weight of five floors but new owners underwent renovations to add four extra floors. As construction on the eighth floor was underway, materials meant to be used for placement of the final top floor formed part of the rubble when the building crumbled.[556] That same year, garment exports from Bangladesh climbed 24%.[557]

The United States ranked near the bottom of the International Trade Union Confederation's (ITUC) 2014 global rights index. On a scale of 1 (best) to 5 (worst), the United States received a score of 4, alongside Yemen, Sierra Leone, Pakistan, Lebanon, and Jordan. The United States ranks alongside countries experiencing extreme poverty and violence, and where the ITUC claims workers face "systematic violations of rights," meaning collective bargaining and labor rights are seriously threatened.[558]

How are we taking care of our community? Are we taking steps to consume products in a mindful way? The American consumer seems willing to purchase cheap foreign imports despite concerns about unsafe work environments and labor exploitation. Consumerism has become an act of searching online for the cheapest product. Homes are decorated with fixtures that fall apart after one season. Kids wear clothes once or twice before making a conscious decision to throw the apparel away as a fast-fashion ritual. The foreign textile industry delivers roughly 16 million tons of clothing and fabric to Americans each year. Of that, approximately two-thirds finds its way into landfills.[559]

Too many U.S. cities fall way short of incorporating modern recycling practices into their community services, and landfill waste often decomposes into soil pollution or greenhouse gases. The toxic waste produced inside landfills should concern families who care about water and air quality. Pumping pollution into the environment leads to worsening health outcomes for all community members.

Environmental regulations impose a cost on companies, and the logical conclusion is that corporate profits underperform when regulations are tight. However, repeated evidence illustrates how countries with high environmental standards outperform their global counterparts. A robust landscape of environmentally friendly policies encourages innovation among companies and the birth of new industries.

Jobs in renewable energy sectors have skyrocketed in number since the turn of the 21st century. Coal mines employ roughly 160,000 workers, but the renewable energy space has given rise to over 4 million jobs.[560] Solar and wind power alone had five times the number of workers as the coal industry, while coal still represents the largest source of greenhouse gas emissions.[561] A

Harvard study unearthed that the external, indirect costs on human health and environmental impacts from using coal sit at around $350-500 billion each year.[562] Renewable sources of electricity represent 10% of America's total energy sources, but the Department of Energy estimates this number could rise to 80%, reducing global warming emissions by roughly 80% as well.[563]

Wages and profit trend higher as investments in environmental-friendly innovations are made. Indirectly, society spends less on health issues when spewing fewer environmental toxins.[564] The Clean Air Act of 1970 will cost companies an estimated $65 billion across the 1990 to 2020 timeframe. During these same three decades, the estimated net benefit accrued for American society will equal $2 trillion. Much of this benefit comes from a reduction in asthma and other pulmonary illnesses.[565]

The loss of auto manufacturing and associated population reduced the tax base in Flint, Michigan. In 2014, austerity measures drove the city to transition its water supply over to the Flint River. Soon, citizens raised alarms over how dirty the drinking water appeared. A year later, a study conducted through Michigan State University discovered elevated levels of lead in blood samples taken from Flint children aged five and younger.[566] The Environmental Protection Agency (EPA) affirms that even low levels of lead exposure can negatively impact mental health and brain acuity.[567] However, the EPA only stipulates volunteer testing for lead in schools despite a 2018 Government Accountability Office report that noted 43% of American school districts have positive lead levels, putting millions of children at risk for mental impairment.[568] A testing kit to look for lead in drinking water costs under $10.

Growing up in Washington State, I remember the backlash inflicted against the fast food restaurant Jack in the Box in 1993 after cases of Escherichia coli 0157:H7 began presenting at the University of Washington medical center, ending with several deaths and dozens of injuries. The fast food organization tried to blame its meat supplier but concerns arose over the temperature at which food was cooked.[569] The "free market" decries regulations and inspections as burdensome, but what was the overall cost to Jack in the Box and Washington State taxpayers as a result of the illnesses, injuries, and deaths caused by tainted beef?

The most profitable companies in the United States use science, mathematics, engineering, and technology (STEM) skills to innovate products. Advanced forms of education, especially in STEM fields, generate a more socioeconomically stable community, but students continue to face burdensome student loan demands in order to obtain critical skills that benefit everyone in society. Output in a modern economy does not come from inefficient manual processes. A company must employ automation, robotics, software, and mechanized equipment to maximize productive gains. Thereafter, advanced logistic systems move products swiftly into the hands of consumers.

Education dollars offer a tremendously high rate of economic return for everyone in the nation. From an economic standpoint, a well-rested, healthy, and properly educated worker has substantial power to innovate. Tolerance of overworked employees who rarely take lunch breaks, let alone a vacation, creates a dearth of innovation. Simply put, shorter work hours in the range of 30 to 40 per week lead to greater overall output for a country—*not* this march toward low pay and longer work schedules.

No other element elevates America's competitive edge in the global economy further and more powerfully than education. Our economy needs an equitable infusion of money to keep education alive for the next generation. A lack of marketable skills upon graduating high school means young adults must either go to college or endure a period of underemployment until requisite job skills can be obtained. All Americans need better access to skills training, especially when unemployed, but the United States ranks almost last among industrialized countries for making job retraining expenditures. A low level of educational attainment corresponds to worse socioeconomic outcomes such as higher rates of crime, imprisonment, drug use, unwanted pregnancy, and homelessness.

The U.S. Conference of Mayors survey indicates that a lack of affordable housing exacerbates the homelessness issue. The "rent burdened," those who spend more than half their incomes on rent, rose to over 25% after the global financial crisis (GFC). This number continues to increase each year as rental costs skyrocket.[570] In a given year, roughly 3.5 million Americans experience homelessness, and many are driven out of their homes without warning because of unemployment or domestic abuse.

The several wars of the modern era, from Vietnam to Iraq and Afghanistan, overused military personnel and left them struggling with homelessness, drug addiction, and suicidality, all the while the Veterans Administration was underfunded.[571] The Opening Doors initiative, launched in 2010 through the Obama Administration, has reportedly reduced homelessness among veterans by 50%.[572]

Younger veterans face an increasing rate of suicide, and approximately 70% use a firearm in the act.[573] Since 1996, the Dickey Amendment, named after Arkansas Representative Jay Dickey, has denied funding to the Centers for Disease Control and Prevention (CDC) for gun violence research, making it more difficult to undertake studies on suicide.[574] Republicans make a false claim about supporting the troops when they put the gun lobby, especially the National Rifle Association, above the interest of United States military veterans—mission not accomplished. Their pro-life agenda does not seem to extend to school shootings, domestic violence, or veteran suicides. Finally, in 2018, as a result of Democrat efforts, the Dickey Amendment was revised and the CDC can now "conduct research on the causes of gun violence" specifically.[575]

Housing and Urban Development (HUD) estimates that the United States needs nearly 6 million affordable rental units to meet demand among low-income persons.[576] Attempts to build more housing, especially in California, run headlong into NIMBY laws, also known as "Not In My Backyard." In most situations, local homeowners show up to city council meetings to fight against property code changes.[577] As such, cities find building high-rises or densifying an area more difficult, and the lack of new housing units forces rents and home values up further. In California, politicians tried repeatedly for years to bring about YIMBY, or "Yes In My Backyard," laws to address the homeless crisis, but each time, the bills met stiff resistance from all sorts of different groups, even housing advocates who oppose statewide property code overrides out of concern for gentrification. Finally, in 2021, California Governor Gavin Newsom signed Senate Bills 9 and 10 into law, which will override single-family zoning rules throughout the state and ease environmental restrictions, respectively.[578]

California's housing crisis is the result of a concerted effort to discriminate. The United States as a whole created this crisis of its own choosing as part of a historical effort to exlude persons of color and low-income residents from living near affluent white families. Exclusionary zoning came about in large part during the Great Depression when suburban living took root. First, the process involved ensuring that no multifamily units could be built among a sea of single-family homes because persons of color and low-income families gravitated toward more affordable multifamily housing. Then, access to home loans was blocked to guarantee that persons of color and low-income residents could definitely not afford a single-family home.

The Fair Housing Administration (FHA) drafted maps of major U.S. cities and color coded areas red where loans would not be underwritten. The so-called redlined areas represented parts of a city where persons of color and low-income families were most likely to inhabit. It was official U.S. federal policy to guarantee racial and wealth divisions. Even if a person of color could afford a single-family home out in the suburb, the FHA encouraged lending standards and zoning restrictions that barred the sale.[579]

California's housing shortage was not random but the byproduct of exclusionary zoning laws left unresolved for decades. A bird's eye view of Los Angeles and San Francisco reveals a high percentage of single-family properties dotting the landscape despite the massive growth in population since the Second World War. More multifamily units would have alleviated the housing crunch decades ago, probably saving California from acting as a factory for homelessness. Instead, both cities became a sprawling trafficjam crisscrossing hyperinflated single-family homes. And because the United States mainly funds primary and secondary schools through property taxes, exclusionary housing laws have helped affluent areas siphon off the most qualified teachers, extending inequality in education to the next generation.

The ability to build equity in a house gives families a means to accrue intergenerational wealth. The equity also serves as a financial underpinning to use in retirement years or instances of unemployment. The ability to buy a single-family home empowers families to build wealth, but can the United States extend this power to multifamily units as well? Singapore, a once British colony in Southeast Asia, boasts the highest rate of homeownership among industrialized nations. As much as 90% of residents own their dwellings. To accomplish this feat, Singapore allows citizens to build equity inside government housing complexes instead of just throwing money away each month in rent, as would happen with U.S. low-income or subsidized housing units.[580]

The United States can learn myriad lessons from global success stories across a range of economic and public policies. The desire to learn about other countries is often met with indifference or a sense of American exceptionalism, and true, having lived in several European countries, it always felt great to return home. The United States has tremendous amenities and amazing features, none more exceptional than American culture. A past wrought with slavery, child labor, worker exploitation, and the indigenous pogrom seems to conflict with the gentle, kind nature found around the country.

America truly has a foundation of greatness but we must build a tower of fairness atop it. The past must not repeat; I explore historical context in this book to help craft a better future for the middle class. Education, healthcare, and labor rights, among all the other key features of a strong middle-class existence must be fortified and expanded in an equitable manner. Most people would argue in favor of this pursuit, but a toxic entity has insidiously emerged with the objective to have us simply argue—you can call it a fox in the hen house.

Fox News seeks to increase viewership with inflammatory content. The media giant uses a "divide and conquer" tactic in which it places Americans onto two very separate political teams, and then demonizes the liberal side. You cannot lump all people into two camps: liberal versus conservative. America's political views are highly diverse, but right-wing media narrows the political spectrum in order to attack a common enemy.

In 1983, 50 companies controlled 90% of the nation's media. In that same year, Ronald Reagan met with media titan Rupert Murdoch in the Oval Office of the White House, kicking off a new era in biased, corporate news. Murdoch, the owner of the Fox News Channel, renounced his Australian citizenship in 1985 because a foreign resident could not own more than 20% of a U.S. media company.[581] As a U.S. citizen, Murdoch could bring his genre of pro-corporate broadcasting to the shores of America. One year later he established the Fox Broadcasting Company.[582]

In 1987, the Federal Communications Commission (FCC) unanimously voted to end the multidecade Fairness Doctrine, which required news stations to cover "important" stories and provide balanced perspective with their reporting.[583] Congress attempted to immediately reinstate the Fairness Doctrine, but President Ronald Reagan vetoed the bill, making way for biased, partisan news programming.

Fox News, owned by the parent corporation Twenty-First Century Fox Inc., purports to deliver "fair and balanced" news to the masses. Anyone with half a brain knows that Fox News has a strong partisan bias. However, how does a news organization, headquartered in the heart of New York City, a liberal bastion, stock its ranks with conservative ideologues? That's just it. Fox News does not really offer a conservative perspective. The news organization pumps out pro-corporate talking points meant to distract voters from focusing on any pro-labor policy. Fox News does the heavy lifting for the ultrawealthy who do not want an organized labor movement.

The American public must see beyond this strong partisan divide that the political establishment loves to fuel. Even President Obama echoed the talking point about a "divided" America on numerous occasions. I can have a mindful discussion with people living in other parts of the country, but then turn on the TV and corporate media blasts the terms "far-left" or "far-right" in the viewers eardrums. It's not that America is strongly divided on issues or there are two extreme political camps; it's that America is being divided by corporate media on purpose.

Media conglomeration grew after Bill Clinton signed into law the Telecommunications Act of 1996. Proponents claimed the law would encourage competition but it lifted the 40-station cap on radio stations and media outlets that one organization could own.[584] Twenty years later, mass consolidation has meant that only six companies now own 90% of America's media, including 70% of cable TV outlets. Clear Channel owns more than 1,200 stations.[585]

Advertisers that provide funding to anger-rich media content should be boycotted. Corporations withdrew from conservative pundit Bill O'Reilly's show upon discovery of his sexual improprieties, but advertisers should have equally shunned his strident bombast. American culture is warm and welcoming, but right-wing corporate media emits a steady stream of confrontational opinion pieces to create addiction among viewers and spur viral reposting of stories. Fox News, Breitbart News Network, OANN, and TheBlaze, among other right-wing media outlets, have hooked Americans on craving anti-liberal ranting. Rational public discourse among opposing political factions becomes untenable in an environment of souped-up anger. It's up to the rational elements of American society to bring awareness to this manipulation and push back against violent or inflammatory news content.

Neuroscientists have recently elucidated the brain pathways in charge of violent or aggressive behavior. Much like an addiction to opioids or cocaine, watching violent events triggers the same dopamine receptors in the human brain.[586] The standard American child, someone who watches an average of 6.5 hours of TV per day, combined with 1.5 hours of social media, sees upwards of 200,000 violent acts before reaching adulthood, all of which trigger the same addiction-prone areas of the brain as heroin.[587] Research clearly has demonstrated how aggressive video games or television promote physical abuse in adulthood, much of which is directed toward women.[588] In Germany, TV violence is censored similar to how American networks edit swear words or sexual content.

Dopamine release can be triggered through anger and violence, but the neurotransmitter also plays a key role in the brain's reward system. Social media giants know that scrolling through multiple condensed posts, along with feedback via comments and likes, triggers this reward system, promoting an addiction to social media platforms.[589] Everyone seems glued to their smartphones nowadays. Try to hang out with a group of people and half will stare like zombies at their device.

In the 2016 presidential election, a Russian troll farm, called Internet Research Agency (IRA), advertised on Twitter and Facebook to mislead American voters with inflammatory posts.[590] Troll farms do not need humans to propagate fake posts; increasingly, automated bots create accounts and post to social media. In the first quarter of 2019, Facebook deleted 2.2 billion accounts it believed were fake.[591] Troll bots post incendiary statements that cause a real user to engage; then, social media algorithms display the post to the real user's followers, disseminating the fake post even further. One study tracked 115 fake posts in the 2016 election cycle and found that these posts "were shared on Facebook a total of 30 million times."[592]

I propose the Broadcasting Real American Information and News Act, otherwise known as the BRAIN Act, to address the so-called fake news that Donald Trump whined about on his Twitter feed. American must reinstate a modernized version of the Fairness Doctrine. It's dangerous to a democracy when outright propaganda poses as public news. Even a disclaimer at the bottom of "news stories" would help Americans realize they are reading or watching biased opinion pieces—*not* objective journalism.

Politicians should pass what I call the Voter Information Act to proactively provide important information about government functions, such as state and federal expenditures, directly inside voter pamphlets. It's vital in a democracy to ensure voters receive accurate facts about how government runs, free of political spin. Currently, political advertisements do not fall under U.S. code governing false advertising.[593] Voter pamphlets contain information about candidates and ballot measures, but voters do not always know how tax dollars are spent.

Maybe it's time we all turn off all the devices and engage with our communities in person. Go encourage modern voting methods in your state similar to Oregon's highly successful automatic voter registration and Vote by Mail system. Sixteen states and Washington, D.C., have passed automatic voter registration laws.[594] Not enough people register to vote; those who are registered, fail to turn out to the polls. At a state or national level, advocate for a voting holiday or reduced work hours to ensure people have enough time to vote on election day. Minnesota boasts the highest voter turnout among all the states, and officials note four key reasons:

1. Early voting period starts 46 days in advance of an election.
2. Residents can register and vote on election day itself.
3. State law guarantees time off work to vote.
4. The Midwest maintains a strong culture around voting.[595]

Liberal-minded people continue to show frustration toward the Electoral College, a system in which the U.S. president is elected indirectly by electorates. However, an effort is underway to allocate electoral votes per the results of the popular vote. The U.S. Constitution permits states to appoint their electors "in such Manner as the Legislature thereof may direct,"[596] including per the national popular vote (NPV). Simply put, encourage your state legislature to switch to the NPV method, or some similar proportional allocation, and the Electoral College can no longer usurp the power of the American public to elect their desired president.

If no candidate embraces the policies you wish to see passed, then run for political office. The American public seems unaware of how, in a democracy, voters get to sway public policy through several mechanisms. Americans can run for political office, write their political leaders, canvass for candidates, donate to campaigns, and vote for candidates. In the 2016 election, voter turnout placed the United States 26th among 32 developed nations, exemplifying the country's chronically low voter engagement.[597] No more complaints about how politics is not your game and the legislative arena is corrupted. Be the spokesperson for change. Hold a house party with your friends and neighbors. Act on a social or economic issue.

The real question is: What will you do after reading this book? What will you decide to accomplish and influence, knowing the game being played behind your back and how economics functions at the most *nano* level?

ENDNOTES

CHAPTER 1

1. Saez, E. (2013). Striking It Richer: The Evolution of Top Incomes in the United States (Updated with 2011 estimates). eml.berkeley.edu/~saez/saez-UStopincomes-2011.pdf.
2. Burkhauser, R., Larrimore, J. and Simon, K. (2011). A "Second Opinion" on the Economic Health of the American Middle Class. Cambridge: National Bureau of Economic Research. www.nber.org/papers/w17164.pdf.
3. U.S. Senator Bob Menendez (2015). Menendez Reacts to SEC Vote Approving CEO-to-Worker Pay Ratio Rule. www.menendez.senate.gov/news-and-events/press/menendez-reacts-to-sec-vote-approving-ceo-to-worker-pay-ratio-rule.
4. Blair Smith, E. and Kuntz, P. (2013). CEO Pay 1,795-to-1 Multiple of Wages Skirts U.S. Law. Bloomberg. www.bloomberg.com/news/articles/2013-04-30/ceo-pay-1-795-to-1-multiple-of-workers-skirts-law-as-sec-delays.
5. Gavett, G. (2014). CEOs Get Paid Too Much, According to Pretty Much Everyone in the World. Harvard Business Review. hbr.org/2014/09/ceos-get-paid-too-much-according-to-pretty-much-everyone-in-the-world.
6. PayScale. (n.d.). CEO Pay: How Much Do CEOs Make Compared to Their Employees? www.payscale.com/data-packages/ceo-pay.
7. Melin, A., Zhao, J. and Perry, J. (2019). Disney Faces Fresh Criticism After Heir Call Iger's Pay 'Insane'. Bloomberg. www.bloomberg.com/graphics/ceo-pay-ratio. Accessed 11 Sep. 2019.
8. Piwowar, M. (2017). Reconsideration of Pay Ratio Rule Implementation. Harvard Law School Forum on Corporate Governance and Financial Regulation. corpgov.law.harvard.edu/2017/02/07/reconsideration-of-pay-ratio-rule-implementation.
9. Sahadi, J. (2015). When an Independent Contractor is Really an Employee. CNNMoney. money.cnn.com/2015/07/16/pf/independent-contractors-employees.
10. Levine, D. (2016). Uber Drivers Remain Independent Contractors as Lawsuit Settled. Reuters. www.reuters.com/article/us-uber-tech-drivers-settlement-idUSKCN0XJ07H.

11. Wong, J. (2017). Uber CEO Travis Kalanick Caught on Video Arguing with Driver about Fares. The Guardian. www.theguardian.com/technology/2017/feb/28/uber-ceo-travis-kalanick-driver-argument-video-fare-prices.
12. Conger, K. (2019). Uber Settles Drivers' Lawsuit for $20 Million. The New York Times. www.nytimes.com/2019/03/12/technology/uber-drivers-lawsuit-settle.html.
13. Numbers based on data maintained by the United States Census Bureau (n.d.).†Statistics of U.S. Businesses (SUSB). www.census.gov/programs-surveys/susb.html [Accessed September 11, 2019].
14. Caruso, A. (2015). Statistics of U.S. Businesses Employment and Payroll Summary: 2012. U.S. Census Bureau.
15. Gavett, G. (2014).
16. Faleye, O., Reis, E. and Venkateswaran, A. (2010). The Effect of Executive-Employee Pay Disparity on Labor Productivity. doi=10.1.1.175.6289.
17. Shin, T. (2012). CEO Compensation and Shareholder Value Orientation among Large U.S. Firms*. The Economic and Social Review, 43(4), pp. 535–559.
18. Ro, S. (2013). CHART OF THE DAY: Here's Who Owns the Stock Market. Business Insider. www.businessinsider.com/chart-stock-market-ownership-2013-3.
19. Clifford, C. (2019). Nearly 68% of the World's Richest People Are 'Self-Made,' Says New Report. CNBC. www.cnbc.com/2019/09/26/majority-of-the-worlds-richest-people-are-self-made-says-new-report.html.
20. Mejia, Z. (2018). Jeff Bezos Got His Parents to Invest Nearly $250,000 in Amazon in 1995—They Might Be Worth $30 Billion Today. CNBC. www.cnbc.com/2018/08/02/how-jeff-bezos-got-his-parents-to-invest-in-amazon--turning-them-into.html.

CHAPTER 2

21. Fleck, S., Glaser, J. and Sprague, S. (2011).†The Compensation-Productivity Gap: A Visual Essay. Monthly Labor Review. www.bls.gov/opub/mlr/2011/01/art3full.pdf.
22. Ro, S. (2013). CHART OF THE DAY: Here's Who Owns the Stock Market. Business Insider. www.businessinsider.com/the-grim-state-of-american-wealth-according-to-the-federal-reserve-2017-11.
23. World Inequality Lab. (2018). Part IV - Trends in Global Wealth Inequality. wir2018.wid.world/part-4.html.
24. Willis, J. and Wroblewski, J. (2007). What Happened to the Gains from Strong Productivity Growth? Federal Reserve Bank of Kansas City. www.kansascityfed.org/publicat/econrev/pdf/1q07will.pdf.
25. Van Dam, A. (2018). Is It Great to Be a Worker in the U.S.? Not Compared with the Rest of the Developed World. The Washington Post. www.washingtonpost.com/news/wonk/wp/2018/07/04/is-it-great-to-be-a-worker-in-the-u-s-not-compared-to-the-rest-of-the-developed-world.
26. Gonzalez-Mulé, E. and Cockburn, B. (2016). Worked to Death: The Relationships of Job Demands and Job Control with Mortality. Personnel Psychology. doi.org/10.1111/peps.12206.
27. Gallup. (2017). State of the American Workplace. www.gallup.com/services/178514/state-american-workplace.aspx.

28. Kasperkevic, J. (2015). Fact-Checking Jeb Bush: If Americans Work More Hours, Economy Will Grow. The Guardian. www.theguardian.com/us-news/reality-check/2015/jul/09/jeb-bush-work-longer-hours-economy.
29. Stech, K. (2015). The Future of Personal Bankruptcy in a Post-Obamacare World. The Wall Street Journal. blogs.wsj.com/bankruptcy/2015/07/01/the-future-of-personal-bankruptcy-in-a-post-obamacare-world.
30. Worstall, T. (2012). The Story of Henry Ford's $5-a-Day Wages: It's Not What You Think. Forbes. www.forbes.com/sites/timworstall/2012/03/04/the-story-of-henry-fords-5-a-day-wages-its-not-what-you-think.
31. PricewaterhouseCoopers LLP (PwC) and the National Venture Capital Association (NVCA) (2016). $58.8 Billion in Venture Capital Invested across U.S. in 2015, According to the MoneyTree Report. www.pwc.com/us/en/press-releases/2016/q4-2015-moneytree-press-release.html.
32. Keegan, P. (2015). Here's What Really Happened at That Company That Set a $70,000 Minimum Wage. Inc. www.inc.com/magazine/201511/paul-keegan/does-more-pay-mean-more-growth.html.
33. Gravity Payments. (n.d.). The Gravity of the $70K Decision. gravitypayments.com/thegravityof70k.
34. Office of the United States Trade Representative. (n.d.). Mexico. ustr.gov/countries-regions/americas/mexico.
35. The Conference Board. (2018). International Comparisons of Hourly Compensation Costs in Manufacturing, 2016 - Summary Tables. www.conference-board.org/ilcprogram/index.cfm?id=38269.
36. Robertson, C. (2013). The best engineers come from Germany. BBC News. www.bbc.com/news/business-2413153.
37. Jacoby, T. (2014). Why Germany Is So Much Better at Training Its Workers. The Atlantic. www.theatlantic.com/business/archive/2014/10/why-germany-is-so-much-better-at-training-its-workers/381550.
38. L. Fulton (2015) Worker Representation in Europe. Labour Research Department and ETUI. Produced with the assistance of the SEEurope Network, www.worker-participation.eu/National-Industrial-Relations/Countries/Germany/Collective-Bargaining.
39. Amounts calculated using average real annual GDP per capita growth rates from 1980 to 2015 according to The World Bank. (n.d.). GDP per capita growth (annual %). data.worldbank.org/indicator/NY.GDP.PCAP.KD.ZG. Accessed September 12, 2019.
40. Amounts calculated using average real annual GDP per capita growth rates from 1980 to 2015 according to the OECD. (n.d.). Growth in GDP per capita, productivity and ULC. stats.oecd.org/Index.aspx?DataSetCode=PDB_GR. Accessed September 12, 2019.
41. Wessner, C. (2013). How Does Germany Do It? The American Society of Mechanical Engineers. www.asme.org/topics-resources/content/how-does-germany-do-it.
42. $100,000 based on a base wage of $69,800 and Consumer Price Index (CPI) of 97.7 in December 1982, adjusted for CPI of 234.9 in January 2015. Bureau of Labor Statistics. (n.d.). Consumer Price Index. www.bls.gov/cpi. Accessed September 12, 2019.
43. U.S. House of Representatives Press Gallery. (2015). Salaries. pressgallery.house.gov/member-data/salaries.

CHAPTER 3

44. Gallaway, L. (2010). Unions, the High-Wage Doctrine, and Employment. Cato Journal, 30(1), pp.197-213. pdfs.semanticscholar.org/8718/8b5e360b699775f7e373e4dd87a1af3cd447.pdf.
45. Gambale, G. (2017). 31st Annual Survey of Corporate Executives: Confidence in U.S. Economy, Need for Investment in Highway Infrastructure and Skilled Labor Reflected - Area Development. Area Development. www.areadevelopment.com/Corporate-Consultants-Survey-Results/Q1-2017/responding-executives-confident-about-Trump-economy-skilled-labor-top-concern.shtml.
46. PricewaterhouseCoopers LLC (2017).Manufacturing Barometer: Business Outlook Report January 2017. www.pwc.com/us/en/industrial-manufacturing/assets/pwc-manufacturing-barometer-q4-2016.pdf.
47. Schwab, K. (2011). The Global Competitiveness Report 2011–2012. World Economic Forum. www3.weforum.org/docs/WEF_GCR_Report_2011-12.pdf.
48. Bartash, J. (2018). Here's Who Owns a Record $21.21 Trillion of U.S. Debt. MarketWatch. www.marketwatch.com/story/heres-who-owns-a-record-2121-trillion-of-us-debt-2018-08-21.
49. Herndon, T., Ash, M. and Pollin, R. (2013). Does High Public Debt Consistently Stifle Economic Growth? A Critique of Reinhart and Rogoff. Cambridge Journal of Economics, 38(2), pp. 257-279.

CHAPTER 4

50. National Labor Relations Board. (n.d.). Employee Rights. www.nlrb.gov/rights-we-protect/employee-rights.
51. Meisburg, R. (2014). Old Fashioned Protected Concerted Activity Stirred Up with a Twist. Labor Relations Update. www.laborrelationsupdate.com/nlrb/old-fashioned-protected-concerted-activity-stirred-up-with-a-twist.
52. National Labor Relations Board. (n.d.). Concerted activity. www.nlrb.gov/rights-we-protect/whats-law/employees/i-am-not-represented-union/concerted-activity.
53. Hirsch, B., Macpherson, D. and Vroman, W. (2001). Estimates of Union Density by State. unionstats.gsu.edu/MLR_7-01_StateUnionDensity.pdf.
54. Bureau of Labor Statistics. (2015). Union Affiliation Data from the Current Population Survey. www.bls.gov/data. Accessed February 27, 2015.
55. Bureau of Labor Statistics. (n.d.). 42. Union Affiliation of Employed Wage and Salary Workers by Occupation and Industry. www.bls.gov/cps/cpsaat42.pdf. Accessed September 14, 2019.
56. Industrial Workers of the World. (n.d.). The Basic Labor Laws (United States of America). www.iww.org/organize/laborlaw/Lynd/Lynd3.shtml.
57. Barbash, J. (2019). Chapter 6: Unions and Rights in the Space Age. U.S. Department of Labor. www.dol.gov/general/aboutdol/history/chapter6.
58. Bureau of Labor Statistics. (2015). Union Affiliation Data from the Current Population Survey. www.bls.gov/data. Accessed February 27, 2015.
59. The Wall Street Journal. (2007). Paycheck Protection End Run. www.wsj.com/articles/SB117936568045105724.

60. Olney, B. (2014). Paycheck Protection or Paycheck Deception? When Government "Subsidies" Silence Political Speech. UC Irvine Law Review, 4(2), p. 908. www.law.uci.edu/lawreview/vol4/no2/Olney.pdf.
61. Brunner, J. (2015). Labor Law Challenged: Freedom Foundation Sues SEIU 925. The Seattle Times. www.seattletimes.com/seattle-news/politics/freedom-foundation-files-suit-against-seiu-925.
62. Kim, H. (2016). Union Leaders Furious over Door-to-Door Tactic Targeting Their Members. Q13 Fox. q13fox.com/2016/08/03/union-leaders-furious-over-door-to-door-tactic-targeting-their-members.
63. Weber, L. and Morath, E. (2018). NLRB Pushes to Rescind Obama-Era Union Ruling. The Wall Street Journal. www.wsj.com/articles/nlrb-pushes-to-rescind-obama-era-union-ruling-1536929983.
64. Wiessner, D. (2018). U.S. Appeals Court Nixes Labor Agency's Obama-Era 'Joint Employment' Test. Reuters. www.reuters.com/article/us-usa-labor/us-appeals-court-nixes-labor-agencys-obama-era-joint-employment-test-idUSKCN1OR1C5.
65. Worker Participation. (2018). European Works Councils. www.worker-participation.eu/European-Works-Councils.
66. Advisory, Conciliation and Arbitration Service. (n.d.). Information and Consultation of Employees (ICE). www.acas.org.uk/index.aspx?articleid=1598
67. Jørgensen, C. (2015). Denmark: Collective Bargaining in Private Sector Gives Way to Some Optimism. Eurofound. www.eurofound.europa.eu/observatories/eurwork/articles/industrial-relations/denmark-collective-bargaining-in-private-sector-gives-way-to-some-optimism.
68. BBC News. (2014). Germany Approves First-Ever National Minimum Wage. www.bbc.com/news/business-28140594.
69. Dale T. Mortensen–Biographical. (n.d.). Nobel Media AB 2020. www.nobelprize.org/prizes/economic-sciences/2010/mortensen/biographical.
70. Budd, J., Chi, W., Wang, Y. and Xie, Q. (2014). What Do Unions in China Do? Provincial-Level Evidence on Wages, Employment, Productivity, and Economic Output. Journal of Labor Research. www.legacy-irc.csom.umn.edu/faculty/jbudd/research/Chinese-Union-Provincial-Effects-final.pdf.
71. Masayuki, M. (2008). What Do Japanese Unions Do for Productivity?: An Empirical Analysis Using Firm-Level Data. Research Institute of Economy, Trade and Industry (RIETI). www.rieti.go.jp/jp/publications/dp/08e027.pdf.
72. Bascia, N. (2003). Triage or Tapestry? Teacher Unions' Work Toward Improving Teacher Quality in an Era of Systemic Reform. Center for the Study of Teaching and Policy.
73. Ingersoll, R. (2011). Do We Produce Enough Mathematics and Science Teachers?. Kappan Magazine, 92(6). www.gse.upenn.edu/pdf/rmi/Enough_Math_Teachers.pdf.
74. Bascia, N. (2003).
75. Coulson, A. (2010). The Effects of Teachers Unions on American Education. Cato Journal, 30(1), p. 165. object.cato.org/sites/cato.org/files/serials/files/cato-journal/2010/1/cj30n1-8.pdf.
76. The Official Website of the City of New York. (2017). Mayor de Blasio Signs Bill Prohibiting All NYC Employers from Inquiring About Salary History of Job Applicants. www1.nyc.gov/office-of-the-mayor/news/285-17/mayor-de-blasio-signs-bill-prohibiting-all-nyc-employers-inquiring-salary-history-job.

77. The Washington Post. (2017). Pay Transparency Could Help Close the 'Wage Gap.' The EEOC Shouldn't Write It Off. www.washingtonpost.com/opinions/pay-transparency-could-help-close-the-wage-gap-the-eeoc-shouldnt-write-it-off/2017/09/09/9d262f44-93f6-11e7-aace-04b862b2b3f3_story.html.

CHAPTER 5

78. History. (2009). Nixon Arrives in China for Talks. www.history.com/this-day-in-history/nixon-arrives-in-china-for-talks.
79. Wang, D. (2013). U.S.-China Trade, 1971–2012: Insights into the U.S.-China Relationship. The Asia-Pacific Journal, 11(24). No 4. apjjf.org/2013/11/24/Dong-Wang/3958/article.html.
80. United States Census Bureau. (2019). Foreign Trade: Trade in Goods with China. www.census.gov/foreign-trade/balance/c5700.html. Accessed September 15, 2019.
81. United States Census Bureau. (2019). Foreign Trade: Historical Series. www.census.gov/foreign-trade/statistics/historical/index.html. Accessed September 15, 2019.
82. Porter, E. (2016). NAFTA May Have Saved Many Autoworkers' Jobs. The New York Times. www.nytimes.com/2016/03/30/business/economy/nafta-may-have-saved-many-autoworkers-jobs.html.
83. China Briefing News. (2017). Investing in China's Free Trade Zones. www.china-briefing.com/news/investing-in-chinas-free-trade-zones.
84. Intel. (2007). Intel to Build 300mm Wafer Fabrication Facility in China. www.intel.com/pressroom/archive/releases/2007/20070326corp.htm.
85. China Briefing News. (2016). China Announces Seven New Free Trade Zones, Signaling Intent to Diversify Economy. www.china-briefing.com/news/2016/09/09/china-seven-new-trade-zones.html.
86. Anonymous. (2016). Main Indicators for Mexico. European Directorate General for Trade. trade.ec.europa.eu/doclib/docs/2006/september/tradoc_111539.pdf.
87. Office of the United States Trade Representative. (n.d.). Mexico: U.S.-Mexico Trade Facts. ustr.gov/countries-regions/americas/Mexico. Accessed September 15, 2019.
88. European Commission. (2019). China. ec.europa.eu/trade/policy/countries-and-regions/countries/china.
89. Freeman, C. (2021). How Will China's Bid to Join a Trans-Pacific Trade Pact Affect Regional Stability? United States Institute of Peace. www.usip.org/publications/2021/10/how-will-chinas-bid-join-trans-pacific-trade-pact-affect-regional-stability.
90. Summers, C. (2016). Inside a Trump Chinese Shoe Factory: 100,000 Pairs of Footwear Branded with Ivanka's Name Have Been Made at Huge Facility (But Now It's Moving to Africa!). Daily Mail. www.dailymail.co.uk/news/article-3824617/Trump-factory-jobs-sent-China-never-come-back.html.
91. Vennochi, J. (2016). Do As Donald Trump Says, Not As Ivanka Trump Does. Boston Globe. www.bostonglobe.com/opinion/2016/12/06/trump-says-not-ivanka-does/Is8q5c2iFaUhVdHVdcVaoO/story.html.
92. Anderson, D. and Flanagan, G. (2018). Inside the Trump 'MAGA' Hat Factory. Business Insider. www.businessinsider.com/inside-trump-maga-hat-factory-california-make-america-great-again-2018-8.

93. DiChristopher, T. (2016). Saudis Threaten $750B Asset Sale, But Experts Question It. CNBC. www.cnbc.com/2016/04/20/saudis-threaten-750b-asset-sale-but-experts-question-it.html.
94. Hiltzik, M. (2016). Saudi Arabia is Threatening to Sell $750 billion in U.S. Assets. Talk about an Empty Threat. Los Angeles Times. www.latimes.com/business/hiltzik/la-fi-hiltzik-saudi-threat-20160418-snap-htmlstory.html.
95. AOL's Steve Case Sells Estate to Saudi Government for $43 Million. The Wall Street Journal. www.wsj.com/articles/aol-s-steve-case-sells-northern-virginia-estate-for-43-million-1527699578.
96. Daniels, J. (2016). Saudi Arabia Buying up Farmland in U.S. Southwest. CNBC. www.cnbc.com/2016/01/15/saudi-arabia-buying-up-farmland-in-us-southwest.html. Taylor, C. (2019).
97. U.S. Consumer Product Safety Commission. (2000). CPSC, Master Lock Co. Announce Recall to Replace Gun Locks. www.cpsc.gov/Recalls/2000/CPSC-Master-Lock-Co-Announce-Recall-to-Replace-Gun-Locks.
98. Schmid, J. (2011). Master Lock Reassessing China. Journal Sentinel. archive.jsonline.com/business/112759524.html.
99. Clifford, S. (2013). Recall Is Expensive Setback for Maker of Yoga Pants. The New York Times. www.nytimes.com/2013/03/22/business/lululemon-says-yoga-pants-mis-hap-will-be-costly.html.
100. U.S. Consumer Product Safety Commission. (2007). Fisher-Price Recalls Licensed Character Toys Due to Lead Poisoning Hazard. www.cpsc.gov/Recalls/2007/Fisher-Price-Recalls-Licensed-Character-Toys-Due-To-Lead-Poisoning-Hazard-.
101. True LEADership Act of 2016. (2016). S. 2821—114th Congress. www.govtrack.us/congress/bills/114/s2821.
102. Patterson, T. (2014). Dreamliner Battery Probe Ends: 8 Questions and Answers. CNN Travel. www.cnn.com/2014/12/11/travel/boeing-787-dreamliner-investigation-report.
103. Premack, R. (2019). Who developed the Boeing 737 Max's Flawed Software? Low-Paid Temp Workers and Recent College Grads, According to Report. Business Insider. www.businessinsider.com/boeing-outsourced-737-max-report-2019-6.
104. Reebok News Stream (2016). Reebok Introduces New Liquid Factory. news.reebok.com/global/latest-news/reebok-introduces-new-liquid-factory/s/8a87d7f7-8a93-49d2-9ddd-efee2d588b76.

CHAPTER 6

105. Kollen Ghizoni, S. (2013). Nixon Ends Convertibility of US Dollars to Gold and Announces Wage/Price Controls. Federal Reserve History. www.federalreservehistory.org/essays/gold_convertibility_ends.
106. Ptacek, F. and Rippy, D. (2013). Owners' Equivalent Rent and the Consumer Price Index: 30 Years and Counting. BLS Beyond the Numbers, 2(4). www.bls.gov/opub/btn/volume-2/pdf/owners-equivalent-rent-and-the-consumer-price-index-30-years-and-counting.pdf.
107. Ibid.

108. Federal Register. (2002). Alternative Mortgage Transaction Parity Act; Preemption. www.federalregister.gov/documents/2002/09/26/02-24407/alternative-mortgage-transaction-parity-act-preemption.
109. Kessler, G. (2013). History Lesson: Who's Responsible for 'Chained CPI'? The Washington Post. www.washingtonpost.com/blogs/fact-checker/post/history-lesson-whos-responsible-for-chained-cpi/2013/04/20/23a002d6-a9d5-11e2-a8e2-5b98cb59187f_blog.html.
110. Frenze, C. (1997). The Consumer Price Index and Public Policy. Joint Economic Committee Republicans. www.jec.senate.gov/public/_cache/files/ed330750-bbe6-4a13-bf78-ff0b09f8cb57/the-consumer-price-index-and-public-policy.pdf.
111. Kessler, G. (2013).
112. Frenze, C. (1997).
113. DeSilver, D. (2018). For Most U.S. Workers, Real Wages Have Barely Budged in Decades. Pew Research Center. www.pewresearch.org/fact-tank/2014/10/09/for-most-workers-real-wages-have-barely-budged-for-decades.
114. Perry, M. (2019). Chart of the DayÖ. or Century? Carpe Diem AEI. www.aei.org/publication/chart-of-the-day-or-century.
115. FRED Economic Data. (2019). S&P/Case-Shiller 20-City Composite Home Price Index. fred.stlouisfed.org/series/SPCS20RSA.

CHAPTER 7

116. History. (2009). Child Labor. www.history.com/topics/child-labor.
117. Berger, N. and Fisher, P. (2013). A Well-Educated Workforce Is Key to State Prosperity. Economic Policy Institute. www.epi.org/publication/states-education-productivity-growth-foundations.
118. Mazerov, M. (2013). Academic Research Lacks Consensus on the Impact of State Tax Cuts on Economic Growth. Center on Budget and Policy Priorities. www.cbpp.org/sites/default/files/atoms/files/6-17-13sfp.pdf.
119. Aghion, P., Akcigit, U., Cage, J. and Kerr, W. (2016). Taxation, Corruption, and Growth. Harvard Business School. www.hbs.edu/faculty/Publication%20Files/AACK-HBSWP-Jan16_520961cd-db29-47b9-a28a-7288d8e43cb1.pdf.
120. Levy, D. (2004). Biography Revisits Fred Terman's Roles in Engineering, Stanford, Silicon Valley. Stanford News. news.stanford.edu/news/2004/november3/Terman-1103.html.
121. Mitroff, S. (2013). If You Want the Real Silicon Valley, Skip Bravo and Tune In to PBS. WIRED. www.wired.com/2013/02/silicon-valley-pbs.
122. Science History Institute. (2017). Gordon E. Moore. www.chemheritage.org/historical-profile/gordon-e-moore. Originally adapted from Christophe Lécuyer and David C. Brock, "Gordon Earle Moore," IEEE Annals of Computing, July–September 2006.
123. Encyclopedia of World Biography. (2010). Robert Noyce Facts. biography.yourdictionary.com/robert-noyce. Accessed September 6, 2019.
124. Dunlop, M. (2016). The College Scorecard and Return on Investment. New England Board of Higher Education. www.nebhe.org/thejournal/the-college-scorecard-and-return-on-investment.

125. Ronald Reagan and a Need for Action. (1966). [film] San Francisco.
126. The Economist. (2017). The Economies of American States and Cities are Diverging. www.economist.com/graphic-detail/2017/10/23/the-economies-of-american-states-and-cities-are-diverging.
127. Langdon, D., McKittrick, G., Beede, D., Khan, B. and Doms, M. (2011). STEM: Good Jobs Now and for the Future. www.commerce.gov/sites/default/files/migrated/reports/stemfinalyjuly14_1.pdf.
128. Fayer, S., Lacey, A. and Watson, A. (2017). STEM Occupations: Past, Present, And Future. U.S. Bureau of Labor Statistics, p. 7. www.bls.gov/spotlight/2017/science-technology-engineering-and-mathematics-stem-occupations-past-present-and-future/pdf/science-technology-engineering-and-mathematics-stem-occupations-past-present-and-future.pdf. Accessed September 17, 2019.
129. Balk, G. (2016). $80,000 Median: Income Gain in Seattle Far Outpaces Other Cities. The Seattle Times. www.seattletimes.com/seattle-news/data/80000-median-wage-income-gain-in-seattle-far-outpaces-other-cities.
130. Johnson, E. (2016). New Year Brings Minimum Wage Hikes for Americans in 14 States. Reuters. www.reuters.com/article/us-usa-minimumwage-idUSKBN0UF1QA20160101.
131. Peterson, P., Woessmann, L., Hanushek, E. and Lastra-AnadÛn, C. (2011). Globally Challenged: Are U.S. Students Ready to Compete? Harvard's Program on Education Policy and Governance & Education Next: Taubman Center for State and Local Government, Harvard Kennedy School, p. viii. sites.hks.harvard.edu/pepg/PDF/Papers/PEPG11-03_GloballyChallenged.pdf.
132. OECD. (2019). Education Spending (Indicator). doi: 10.1787/ca274bac-en. Accessed September 17, 2019.
133. Trostel, P. (2008). High Returns: Public Investment in Higher Education. Federal Reserve Bank of Boston: This Communities & Banking, pp. 31-32.
134. Rephann, T., Knapp, J. and Shobe, W. (2010). Study of the Economic Impact of Virginia Public Higher Education. Center for Economic and Policy Studies. www.researchgate.net/publication/46468694_Study_of_the_Economic_Impact_of_Virginia_Public_Higher_Education.
135. Rephann, T. (2013). Study of the Economic Impact of Virginia Public Higher Education: 2013 Update for the Virginia Business Higher Education Council. Weldon Cooper Center for Public Service, University of Virginia. www.researchgate.net/publication/269393943_Study_of_the_Economic_Impact_of_Virginia_Public_Higher_Education_2013_Update_for_the_Virginia_Business_Higher_Education_Council.
136. Bureau of Labor Statistics, U.S. Department of Labor. (2012). International Comparisons of Hourly Compensation Costs in Manufacturing, 2011. www.bls.gov/news.release/pdf/ichcc.pdf.
137. Woessmann L. (2016). The Economic Case for Education. Education Economics, 24:1, 3-32, Available online at: DOI: 10.1080/09645292.2015.1059801.
138. OECD (2016). PISA 2015 Results (Volume I): Excellence and Equity in Education. Paris: OECD, p. 44. doi.org/10.1787/9789264266490-en.
139. World Bank, International Comparison Program database. (n.d.). GDP per capita, PPP (current international $). data.worldbank.org/indicator/NY.GDP.PCAP.PP.CD. Accessed September 17, 2019.

140. Jackson, A. and Kiersz, A. (2016). The Latest Ranking of Top Countries in Math, Reading, and Science is Out—and the U.S. Didn't Crack the Top 10. Business Insider. www.businessinsider.com/pisa-worldwide-ranking-of-math-science-reading-skills-2016-12.
141. Schwab, K. (2016). The Global Competitiveness Report 2016–2017. Geneva: World Economic Forum, p. 357. www3.weforum.org/docs/GCR2016-2017/05FullReport/TheGlobalCompetitivenessReport2016-2017_FINAL.pdf.
142. Engineering and Economic Growth: A Global View. (2016). Centre for Economics and Business Research for the Royal Academy of Engineering. www.raeng.org.uk/publications/reports/engineering-and-economic-growth-a-global-view.
143. OECD (2017). OECD Science, Technology and Industry Scoreboard 2017: The Digital Transformation. Paris: OECD, p. 102.
144. DeSilver, D. (2015). Growth from Asia Drives Surge in U.S. Foreign Students. Pew Research Center. www.pewresearch.org/fact-tank/2015/06/18/growth-from-asia-drives-surge-in-u-s-foreign-students.
145. Ross, K. (2016). Study: Interest in STEM Fuels Growth in Number of International Students in U.S. U.S. News and World Report: Education. www.usnews.com/education/best-colleges/articles/2016-11-14/study-interest-in-stem-fuels-growth-in-number-of-international-students-in-us.
146. Strauss, V. (2016). U.S. High School Graduation Rate is Up—But There's a Warning Label Attached. The Washington Post. www.washingtonpost.com/news/answer-sheet/wp/2016/10/27/u-s-high-school-graduation-rate-is-up-but-theres-a-warning-label-attached.
147. Sirkin, H. (2013). What Germany Can Teach the U.S. about Vocational Education. Bloomberg. www.bloomberg.com/news/articles/2013-04-29/what-germany-can-teach-the-u-dot-s-dot-about-vocational-education.
148. Bureau of Labor Statistics (2015). High Tech Industries in the U.S. Economy. Workforce Information Council High-Tech Study Group. www.bls.gov/advisory/bloc/high-tech-industries.pdf.
149. Commonwealth of Pennsylvania: Department of Education. (n.d.). Career and Technical Education. www.education.pa.gov/K-12/Career%20and%20Technical%20Education/Pages/default.aspx. Accessed September 17, 2019.
150. Lehigh Career & Technical Institute (2018). Career & Technical Education Program Guide. p. 2. www.lcti.org/uploads/2019/02/CTE-Program-Guide-NACCI.pdf.
151. NOCTI. (n.d.). State Programs. www.nocti.org/StateCustomized.cfm. Accessed September 17, 2019.
152. Republic of France: Ministry for National Education (2010). National Education and Vocational Education in France. media.eduscol.education.fr/file/dossiers/61/8/formation_professionnelle_VA_151618.pdf.
153. Semuels, A. (2016). Good School, Rich School; Bad School, Poor School. The Atlantic. www.theatlantic.com/business/archive/2016/08/property-taxes-and-unequal-schools/497333.
154. Colorado Department of Education. (2019). 2018-2019 Teachers FTE and Average Salary. www.cde.state.co.us/cdereval/2018-19averagesalariesforteacherspdf.
155. National Science Board. (2018). Science & Engineering Indicators 2018, p. 28. www.nsf.gov/statistics/2018/nsb20181/assets/nsb20181.pdf.

156. Berman, J. (2016). Watch America's Student-Loan Debt Grow $2,726 Every Second. MarketWatch. www.marketwatch.com/story/every-second-americans-get-buried-under-another-3055-in-student-loan-debt-2015-06-10.
157. Brown, M. and Caldwell, S. (2013). Young Student Loan Borrowers Retreat from Housing and Auto Markets. Federal Reserve Bank of New York: Liberty Street Economics. libertystreeteconomics.newyorkfed.org/2013/04/young-student-loan-borrowers-retreat-from-housing-and-auto-markets.html.
158. Bureau of Labor Statistics: The Economics Daily. (2013). The Job Market for Recent College Graduates in the United States. www.bls.gov/opub/ted/2013/ted_20130405.htm.
159. Bureau of Labor Statistics: The Economics Daily. (2013).
160. Applegate, J. and Fulton, M. (2016). Wiping the Slate Clean: A New Federalism for the 21st Century Student. Education Commission of the States, p. 9. www.ecs.org/ec-content/uploads/ECS_FundingReports_ApplegateFulton_F.pdf.
161. Dickler, J. (2017). Women Carry Bigger Burden of Student Loan Debt Than Men. CNBC. www.cnbc.com/2017/01/25/women-carry-bigger-burden-of-student-loan-debt-than-men.html.
162. Insler, S. (2017). The Mental Toll of Student Debt: What Our Survey Shows. Student Loan Hero. studentloanhero.com/featured/psychological-effects-of-debt-survey-results.
163. SoFi. (2017). Data Suggests Student Loan Stress More Extreme Than You Thought. www.sofi.com/blog/refi-and-relax.
164. Walsemann, K., Gee, G. and Gentile, D. (2015). Sick of Our Loans: Student Borrowing and the Mental Health of Young Adults in the United States. Social Science & Medicine, 124, pp. 85-93. doi.org/10.1016/j.socscimed.2014.11.027.
165. Brown, M., Haughwout, A., Lee, D., Scally, J. and van der Klaauw, W. (2015). Looking at Student Loan Defaults through a Larger Window. Federal Reserve Bank of New York: Liberty Street Economics. libertystreeteconomics.newyorkfed.org/2015/02/looking_at_student_loan_defaults_through_a_larger_window.html.
166. Tanzi, A. (2019). U.S. Student Debt in 'Serious Delinquency' Tops $166 Billion. Bloomberg. www.bloomberg.com/news/articles/2019-02-16/u-s-student-debt-in-serious-delinquency-tops-166-billion.
167. Total Wage Garnishments Calculated Using Quarterly Data for 2016 Default Recoveries by Private Collection Agencies. U.S. Department of Education: Federal Student Aid. (n.d.). Default Rates. studentaid.ed.gov/sa/about/data-center/student/default. Accessed September 17, 2019.
168. Amounts Found by Examination of Private Collection Agency Contracts. U.S. Department of Education: Federal Student Aid. (n.d.). Private Collection Agency Contracts. studentaid.ed.gov/sa/about/data-center/business-info/contracts/collection-agency#. Accessed September 17, 2019.
169. Sullivan, B. (2014). 4 Student Loan Debt Collection Tricks. CBS News. www.cbsnews.com/media/4-student-loan-debt-collection-tricks.
170. Kim, A. (2018). Innovating Out of Student Debt. Progressive Policy Institute. www.progressivepolicy.org/publications/policy-memo/innovating-out-of-student-debt.
171. Mitchell, J. and Kusisto, L. (2019). Fed Says Student Debt Has Hurt the U.S. Housing Market. The Wall Street Journal. www.wsj.com/articles/fed-says-student-debt-is-u-s-hurting-housing-market-11547657473.

172. U.S. Department of Labor: Bureau of Labor Statistics. (n.d.). Labor Force Statistics from the Current Population Survey. www.bls.gov/cps. Accessed March 21, 2017.
173. Wolf Harlow, C. (2003). Education and Correctional Populations. NCJ 195670. U.S. Department of Justice, Bureau of Justice Statistics. www.bjs.gov/content/pub/pdf/ecp.pdf.

CHAPTER 8

174. U.S. Department of Labor: Wage & Hour Divisions. (2019). Minimum Wages for Tipped Employees. www.dol.gov/whd/state/tipped.htm. Accessed September 25, 2019.
175. Statistics calculated using data from the U.S. Census Bureau's Small Area Income and Poverty Estimates database compared to the Department of Labor's January 1, 2017 Table of Minimum Hourly Wages for Tipped Employees, by State.
176. Restaurant Opportunities Centers United (2015). Picking Up the NRA's Tab: The Public Cost of Low Wages in the Full-Service Restaurant Industry. New York: Restaurant Opportunities Centers United, p. 5. rocunited.org/wp2015b/wp-content/uploads/2015/04/REPORT_Public-Cost-of-Low-Wages-in-Full-Service-Restaurant-Industry.pdf.
177. Wann, E. (2016). American Tipping is Rooted in Slavery—and It Still Hurts Workers Today. Ford Foundation. www.fordfoundation.org/ideas/equals-change-blog/posts/american-tipping-is-rooted-in-slavery-and-it-still-hurts-workers-today.
178. Allegretto, S. and Cooper, D. (2014). Twenty-Three Years and Still Waiting for Change: Why It's Time to Give Tipped Workers the Regular Minimum Wage. Washington, DC: Economic Policy Institute, p.18. www.epi.org/files/2014/EPI-CWED-BP379.pdf.
179. Greenspan, R. (2018). 'It's the Legacy of Slavery': Here's the Troubling History Behind Tipping Practices in the U.S. Time. time.com/5404475/history-tipping-american-restaurants-civil-war.
180. Lynn, M., Sturman, M., Ganley, C., Adams, E. and Douglas, M. (2008). Consumer Racial Discrimination in Tipping: A Replication and Extension. Cornell University, School of Hospitality Administration. scholarship.sha.cornell.edu/articles/27.
181. Brewster, Z. and Lynn, M. (2014). Black-White Earnings Gap among Restaurant Servers: A Replication, Extension, and Exploration of Consumer Racial Discrimination in Tipping. Sociological Inquiry, 84(4), pp. 545-569.
182. U.S. Department of Labor, Wage and Hour Division. (n.d.). Final Rule: Overtime Update. www.dol.gov/whd/overtime2019.
183. Kennedy, John F. Remarks of Senator John F. Kennedy, Municipal Auditorium, Canton, Ohio Online by Gerhard Peters and John T. Woolley, The American Presidency Project. www.presidency.ucsb.edu/node/274665.
184. The Economist. (2011). Cutting the Cake. www.economist.com/blogs/dailychart/2011/09/us-household-income.
185. Monaco, K. and Pierce, B. (2015). Compensation Inequality: Evidence from the National Compensation Survey. Monthly Labor Review. U.S. Department of Labor, Bureau of Labor Statistics.

186. U.S. Department of Agriculture, Food and Nutrition Service. (2018). A Short History of SNAP. www.fns.usda.gov/snap/short-history-snap.
187. Farson Gray, K., Fisher, S. and Lauffer, S. (2016). Characteristics of Supplemental Nutrition Assistance Program Households: Fiscal Year 2015. Alexandria, VA: U.S. Department of Agriculture, Food and Nutrition Service, Office of Policy Support, p. xvi. www.fns.usda.gov/ops/research-and-analysis].
188. U.S. Department of Agriculture, Food and Nutrition Service. (2019). SNAP Eligibility. www.fns.usda.gov/snap/eligibility#Employment Requirements. Accessed September 25, 2019.
189. U.S. Department of Agriculture, Food and Nutrition Service. (2018). Able-Bodied Adults Without Dependents (ABAWDs). www.fns.usda.gov/snap/able-bodied-adults-without-dependents-abawds. Accessed September 25, 2019.
190. U.S. Department of Agriculture, Food and Nutrition Service. (2013). Students. www.fns.usda.gov/snap/students. Accessed September 25, 2019.
191. Jacobs, K., Perry, I. and MacGillvary, J. (2015). The High Public Cost of Low Wages: Poverty-Level Wages Cost U.S. Taxpayers $152.8 Billion Each Year in Public Support for Working Families. Berkeley, CA: UC Berkeley Center for Labor Research and Education, p. 2-3. laborcenter.berkeley.edu/pdf/2015/the-high-public-cost-of-low-wages.pdf.
192. Warren E. (2015). Senator Warren's Remarks at AFL-CIO National Summit on Raising Wages. www.warren.senate.gov/newsroom/press-releases/senator-warren-and-039s-remarks-at-afl-cio-national-summit-on-raising-wages.
193. Restaurant Opportunities Centers United (2015). Picking Up the NRAís Tab: The Public Cost of Low Wages in the Full-Service Restaurant Industry.
194. Allegretto S.A., Doussard M., Graham-Squire D., Jacobs K., Thompson D., and Thompson J. (2013). Fast Food, Poverty Wages: The Public Cost of Low-Wage Jobs in the Fast-Food Industry. Berkeley, CA: UC Berkeley Center for Labor Research and Education, p. 1. laborcenter.berkeley.edu/pdf/2013/fast_food_poverty_wages.pdf. Accessed September 25, 2019.
195. Restaurant Opportunities Centers United (2015). Picking Up the NRA's Tab: The Public Cost of Low Wages in the Full-Service Restaurant Industry.
196. Kim, S. (2013). McDonald's Pulls Worker Website That Warned about Fast Food. ABC News. abcnews.go.com/Business/mcdonalds-takes-mcresource-website/story?id=21338832.
197. Food Marketing Institute vs. Argus Leader Media, dba Argus Leader [2019] U.S. 558 (Supreme Court of the United States), p. 18.
198. U.S. House of Representatives (2013). The Low-Wage Drag on Our Economy: Wal-Mart's Low Wages and Their Effect on Taxpayers and Economic Growth. Washington, D.C.: Democratic staff of the U.S. House Committee on Education and the Workforce, p. 1. edlabor.house.gov/imo/media/doc/WalMartReport-May2013.pdf.
199. Talk Business & Politics. (2013). Wal-Mart Downplays SNAP Cuts. talkbusiness.net/2013/10/wal-mart-downplays-snap-cuts-updated.
200. Americans for Tax Fairness (2014). Walmart on Tax Day: How Taxpayers Subsidize America's Biggest Employer and Richest Family. Washington, D.C, p. 4. americansfortaxfairness.org/files/Walmart-on-Tax-Day-Americans-for-Tax-Fairness-11.pdf.

201. Shiller, Z. (2018). More Ohio Amazon Workers Relying on Food Aid. Policy Matters Ohio. www.policymattersohio.org/press-room/2018/01/05/more-ohio-amazon-workers-relying-on-food-aid.
202. Green, D. (2018). Data from States Shows Thousands of Amazon Employees Are on Food Stamps. Business Insider. www.businessinsider.com/amazon-employees-on-food-stamps-2018-8.
203. Jacobs, K., Perry, I. and MacGillvary, J. (2015).
204. Ibid.
205. Congressional Budget Office (2014). The Effects of a Minimum-Wage Increase on Employment and Family Income. Washington, D.C.: Congress of the United States, p. 16. www.cbo.gov/sites/default/files/113th-congress-2013-2014/reports/44995-MinimumWage.pdf.
206. Tu, J. (2016). Voters Approve Minimum Wage Increase to $13.50 in Washington State. The Seattle Times. www.seattletimes.com/seattle-news/politics/washington-state-minimum-wage-initiative-1433.
207. Office of the Mayor, Mayor Edward B. Murray. (n.d.). $15 Minimum Wage. murray.seattle.gov/minimumwage. Accessed September 25, 2019.
208. U.S. Department of Labor, Bureau of Labor Statistics. (n.d.). Seattle-Tacoma-Bellevue, WA Economy at a Glance. www.bls.gov/eag/eag.wa_seattle_msa.htm. Accessed September 25, 2019.
209. Winkler, M. (2019). States with High Minimum Wages Are Doing Just Fine. Bloomberg. www.bloomberg.com/opinion/articles/2019-07-26/minimum-wage-hikes-don-t-stifle-state-economic-booms.
210. D'Onfro, J. (2018). Bernie Sanders Introduces the Bezos Act, Slamming Amazon's Low Wages. CNBC. www.cnbc.com/2018/09/05/bernie-sanders-introduces-the-bezos-act-slamming-amazon-low-wages.html.
211. Sanders B. (2018). Sanders, Khanna Introduce the Stop WALMART Act to Put Workers Over Shareholders. www.sanders.senate.gov/newsroom/press-releases/sanders-khanna-introduce-the-stop-walmart-act-to-put-workers-over-shareholders.
212. Americans for Tax Fairness (2014). Walmart on Tax Day: How Taxpayers Subsidize America's Biggest Employer and Richest Family.

CHAPTER 9

213. PBS. (2007). War Production. www.pbs.org/thewar/at_home_war_production.htm.
214. Daggett, S. (2010). Costs of Major U.S. Wars. Washington, D.C: Congressional Research Service, p. 2. fas.org/sgp/crs/natsec/RS22926.pdf.
215. Bonacum, L., Scott, E. and Au, B. (2013). 2013 CCH Whole Ball of Tax. CCH Incorporated. www.cch.com/WBOT2013/029IncomeTaxRates.asp.
216. Internal Revenue Service. (2019). SOI Tax Stats - Historical Table 23. www.irs.gov/statistics/soi-tax-stats-historical-table-23.
217. Ibid.
218. Social Security Administration. (n.d.). Social Security & Medicare Tax Rates. www.ssa.gov/oact/progdata/taxRates.html.
219. Tax Foundation. (2012). Federal Corporate Income Tax Rates, Income Years 1909-2012. taxfoundation.org/federal-corporate-income-tax-rates-income-years-1909-2012.

220. Congressional Budget Office (2017). The Budget and Economic Outlook: 2017 to 2027: Data and Supplemental Information. www.cbo.gov/publication/52370.
221. History. (2019). Johnson Asks for More Funding for Vietnam War. www.history.com/this-day-in-history/johnson-asks-for-more-funding-for-vietnam-war.
222. Intuit, Inc. (2018). How an S-Corp Can Reduce Your Self-Employment Taxes. turbotax.intuit.com/tax-tips/small-business-taxes/how-an-s-corp-can-reduce-your-self-employment-taxes/L4abUcaRn.
223. Califano Jr., J. (1995). Balancing the Budget, L.B.J. Style. The New York Times, Section 4, p. 9. www.nytimes.com/1995/12/31/opinion/balancing-the-budget-lbj-style.html.
224. Brownstein, R. (2003). Bush Breaks With 140 Years of History in Plan for Wartime Tax Cut. Los Angeles Times. www.latimes.com/archives/la-xpm-2003-jan-13-na-outlook13-story.html.
225. Lewandoski, M. (2008). The Bush Tax Cuts of 2001 and 2003. Federal Budget Policy Seminar. A Brief Legislative History., Harvard Law School. Briefing Paper No. 37.
226. Ensor, D. (2003). Fake Iraq Documents 'Embarrassing' for U.S. CNN. www.cnn.com/2003/US/03/14/sprj.irq.documents.
227. Hanley, R. (2004). Bulletproof Vests Collected to Help a Son's Unit in Iraq. The New York Times. www.nytimes.com/2004/05/22/nyregion/bulletproof-vests-collected-to-help-a-son-s-unit-in-iraq.html.
228. Fox News. (2003). U.S. Troops in Iraq Have Limited Body Armor. www.foxnews.com/story/2003/10/24/us-troops-in-iraq-have-limited-body-armor.html.
229. Associated Press. (2004). Troops in Iraq Still Buying Their Own Body Armor. usatoday30.usatoday.com/news/world/iraq/2004-03-26-body-armor_x.htm.
230. Cox, J. (2017). Companies Have Big Plans for Trillions in Overseas Cash—If Tax Reform Ever Happens. CNBC. www.cnbc.com/2017/07/13/companies-have-big-plans-foroverseas-cash--if-tax-reform-ever-happens.html.
231. Fox News. (2009). Conclusion of Hannity-Moore Showdown. www.foxnews.com/transcript/conclusion-of-hannity-moore-showdown.
232. The Economist. (2016). The Avengers: A Network of Wealthy Donors Has a Mission to Push Politics to the Right. www.economist.com/news/books-and-arts/21689522-network-wealthy-donors-has-mission-push-politics-right-avengers.
233. Mayer, J. (2017). Dark Money: The Hidden History of the Billionaires Behind the Rise of the Radical Right. 1st ed. New York: Anchor Books, pp. 88-98.
234. Valentine, P. (2014). Richard Mellon Scaife, Billionaire Who Funded Anti-Liberal Causes, Dies at 82. The Washington Post. www.washingtonpost.com/national/richard-mellon-scaife-billionaire-famous-for-attacks-against-bill-clinton-has-died/2014/07/04/9e2fcace-458c-11e3-bf0c-cebf37c6f484_story.html.
235. Adeniji, A. (2015). How the Hoover Institution Vacuums Up Big Conservative Bucks. Inside Philanthropy. www.insidephilanthropy.com/home/2015/4/21/how-the-hoover-institution-vacuums-up-big-conservative-bucks.html.
236. Mayer, J. (2010). The Koch Brothers' Covert Ops. The New Yorker. www.newyorker.com/magazine/2010/08/30/covert-operations.
237. Hertel-Fernandez, A., C. Tervo, and T. Skocpol. (2018). How the Koch Brothers Built the Most Powerful Rightwing Group You've Never Heard of. The Guardian. www.theguardian.com/us-news/2018/sep/26/koch-brothers-americans-for-prosperity-rightwing-political-group.

238. Koch Industries: Secretly Funding the Climate Denial Machine. (n.d.). Greenpeace. www.greenpeace.org/usa/global-warming/climate-deniers/koch-industries. Accessed September 26, 2019.
239. Myers, J. (2016). Nonprofit Backed by Koch Brothers Won't Have to Reveal Its Donors to Atty. Gen. Kamala Harris. Los Angeles Times. www.latimes.com/politics/la-pol-sac-koch-brothers-group-donors-kamala-harris-20160421-story.html.
240. U.S. News & World Report. (n.d.). Best States Rankings: Measuring Outcomes for Citizens Using More Than 70 Metrics. www.usnews.com/news/best-states/rankings. Accessed September 26, 2019.
241. Gravelle, J. and Marples, D. (2014). Tax Rates and Economic Growth. Washington, D.C.: Congressional Research Service, p. 5. fas.org/sgp/crs/misc/R42111.pdf.
242. Offshore Profit Shifting and the U.S Tax Code—Part 2 (Apple Inc.), 103rd Cong. 35 (2013) (Testimony of Timothy Cook). www.gpo.gov/fdsys/pkg/CHRG-113shrg81657/pdf/CHRG-113shrg81657.pdf.
243. Ibid.
244. Ibid.
245. Taylor, H. (2016). How Apple Managed to Pay a 0.005 Percent Tax Rate in 2014. CNBC. www.cnbc.com/2016/08/30/how-apples-irish-subsidiaries-paid-a-0005-percent-tax-rate-in-2014.html.
246. Offshore Profit Shifting and the U.S Tax Code—Part 2 (Apple Inc.), 103rd Cong. 35 (2013) (Testimony of Timothy Cook).
247. Arnold, C. (2012). How Many U.S. Jobs Does Apple Really Create? NPR. www.npr.org/2012/03/06/148049517/how-many-u-s-jobs-does-apple-really-create.
248. Duhigg, C. and Kocieniewski, D. (2012). Apple's Tax Strategy Aims at Low-Tax States and Nations. The New York Times. www.nytimes.com/2012/04/29/business/apples-tax-strategy-aims-at-low-tax-states-and-nations.html.
249. Kahn, J. and Drucker, J. (2016). Google Lowered Taxes by $2.4 Billion Using European Subsidiaries. Bloomberg. www.bloomberg.com/news/articles/2016-02-19/google-lowered-taxes-by-2-4-billion-using-european-subsidiaries.
250. Sterling, T. and Bergin, T. (2016). Google Accounts Show 11 Billion Euros Moved via Low Tax 'Dutch Sandwich' in 2014. Reuters. www.reuters.com/article/us-google-tax-idUSKCN0VS1GP.
251. Kahn, J. and Van Der Starre, M. (2016). Google Lowered 2015 Taxes by $3.6 Billion Using 'Dutch Sandwich'. Bloomberg. www.bloomberg.com/news/articles/2016-12-21/google-lowered-2015-taxes-by-3-6-billion-using-dutch-sandwich.
252. Phillips Erb, K. (2014). Ireland Declares 'Double Irish' Tax Scheme Dead. Forbes. www.forbes.com/sites/kellyphillipserb/2014/10/15/ireland-declares-double-irish-tax-scheme-dead.
253. Drawbaugh, K. and Sullivan, A. (2013). How a Massive U.S. Treasury Tax Loophole Saves Companies Billions Each Year. Business Insider. www.businessinsider.com/how-a-massive-us-treasury-tax-loophole-saves-companies-billions-each-year-2013-5.
254. Gravelle, J. (2015). Tax Havens: International Tax Avoidance and Evasion. Congressional Research Service. fas.org/sgp/crs/misc/R40623.pdf.
255. U.S. Congress. House. Sequester Delay and Stop Tax Haven Abuse Act. HR 3666. 113th Cong., 1st sess. Introduced in House December 05, 2013. www.congress.gov/bill/113th-congress/house-bill/3666/related-bills.

256. Internal Revenue Service. (2007). Internal Revenue Bulletin: 2007-7. www.irs.gov/irb/2007-07_IRB.
257. Congressional Budget Office (2013). Modify the Rules for the Sourcing of Income From Exports. www.cbo.gov/budget-options/2013/44851.
258. Chicago Tribune. (1994). U.S. Tax Court Upholds `Passage-of-Title' Break for Multinationals. articles.chicagotribune.com/1994-12-18/business/9412180037_1_tax-code-foreign-source-income-computer-chips.
259. Bowers, S. (2014). Luxembourg Tax Files: How Tiny State Rubber-Stamped Tax Avoidance on an Industrial Scale. The Guardian. www.theguardian.com/business/2014/nov/05/-sp-luxembourg-tax-files-tax-avoidance-industrial-scale.
260. Drucker, J. and Dudley, R. (2015). Wal-Mart Has $76 Billion in Undisclosed Overseas Tax Havens. Bloomberg. www.bloomberg.com/news/articles/2015-06-17/wal-mart-has-76-billion-in-overseas-tax-havens-report-says.
261. Picchi, A. (2015). Report: Walmart has $76 Billion in Offshore Tax Havens. CBS News. www.cbsnews.com/news/report-walmart-has-76-billion-in-offshore-tax-havens.
262. The Official Portal of the Grand Duchy of Luxembourg. (2019). Population and Multiculturality. www.luxembourg.public.lu/en/le-grand-duche-se-presente/luxembourg-tour-horizon/population-et-multiculturalite. Accessed September 26, 2019.
263. The World Bank, Data. (n.d.). GDP per capita, PPP (current international $). data.worldbank.org/indicator/NY.GDP.PCAP.PP.CD.
264. Kleinnijenhuis, J. (2014). Is Your Head Spinning? 5 Tips to Understand the 'Lux Leaks' Files. The International Consortium of Investigative Journalists. www.icij.org/investigations/luxembourg-leaks/your-head-spinning-5-tips-understand-lux-leaks-files.
265. PricewaterhouseCoopers, LLP. (2019). Luxembourg, Corporate - Withholding Taxes. taxsummaries.pwc.com/ID/Luxembourg-Corporate-Withholding-taxes. Accessed September 26, 2019.
266. PricewaterhouseCoopers, LLP (2016). Luxembourg Issues New TP Circulaire for the Fiscal Treatment of Intra-Group Financial Transactions. www.pwc.lu/en/transfer-pricing/docs/pwc-tp-281216.pdf.
267. Scott, M. (2016). Tim Cook, Apple Chief, Defends Tax Practices and Says Cash Will Return to U.S. The New York Times. www.nytimes.com/2016/09/02/technology/apple-tax-ireland-tim-cook.html.
268. Silvia, A. (2020). Apple wins tax battle with EU as court annuls 2016 order to pay $15 billion in taxes. CNBC. www.cnbc.com/2020/07/15/apple-wins-backing-of-eu-court-over-13-billion-euros-in-unpaid-taxes.html.
269. Phillips, R., Gardner, M., Kitson, K., Robins, A. and Surka, M. (2016). Offshore Shell Games 2016: The Use of Offshore Tax Havens by Fortune 500 Companies. Citizens for Tax Justice, Institute on Taxation and Economic Policy and U.S. PIRG Education Fund, p. 2. www.ctj.org/pdf/offshoreshellgames2016.pdf.
270. Petroff, A. (2016). Top 50 U.S. Companies Hold $1.4 Trillion in Cash Offshore. CNN Money. money.cnn.com/2016/04/14/news/tax-us-companies-offshore-cash.
271. Wong, A. (2016). A $2.6 Trillion Myth: For the Dollar, Trump Tax Holiday Is a Dud. Bloomberg. www.bloomberg.com/news/articles/2016-11-17/a-2-6-trillion-myth-for-the-dollar-trump-tax-holiday-is-a-dud.
272. Wong, A. (2016). Americans Are Paying Apple Millions to Shelter Overseas Profits. Bloomberg. www.bloomberg.com/graphics/2016-apple-profits.

273. Johnston, D.C. (2000). Taking Aim at Tax Havens, I.R.S. Seeks Credit Card Slips. The New York Times. www.nytimes.com/2000/10/20/business/taking-aim-at-tax-havens-irs-seeks-credit-card-slips.html.
274. Ernst & Young, LLP. (2010). Six Strategies for Restructuring Intercompany Loans.
275. CBS News. (2013). U.S. Disallows $2.86B in Deductions Taken by Tyco. www.cbsnews.com/news/us-disallows-286b-in-deductions-taken-by-tyco.
276. Gregory, D. and McManus, E. (2016). Tyco, Spun-off Affiliates Settle Remaining Tax Issues. Bloomberg BNA. www.bna.com/tyco-spunoff-affiliates-n57982073821.
277. Kocieniewski, D. (2011). Companies Push for Tax Break on Foreign Cash. The New York Times. www.nytimes.com/2011/06/20/business/20tax.html.
278. Dharmapala, D., Fritz Foley, C. and Forbes, K. (2009). Watch What I Do, Not What I Say: The Unintended Consequences of the Homeland Investment Act. NBER Working Paper No. 15023. Cambridge, MA, pp. 1,6,17. www.nber.org/papers/w15023.pdf.
279. U.S. Congress. Committee on Homeland Security and Governmental Affairs U.S. Senate. Permanent Subcommittee on Investigations. Repatriating Offshore Funds: 2004 Tax Windfall for Select Multinationals: A Report. 112th Cong., 1st sess., 2011. Senate Print 112-27. www.gpo.gov/fdsys/pkg/CPRT-112SPRT70710/pdf/CPRT-112SPRT70710.pdf.
280. Norris, F. (2009). Tax Break for Profits Went Awry. The New York Times. www.nytimes.com/2009/06/05/business/05norris.html.
281. Cox, J. (2017). Companies Have Big Plans for Trillions in Overseas Cash—If Tax Reform Ever Happens.
282. Lohman, J. (2012). Corporation Tax Income Apportionment Formulas. CCH, State Tax Guide. www.cga.ct.gov/2012/rpt/2012-R-0414.htm.
283. Newton, R. (2017). S&P Says Kansas Credit Rating Outlook 'Negative'. KSN. ksn.com/2017/02/09/sp-says-kansas-credit-rating-outlook-negative.
284. Hanna, J. (2016). S&P Downgrades Kansas Credit Rating, Citing Ongoing Budget Issues. The Topeka Capital-Journal. www.cjonline.com/news/2016-07-26/sp-downgrades-kansas-credit-rating-citing-ongoing-budget-issues.
285. Picchi, A. (2015). How Low-Wage Employers Cost Taxpayers $153B a Year. CBS News. www.cbsnews.com/news/how-low-wage-employers-cost-taxpayers-153-billion-a-year.

CHAPTER 10

286. Klein, C. (2016). The Epic Road Trip That Inspired the Interstate Highway System. History. www.history.com/news/the-epic-road-trip-that-inspired-the-interstate-highway-system.
287. Ibid.
288. U.S. President. Toll Roads and Free Roads. Message from the President of the United States Transmitting a Letter from the Secretary of Agriculture, Concurred in by the Secretary of War, Enclosing a Report of the Bureau of Public Roads, United States Department of Agriculture, on the Feasibility of a System of Transcontinental Toll Roads and a Master Plan for Free Highway Development. 76th Cong., 1st sess., 1939. H. Doc. 272. hdl.handle.net/2027/wu.89090507302.

289. History. (2010). The Interstate Highway System. www.history.com/topics/interstate-highway-system.
290. U.S. Department of Transportation, Federal Highway Administration. (2019). Interstate System: Dwight D. Eisenhower National System of Interstate and Defense Highways. www.fhwa.dot.gov/programadmin/interstate.cfm.
291. The United States Postal Service. (2012). Publication 100, An American History 1775 - 2006: Rural Free Delivery (RFD). about.usps.com/publications/pub100/pub100_020.htm.
292. Chambers, M., Goworowska, J., Rick, C. and Sedor, J. (2015). Freight Facts and Figures 2015. U.S. Department of Transportation, Bureau of Transportation Statistics, p. 3. doi.org/10.21949/1501678.
293. Freight Shipments In America: Preliminary Highlights from the 2002 Commodity Flow Survey. (2004). U.S. Department of Transportation, Bureau of Transportation Statistics. www.bts.gov/archive/publications/freight_shipments_in_america/index.
294. Weisbrod, G. and Fitzroy, S. (2011). Traffic Congestion Effects on Supply Chains: Accounting for Behavioral Elements in Planning and Economic Impact Models. Ch. 16 in Sanda Renko (Eds.), Supply Chain Management—New Perspectives. InTechOpen, p. 343. doi.org/10.5772/23057.
295. The American Society of Civil Engineers. (2017). 2017 American Infrastructure Report Card: A Comprehensive Assessment of America's Infrastructure. www.infrastructurereportcard.org.
296. Handy, S. (2015). Increasing Highway Capacity Unlikely to Relieve Traffic Congestion. Policy Brief. National Center for Sustainable Transportation. escholarship.org/uc/item/58x8436d.
297. Downs, A. (1962). The Law of Peak-Hour Expressway Congestion. Traffic Quarterly, 16(3), pp. 393-409. hdl.handle.net/2027/uc1.$b3477.
298. HCM 2010: Highway Capacity Manual. 5th ed. Washington, D.C.: Transportation Research Board, 2010.
299. Transportation Research Circular E-C213 (2016). 13th National Light Rail and Streetcar Conference: Transforming Urban Areas. Washington, D.C.: Transportation Research Board, p. 234. onlinepubs.trb.org/onlinepubs/circulars/ec213.pdf.
300. Transportation Research Circular E-C112 (2007). Joint International Light Rail Conference: A World of Applications and Opportunities. Washington, D.C.: Transportation Research Board, p. 730. onlinepubs.trb.org/onlinepubs/circulars/ec112.pdf. Cost per miles were reported as $12.7 million in Sacramento, CA, and $118.8 million in Buffalo, NY, for the year 2000. Amounts were adjusted for inflation and set in 2018 dollars using the CPI Inflation Calculator at bls.gov.
301. Arkansas Department of Transportation. (2014). Estimated Costs per Mile. www.arkansashighways.com/roadway_design_division/Cost%20per%20Mile%20(JULY%20 2014).pdf.
302. Washington State Department of Transportation. (2014). Highway Construction Costs: Are WSDOT's Highway Construction Costs in Line with National Experience? p. 8. www.vtpi.org/WSDOT_HighwayCosts_2004.pdf.
303. Transportation Research Circular E-C112 (2007). Joint International Light Rail Conference: A World of Applications and Opportunities.

304. Clarke, R. (2005). Cost Effective Program Management Strategies For the T-REX Project in Denver. In: Rail Transit Conference. Washington, D.C.: American Public Transportation Association. trid.trb.org/view.aspx?id=758051.
305. Transportation Research Circular E-C112 (2007). Joint International Light Rail Conference: A World of Applications and Opportunities. Cost was reported as $1.245 billion in Portland, OR, for the year 2000. Amounts were adjusted for inflation and set in 2018 dollars using the CPI Inflation Calculator at bls.gov.
306. Clackamas County. (2015). I-205 Operational Enhancements Project. [pdf]. westlinn.granicus.com/MetaViewer.php?view_id=&clip_id=598&meta_id=24364.
307. Lindblom, M. (2016). Sound Transit's Cost Overruns for First Phase Hit About 86 Percent. The Seattle Times. www.seattletimes.com/seattle-news/transportation/sound-transits-cost-overruns-for-first-phase-hit-about-86-percent.
308. Washington State Department of Transportation. (2014). Highway Construction Costs: Are WSDOT's Highway Construction Costs in Line with National Experience?
309. Lindblom, M. (2016). Sound Transit Keeping Close Eye on Crowded Light-Rail Trains. The Seattle Times. www.seattletimes.com/seattle-news/transportation/sound-transit-keeping-close-eye-on-crowded-light-rail-trains.
310. Chambers, M., Goworowska, J., Rick, C. and Sedor, J. (2015). Freight Facts and Figures 2015. U.S. Department of Transportation, Bureau of Transportation Statistics, p. 45. doi.org/10.21949/1501678.
311. Begley, D. (2015). Congestion Costs Nearly $1,500 Each for Area Commuters. Houston Chronicle. www.houstonchronicle.com/news/transportation/article/Congestion-costs-nearly-1-500-each-for-area-6465411.php.
312. American Transportation Research Institute. (2016). Trucking Industry Congestion Costs Top $49.6 Billion in 2014. atri-online.org/2016/04/19/trucking-industry-congestion-costs-top-49-6-billion-in-2014.
313. INRIX, Inc. (2017). Congestion Cost U.S. Drivers Nearly $300 Billion in 2016, An Average of $1,400 per Driver. inrix.com/press-releases/los-angeles-tops-inrix-global-congestion-ranking.
314. McGinn, B. (2019). ARTBA Forecasts Modest 2015 Growth for U.S. Transportation Infrastructure Market. American Road & Transportation Builders Association. www.artba.org/2014/12/03/artba-forecasts-modest-2015-growth-for-u-s-transportation-infrastructure-market.
315. Forkenbrock, D. and March, J. (2005). Issues in The Financing of Truck-Only Lanes. U.S. Department of Transportation, Federal Highway Administration. www.fhwa.dot.gov/publications/publicroads/05sep/02.cfm.
316. Dovell, E. (2012). U.S. Rail Infrastructure. Council on Foreign Relations. www.cfr.org/backgrounder/us-rail-infrastructure.
317. U.S. Department of Commerce, International Trade Administration. (2019). China—Rail and Urban Rail. www.export.gov/article?id=China-Rail-and-Urban-Rail. Accessed September 27, 2019.
318. KPMG Global China Practice (2016). The 13th Five-Year Plan—China's Transformation and Integration with the World Economy: Opportunities for Chinese and Foreign Businesses. p. 86. assets.kpmg/content/dam/kpmg/cn/pdf/en/2016/10/13fyp-opportunities-analysis-for-chinese-and-foreign-businesses.pdf.

319. The European Rail Research Advisory Council. (2009). Metro, Light Rail and Tram Systems in Europe. p. 34. www.uitp.org/sites/default/files/cck-focus-papers-files/errac_metrolr_tramsystemsineurope.pdf. Cost was reported as Ä15.8 million per kilometer for the year 2009. Amounts were adjusted into miles and reset for inflation into 2018 dollars terms using the euro inflation calculator at inflationtools.com.
320. Yglesias, M. (2017). Someone Killed a Congressional Inquiry into America's Sky-High Transit Construction Costs: The Life and Death of Great American GAO Reports. Vox. www.vox.com/policy-and-politics/2017/5/24/15681560/gao-report-transit-construction-costs.

CHAPTER 11

321. Scofea, L. (1994). The Development and Growth of Employer-Provided Health Insurance. Monthly Labor Review, p. 6. www.bls.gov/opub/mlr/1994/03/art1full.pdf
322. Henning Schumann, J. (2016). A Bygone Era: When Bipartisanship Led to Health Care Transformation. NPR. www.npr.org/sections/health-shots/2016/10/02/495775518/a-bygone-era-when-bipartisanship-led-to-health-care-transformation.
323. U.S. Health Resources & Services Administration. (2019). Hill-Burton Free and Reduced-Cost Health Care. www.hrsa.gov/get-health-care/affordable/hill-burton/index.html.
324. Melhado, E. (2006). Health Planning in the United States and the Decline of Public-Interest Policymaking. The Milbank Quarterly, 84(2), pp. 359-440. www.ncbi.nlm.nih.gov/pmc/articles/PMC2690168.
325. Government of Canada. (n.d.). Canada's Health Care System. www.canada.ca/en/health-canada/services/health-care-system/reports-publications/health-care-system/canada.html.
326. Angell, M. (2008). Privatizing Health Care is Not the Answer: Lessons from the United States. Canadian Medical Association Journal, 179(9), pp. 916-919. www.ncbi.nlm.nih.gov/pmc/articles/PMC2565716.
327. Baker, J. (1988). The Antitrust Analysis of Hospital Mergers and the Transformation of the Hospital Industry. Law and Contemporary Problems, 51(2), pp. 93-164. scholarship.law.duke.edu/cgi/viewcontent.cgi?article=3949&context=lcp.
328. Melhado, E. (2006). Health Planning in the United States and the Decline of Public-interest Policymaking.
329. Social Security Bulletin. (1974). Health Maintenance Organization Act of ,1973, pp. 35-39. www.ssa.gov/policy/docs/ssb/v37n3/v37n3p35.pdf. Accessed September 28, 2019.
330. Morrison, E. and Luft, H. (1990). Health Maintenance Organization Environments in the 1980s and Beyond. Health Care Financing Review, 12(1), pp. 81–90. www.ncbi.nlm.nih.gov/pmc/articles/PMC4193099.
331. Frakt, A. (2018). Reagan, Deregulation and America's Exceptional Rise in Health Care Costs. The New York Times. www.nytimes.com/2018/06/04/upshot/reagan-deregulation-and-americas-exceptional-rise-in-health-care-costs.html.
332. The New York Times. (1984). Women and Children Last. p. 22. www.nytimes.com/1984/02/04/opinion/women-and-children-last.html?mcubz=1.

333. Central Intelligence Agency. (n.d.). The World Factbook, Country Comparison: Infant Mortality Rate. www.cia.gov/library/publications/the-world-factbook/rankorder/2091rank.html. Accessed September 28, 2019.
334. Fox, P. and Kongstvedt, P. (2007). A History of Managed Health Care and Health Insurance in the United States. In: P. Kongstvedt, ed., Essentials of Managed Health Care, 5th ed. Sudbury, MA: Jones and Bartlett, p. 11.
335. Rovner, J. (2019). The Affordable Care Act Is Back In Court: 5 Facts You Need To Know. NPR. www.npr.org/sections/health-shots/2019/07/09/739653482/the-affordable-care-act-is-back-in-court-5-facts-you-need-to-know.
336. The World Bank, Data. (n.d.). Current Health Expenditure (% of GDP)—United States. data.worldbank.org/indicator/SH.XPD.CHEX.GD.ZS?locations=US. Accessed September 28, 2019.
337. Federal Reserve Bank of St. Louis. (n.d.). Consumer Price Index: Medical Care in U.S. City Average, All Urban Consumers (CPIMEDSL). fred.stlouisfed.org/series/CPIMEDSL. Units on graph edited to show "Percent Change from Year Ago, Seasonally Adjusted."
338. Bryan, B. (2016). Americans' Out-of-Pocket Healthcare Costs are Skyrocketing. Business Insider. www.businessinsider.com/out-of-pocket-healthcare-payments-skyrocketing-2016-9.
339. Congressional Budget Office. (2017). American Health Care Act: Budget Reconciliation Recommendations of the House Committees on Ways and Means and Energy and Commerce, March 9, 2017. p. 3. www.cbo.gov/system/files/115th-congress-2017-2018/costestimate/americanhealthcareact.pdf.
340. Himmelstein, D., Thorne, D., Warren, E. and Woolhandler, S. (2009). Medical Bankruptcy in the United States, 2007: Results of a National Study. The American Journal of Medicine, 122(8), pp. 741-746. www.amjmed.com/article/S0002-9343(09)00404-5/pdf.
341. Andrews, M. (2017). Overhauling Obamacare Could Lead to Spike in Medical Debt Collections. CNN Money. money.cnn.com/2017/01/26/pf/medical-debt-collections-obamacare.
342. Picchi, A. (2015). How Obamacare is Affecting Americans' Medical Bills. CBS News. www.cbsnews.com/news/how-obamacare-is-affecting-medical-bills.
343. Ibid.
344. Board of Governors of the Federal Reserve System (2016). Report on the Economic Well-Being of U.S. Households in 2015. Washington, D.C.: Federal Reserve Board, p. 24. www.federalreserve.gov/2015-report-economic-well-being-us-households-201605.pdf.
345. Sanger-Katz, M. (2016). Obamacare Seems to Be Reducing People's Medical Debt. The New York Times. www.nytimes.com/2016/04/21/upshot/obamacare-seems-to-be-reducing-peoples-medical-debt.html?mcubz=1.
346. Johnson, C. (2016). Americans are Shouldering More and More of Their Health-Care Costs. The Washington Post. www.washingtonpost.com/news/wonk/wp/2016/06/27/one-reason-a-historic-slowdown-in-health-spending-didnt-feel-like-it.
347. National Conference of State Legislatures. (2018). Health Insurance: Premiums and Increases. www.ncsl.org/research/health/health-insurance-premiums.aspx. Accessed September 28, 2019.

348. The World Bank, Data. (n.d.). Current Health Expenditure (% of GDP). data.worldbank.org/indicator/SH.XPD.CHEX.GD.ZS. Accessed September 28, 2019.
349. Himmelstein, D., Jun, M., Busse, R., Chevreul, K., Geissler, A., Jeurissen, P., Thomson, S., Vinet, M. and Woolhandler, S. (2014). A Comparison of Hospital Administrative Costs in Eight Nations: U.S. Costs Exceed All Others by Far. Health Affairs, 33(9), pp. =1586-1594. www.ncbi.nlm.nih.gov/pubmed/25201663.
350. Institute of Medicine. (2010). The Healthcare Imperative: Lowering Costs and Improving Outcomes: Workshop Series Summary. Washington, D.C.: The National Academies Press. doi.org/10.17226/12750.
351. Woolhandler, S. and Himmelstein, D. (2004). The High Costs of For-Profit Care. Canadian Medical Association Journal, 170(12), pp. 1814-1815. www.ncbi.nlm.nih.gov/pmc/articles/PMC419771.
352. Himmelstein, D.U. and Woolhandler, S. (2002). Taking Care of Business: HMOs That Spend More on Administration Deliver Lower-Quality Care. International Journal of Health Services, 32(4), pp. 657-667. www.ncbi.nlm.nih.gov/pubmed/12456120.
353. Institute of Medicine. (1989). Controlling Costs and Changing Patient Care?: The Role of Utilization Management. Washington, D.C.: The National Academies Press, p. 44. doi.org/10.17226/1359.
354. Rosenthal, E. (2014). Medicine's Top Earners Are Not the M.D.s. The New York Times. www.nytimes.com/2014/05/18/sunday-review/doctors-salaries-are-not-the-big-cost.html.
355. Jiwani, A., Himmelstein, D., Woolhandler, S. and Kahn, J. (2014). Billing and Insurance-Related Administrative Costs in United States' Health Care: Synthesis of Micro-Costing Evidence. BMC Health Services Research, 14(556). www.ncbi.nlm.nih.gov/pmc/articles/PMC4283267.
356. Casalino, L., Nicholson, S., Gans, D., Hammons, T., Morra, D., Karrison, T. and Levinson, W. (2009). What Does It Cost Physician Practices to Interact with Health Insurance Plans? Health Affairs, 28(4), pp. w533-w543. www.healthaffairs.org/doi/pdf/10.1377/hlthaff.28.4.w533.
357. Institute of Medicine. (2010). The Healthcare Imperative: Lowering Costs and Improving Outcomes: Workshop Series Summary.
358. Woolhandler, S. and Himmelstein, D.U. (2014). Administrative Work Consumes One-Sixth of U.S. Physicians' Working Hours and Lowers Their Career Satisfaction. International Journal of Health Services, 44(4), pp. 635-642. www.ncbi.nlm.nih.gov/pubmed/25626223.
359. Petersen, M. (2017). Young Doctors Can Work 28 Hours Straight Under New Rules. Los Angeles Times. www.latimes.com/business/la-fi-medical-resident-hours-20170310-story.html.
360. Christino, M., Matson, A., Fischer, S., Reinert, S., DiGiovanni, C. and Fadale, P. (2013). Paperwork Versus Patient Care: A Nationwide Survey of Residents' Perceptions of Clinical Documentation Requirements and Patient Care. Journal of Graduate Medical Education, 5(4), pp. 600-604. www.ncbi.nlm.nih.gov/pmc/articles/PMC3886458.

361. Skinner, J. and Fisher, E. (2010). Reflections on Geographic Variations in U.S. Health Care, Lebanon, NH: The Dartmouth Institute for Health Policy and Clinical Practice, p. iii. www.dartmouthatlas.org/downloads/press/Skinner_Fisher_DA_05_10.pdf.
362. Fisher, E., Wennberg, D., Stukel, T., Gottlieb, D., Lucas, F. and Pinder, É. (2003). The Implications of Regional Variations in Medicare Spending. Part 1: The Content, Quality, and Accessibility of Care. Annals of Internal Medicine, 138(4), p. 273. annals.org/aim/fullarticle/716066/implications-regional-variations-medicare-spending-part-1-content-quality-accessibility.
363. National Academies. (2012). Transformation of Health System Needed to Improve Care and Reduce Costs. www8.nationalacademies.org/onpinews/newsitem.aspx?RecordID=13444.
364. Jagannathan, M. (2019). In a Review of 337,000 Patient Cases, This Was the No. 1 Most Common Preventable Medical Error. MarketWatch. www.marketwatch.com/story/in-a-review-of-337000-patient-cases-this-was-the-no-1-most-common-medical-error-2019-07-22.
365. John Hopkins. (2016). Study Suggests Medical Errors Now Third-Leading Cause of Death in the U.S. www.hopkinsmedicine.org/news/media/releases/study_suggests_medical_errors_now_third_leading_cause_of_death_in_the_us.
366. Katz, J. (2019). Drug Deaths in America Are Rising Faster Than Ever. The New York Times. www.nytimes.com/interactive/2017/06/05/upshot/opioid-epidemic-drug-overdose-deaths-are-rising-faster-than-ever.html.
367. Michas, F. (2021). Cesarean sections in OECD countries 2018. Statista. www.statista.com/statistics/283123/cesarean-sections-in-oecd-countries.
368. Centers for Disease Control and Prevention. (2019). Health and Economic Costs of Chronic Diseases. www.cdc.gov/chronicdisease/about/costs/index.htm. Accessed September 29, 2019. Smoking, alcohol, and inactivity contribute $536 billion in healthcare costs out of $3.3 trillion in total, or 16%.
369. Centers for Disease Control and Prevention. (2019). Poor Nutrition. www.cdc.gov/chronicdisease/resources/publications/factsheets/nutrition.htm. Accessed September 29, 2019. Obesity contributes $147 billion in healthcare costs out of $3.3 trillion in total, or 4%.
370. Adams, K., Butsch, W. and Kohlmeier, M. (2015). The State of Nutrition Education at U.S. Medical Schools. Journal of Biomedical Education, 2015, pp. 1-7. www.hindawi.com/journals/jbe/2015/357627.
371. Schwartz, N. (2009). Swiss Model for Health Care Is Gaining Admirers. The New York Times. www.nytimes.com/2009/10/01/health/policy/01swiss.html.
372. Biller-Andorno, N. and Jüni, P. (2014). Abolishing Mammography Screening Programs? A View from the Swiss Medical Board. New England Journal of Medicine, 370(21), pp. 1965-1967. www.nejm.org/doi/full/10.1056/NEJMp1401875.
373. Reid, T. (2008). Japanese Pay Less for More Health Care. NPR. www.npr.org/templates/story/story.php?storyId=89626309.
374. World Health Organization. (2017). World Health Statistics 2017: Monitoring Health for the SDGs, Sustainable Development Goals. Geneva: CC BY-NC-SA 3.0 IGO, p. 54. apps.who.int/iris/bitstream/10665/255336/1/9789241565486-eng.pdf.

375. Healthcare Access and Quality Index Based on Mortality from Causes Amenable to Personal Health Care in 195 Countries and Territories, 1990–2015: A Novel Analysis from the Global Burden of Disease Study 2015. (2017). The Lancet, 390, p. 238. www.thelancet.com/pdfs/journals/lancet/PIIS0140-6736(17)30818-8.pdf.
376. World Health Organization. (2017). World Health Statistics 2017: Monitoring Health for the SDGs, Sustainable Development Goals. Geneva: CC BY-NC-SA 3.0 IGO, pp. 89-93. apps.who.int/iris/bitstream/10665/255336/1/9789241565486-eng.pdf.
377. Taylor, A., Whelan Parento, E. and Schmidt, L. (2014). The Increasing Weight of Regulation: Countries Combat the Global Obesity Epidemic. Indiana Law Journal, 90, p. 28. ssrn.com/abstract=2422508.
378. Harden, B. (2009). Japan's Health-Care System Has Many Advantages, but May Not Be Sustainable. Washington Post Foreign Service. www.washingtonpost.com/wp-dyn/content/article/2009/09/06/AR2009090601630_4.html.
379. Environmental Working Group. (2019). EWG's Farm Subsidy Database. farm.ewg.org/progdetail.php?fips=00000&progcode=corn. Accessed September 29, 2019.
380. Li, B., Andrews, K. and Pehrsson, P. (2002). Individual Sugars, Soluble, and Insoluble Dietary Fiber Contents of 70 High Consumption Foods. Journal of Food Composition and Analysis, 15(6), pp. 715-723. www.ars.usda.gov/ARSUserFiles/80400525/Articles/jfca15_715-723.pdf.
381. Imamura, F., O'Connor, L., Ye, Z., Mursu, J., Hayashino, Y., Bhupathiraju, S. and Forouhi, N. (2015). Consumption of Sugar Sweetened Beverages, Artificially Sweetened Beverages, and Fruit Juice and Incidence of Type 2 Diabetes: Systematic Review, Meta-Analysis, and Estimation of Population Attributable Fraction. BMJ, 351, p. h3576. www.ncbi.nlm.nih.gov/pubmed/26199070.
382. Greger, M. (2013). Eating Healthy on a Budget. [video] nutritionfacts.org/video/eating-healthy-on-a-budget.
383. U.S. Department of Agriculture, Office of the Chief Economist. (n.d.). U.S. Food Waste Challenge FAQs. www.usda.gov/oce/foodwaste/faqs.htm.
384. Brugger, K. (2017). Labor Shortage Leaves $13 Million in Crops to Rot in Fields. The Santa Barbara Independent. www.independent.com/news/2017/jun/22/labor-shortage-leaves-13-million-crops-rot-fields.
385. Centers for Disease Control and Prevention. (2016). Worker Productivity Measures. www.cdc.gov/workplacehealthpromotion/model/evaluation/productivity.html.
386. Ward, A. (2014). Companies wake up to cost of ill employees. Financial Times. www.ft.com/content/a0198856-4d93-11e4-bf60-00144feab7de.
387. Hancock, L. (2011). Why Are Finland's Schools Successful? Smithsonian Magazine. www.smithsonianmag.com/innovation/why-are-finlands-schools-successful-49859555.
388. Erickson, K., Hillman, C. and Kramer, A. (2015). Physical Activity, Brain, and Cognition. Current Opinion in Behavioral Sciences, 4, pp. 27-32. www.sciencedirect.com/science/article/pii/S2352154615000157.
389. Gerhardt, W., Korenda, L., Morris, M. and Vadnerkar, G. (2015). The Road to Value-Based Care. Deloitte Insights. dupress.deloitte.com/dup-us-en/industry/life-sciences/value-based-care-market-shift.html.

390. Porter, M. and Lee, T. (2013). The Strategy That Will Fix Health Care. Harvard Business Review. hbr.org/2013/10/the-strategy-that-will-fix-health-care.
391. Bundled Payments: Market Trends and Markers of Success. (2019). American Hospital Association. www.aha.org/system/files/2019-01/Bundled-Payments_January-2019_final.pdf.
392. Utah Alliance for the Determinants of Health Story. (n.d.). Intermountain Healthcare. www.intermountainhealthcare.org/about/who-we-are/community-benefit/community/utah-alliance-for-the-determinants-of-health-story. Accessed January 24, 2020.
393. Willett, W., Koplan, J., Nugent, R., Dusenbury, C., Puska, P., and Gaziano, T. (2006). Prevention of Chronic Disease By Means Of Diet And Lifestyle Changes. In Disease Control Priorities in Developing Countries, 2nd ed., p. 837., Washington, D.C.: The World Bank, International Bank for Reconstruction and Development. www.ncbi.nlm.nih.gov/books/NBK11795

CHAPTER 12

394. History. (2009). Child Labor. www.history.com/topics/child-labor
395. Grossman, J. (n.d.). Fair Labor Standards Act of 1938: Maximum Struggle for a Minimum Wage. U.S. Department of Labor. www.dol.gov/general/aboutdol/history/flsa1938.
396. Ibid.
397. Drobnic Holan, A. (2009). Obama Right that Roosevelt Was Called a Socialist and a Communist. PolitiFact. www.politifact.com/truth-o-meter/statements/2009/sep/22/barack-obama/obama-roosevelt-socialist-communist.
398. Robinson, S. (2012). Bring Back the 40-Hour Work Week. Salon. www.salon.com/test/2012/03/14/bring_back_the_40_hour_work_week.
399. OECD. (2019). Hours Worked (Indicator). data.oecd.org/emp/hours-worked.htm. Accessed September 29, 2019.
400. The World Bank, Data. (n.d.). GDP per capita, PPP (current international $). data.worldbank.org/indicator/NY.GDP.PCAP.PP.CD. Accessed September 29, 2019.
401. Lane, E. (2017). The Young Japanese Working Themselves to Death. BBC News. www.bbc.com/news/business-39981997.
402. Kullander, M. and Danielsson, P. (2015). Sweden: Gothenburg Municipality Implements 30-Hour Working Week. Eurofound. www.eurofound.europa.eu/observatories/eurwork/articles/working-conditions-industrial-relations-law-and-regulation/sweden-gothenburg-municipality-implements-30-hour-working-week.
403. Alderman, L. (2016). In Sweden, an Experiment Turns Shorter Workdays into Bigger Gains. The New York Times. www.nytimes.com/2016/05/21/business/international/in-sweden-an-experiment-turns-shorter-workdays-into-bigger-gains.html.
404. Saad, L. (2014). The "40-Hour" Workweek Is Actually Longer—by Seven Hours. Gallup. www.gallup.com/poll/175286/hour-workweek-actually-longer-seven-hours.aspx.
405. Savage, M. (2015). The Truth about Sweden's Short Working Hours. BBC News. www.bbc.com/news/business-34677949.

406. Perpetual Guardian. (2019). White Paper: The Four-Day Week: Guidelines for an Outcome-Based Trial -- Raising Productivity and Engagement. 4dayweek.com/research. Results are displayed via infographics at 4dayweek.com.
407. Venturi, R. (2014). Busting the Myth of France's 35-Hour Workweek. BBC Worklife. www.bbc.com/worklife/article/20140312-frances-mythic-35-hour-week.
408. Fact Sheet #17A: Exemption for Executive, Administrative, Professional, Computer & Outside Sales Employees under the Fair Labor Standards Act (FLSA). (2019). Washington, D.C.: U.S. Department of Labor, Wage and Hour Division. www.dol.gov/whd/overtime/fs17a_overview.pdf.
409. OECD.Stat. (n.d.). Average Annual Hours Actually Worked per Worker. stats.oecd.org/index.aspx?DataSetCode=ANHRS. Accessed September 29, 2019.
410. U.S. Bureau of Economic Analysis. (2019). 2018 Trade Gap is $621.0 Billion. www.bea.gov/news/blog/2019-03-06/2018-trade-gap-6210-billion.
411. Nienaber, M. and Wagner, R. (2019). Germany, with Bumper Current Account Surplus, Frets about Car Tariffs. Reuters. www.reuters.com/article/us-germany-economy-trade-surplus/germany-with-bumper-current-account-surplus-frets-about-car-tariffs-idUSKCN1Q80L0.
412. W, C. (2014). Proof That You Should Get a Life. The Economist. www.economist.com/free-exchange/2014/12/09/proof-that-you-should-get-a-life.
413. U.S. Department of Transportation, National Highway Traffic Safety Administration. (n.d.). Research on Drowsy Driving. one.nhtsa.gov/Driving-Safety/Drowsy-Driving/scope-of-the-problem.
414. Fryer, B. (2006). Sleep Deficit: The Performance Killer. Harvard Business Review. hbr.org/2006/10/sleep-deficit-the-performance-killer. Accessed September 29, 2019.
415. Federal Motor Carrier Safety Administration. (2013). New Hours-of-Service Safety Regulations to Reduce Truck Driver Fatigue Begin Today. www.prnewswire.com/news-releases/new-hours-of-service-safety-regulations-to-reduce-truck-driver-fatigue-begin-today-213821351.html.
416. Söderström, M., Jeding, K., Ekstedt, M., Perski, A. and ≈kerstedt, T. (2012). Insufficient Sleep Predicts Clinical Burnout. Journal of Occupational Health Psychology, 17(2), pp. 175-183. doi:10.1037/a0027518.
417. Yang, G. (2014). China's Forty-Hour Work Week Is Mandatory. Except When It's Not. Part III. China Law Blog. www.chinalawblog.com/2014/08/chinas-forty-hour-work-week-is-mandatory-except-when-its-not-part-iii.html.
418. Boquen, A. (2018). What You Need to Know About Overtime in China. New Horizons Global Partners. nhglobalpartners.com/overtime-in-china.
419. China Labor Watch. (2015). Something's Not Right Here: Poor Working Conditions Persist at Apple Supplier Pegatron. www.chinalaborwatch.org/report/109.
420. China Labor Watch. (2016). Study Casts Doubts on Apple's Ethical Standards. www.chinalaborwatch.org/report/113.
421. Tsukayama, H. (2013). Sony, Foxconn Report Reminds Us Apple Isn't the Only Firm with Labor Issues. The Washington Post. www.washingtonpost.com/news/the-switch/wp/2013/10/11/sony-foxconn-report-reminds-us-apple-isnt-the-only-firm-with-labor-issues.
422. Apple Inc. "2015 Form 10-K Annual Report." 2015. Annual Reports. www.annualreports.com/HostedData/AnnualReportArchive/a/NASDAQ_AAPL_2015.pdf.

423. China Labor Watch. (2015). Something's Not Right Here: Poor Working Conditions Persist at Apple Supplier Pegatron.
424. Duhigg, D. and Barboza, C. (2012). Apple's iPad and the Human Costs for Workers in China. The New York Times. www.nytimes.com/2012/01/26/business/ieconomy-apples-ipad-and-the-human-costs-for-workers-in-china.html.
425. Keizer, G. (2012). Apple Confirms Aluminum Dust Caused Chinese Factory Explosions. Computerworld. www.computerworld.com/article/2501382/apple-mac/apple-confirms-aluminum-dust-caused-chinese-factory-explosions.html.
426. U.S. Chemical Safety and Hazard Investigation Board. (2011). Hoeganaes Corporation: Gallatin, TN: Metal Dust Flash Fires and Hydrogen Explosion. www.csb.gov/hoeganaes-corporation-fatal-flash-fires.
427. U.S. Bureau of Labor Statistics, National Safety Council (2019). Workplace Injuries by the Numbers. [image] www.nsc.org/work-safety/tools-resources/infographics/workplace-injuries.
428. Pesce, N. (2019). Alarming Research Shows That Serious Workplace Injuries May Increase the Risk of Suicide and Drug Overdose Deaths. MarketWatch. www.marketwatch.com/story/alarming-research-shows-that-serious-workplace-injuries-may-have-dire-implications-beyond-work-and-be-linked-to-suicide-rates-2019-07-23.
429. Applebaum, K., Asfaw, A., O'Leary, P., Busey, A., Tripodis, Y. and Boden, L. (2019). Suicide and Drug?Related Mortality Following Occupational Injury. American Journal of Industrial Medicine, 62(9), pp. 733-741. onlinelibrary.wiley.com/doi/pdf/10.1002/ajim.23021.
430. NAV. (2014). Work Combined with Disability Benefit. www.nav.no/en/Home/Benefits+and+services/Relatert+informasjon/work-combined-with-disability-benefit. Accessed September 29, 2019.
431. Sickness, Disability and Work: Improving Social and Labour-Market Integration of People with Disability. (2010). OECD. www.oecd.org/social/soc/46488022.pdf.
432. Montana Department of Labor & Industry. (n.d.). Frequently Asked Questions. dli.mt.gov/resources/faq. Accessed September 29, 2019.
433. U.S. Department of Labor, Bureau of Labor Statistics. (2012). Leave Benefits: Access Private Industry Workers, National Compensation Survey, March 2012. www.bls.gov/ncs/ebs/benefits/2012/ownership/private/table21a.htm.
434. Alchemy Systems. (2019). The Mind of the Food Worker: Behaviors and Perceptions That Impact Safety and Operations. Center for Research & Public Policy, p. 5.
435. Hemp, P. (2004). Presenteeism: At Work—But Out of It. Harvard Business Review. hbr.org/2004/10/presenteeism-at-work-but-out-of-it.
436. Thosar, S., Bielko, S., Mather, K., Johnston, J. and Wallace, J. (2015). Effect of Prolonged Sitting and Breaks in Sitting Time on Endothelial Function. Medicine & Science in Sports & Exercise, 47(4), pp. 843-849. www.ncbi.nlm.nih.gov/pubmed/25137367.
437. van Uffelen, J., Wong, J., Chau, J., van der Ploeg, H., Riphagen, I., Gilson, N., Burton, N., Healy, G., Thorp, A., Clark, B., Gardiner, P., Dunstan, D., Bauman, A., Owen, N. and Brown, W. (2010). Occupational Sitting and Health Risks. American Journal of Preventive Medicine, 39(4), pp. 379-388. www.ncbi.nlm.nih.gov/pubmed/20837291.

438. Thorp, A., Kingwell, B., Owen, N. and Dunstan, D. (2014). Breaking up Workplace Sitting Time with Intermittent Standing Bouts Improves Fatigue and Musculoskeletal Discomfort in Overweight/Obese Office Workers. Occupational and Environmental Medicine, 71(11), pp. 765-771. www.ncbi.nlm.nih.gov/pubmed/25168375.
439. Ballman, D. (2014). States with Pro-Employee Laws: Work Breaks for Employees. LexisNexis® Legal Newsroom. www.lexisnexis.com/legalnewsroom/labor-employment/b/labor-employment-top-blogs/posts/states-with-pro-employee-laws-work-breaks-for-employees.
440. Staples Advantage (2014). Staples Survey Reveals Many Employees Feel Too Guilty to Take Breaks, Despite Spending Longer Hours at Work. investor.staples.com/phoenix.zhtml?c=96244&p=irol-newsArticle&ID=1928035.
441. OfficeTeam (2018). More Than Half of Workers Take 30 Minutes or Less for Lunch, Survey Says. rh-us.mediaroom.com/2018-09-10-More-Than-Half-Of-Workers-Take-30-Minutes-Or-Less-For-Lunch-Survey-Says.
442. U.S. Only Advanced Economy That Does Not Guarantee Paid Vacation or Holidays. (n.d.). Washington, D.C.: Center for Economic and Policy Research. cepr.net/documents/publications/nvn-summary.pdf.
443. Oxford Economics. (2014). An Assessment of Paid Time Off in the U.S.: Implications for Employees, Companies, and the Economy. p. 6. www.oxfordeconomics.com/my-oxford/projects/280061. Accessed September 29, 2019.
444. The FMLA at 25: Building on the Family and Medical Leave Act. (n.d.). Washington, D.C.: Committee on Education and the Workforce Democrats. edlabor.house.gov/imo/media/doc/Paid%20Leave%20Fact%20Sheet.pdf.
445. Campbell-Yeo, M., Disher, T., Benoit, B. and Johnston, C. (2015). Understanding Kangaroo Care and Its Benefits to Preterm Infants. Pediatric Health, Medicine and Therapeutics, 6, p. 15. www.ncbi.nlm.nih.gov/pmc/articles/PMC5683265.
446. Dube, R. and Raeburn, P. (2014). Mets Player Criticized for Paternity Leave: It Was 'Best Thing for Our Family'. TODAY. www.today.com/parents/mets-player-criticized-paternity-leave-it-was-best-thing-our-2D79480866.
447. Adamczyk, A. (2015). These Are the Companies with the Best Parental Leave Policies. Money. money.com/money/4098469/paid-parental-leave-google-amazon-apple-facebook.
448. Marcario, R. (2016). Why Should Employers Care about Families? Patagonia, The Cleanest Line. tcl.patagonia.com/2016/08/why-should-employers-care-about-families.
449. Strang, L. and Broeks, M. (2016). Maternity Leave Policies: Trade-Offs Between Labour Market Demands and Health Benefits for Children. RAND Europe. www.rand.org/pubs/research_reports/RR1734.html.
450. World Bank, Data. (n.d.). Proportion of Seats Held by Women in National Parliaments (%). data.worldbank.org/indicator/SG.GEN.PARL.ZS. Accessed September 29, 2019.
451. DeSilver, D. (2018). A Record Number of Women Will Be Serving in the New Congress. Pew Research Center. www.pewresearch.org/fact-tank/2018/12/18/record-number-women-in-congress.
452. Peters, A. (2015). Why Sweden Is Shifting to a 6-Hour Workday. Fast Company. www.fastcompany.com/3051448/why-sweden-is-shifting-to-a-6-hour-work-day.

453. Green Carmichael, S. (2015). The Research Is Clear: Long Hours Backfire for People and for Companies. Harvard Business Review. hbr.org/2015/08/the-research-is-clear-long-hours-backfire-for-people-and-for-companies.
454. Mattingly, M., Schaefer, A. and Carson, J. (2016). Child Care Costs Exceed 10 Percent of Family Income for One in Four Families. The Carsey School of Public Policy at the Scholars' Repository. scholars.unh.edu/carsey/288.
455. National Women's Law Center. (2017). Child Care is Out of Reach for Many Low-Income Families, New NWLC Report Shows. nwlc.org/press-releases/child-care-is-out-of-reach-for-many-low-income-families-new-nwlc-report-shows.

CHAPTER 13

456. Seburn, P. (1991). Evolution of Employer-Provided Defined Benefit Pensions. Monthly Labor Review, p. 18-20. www.bls.gov/mlr/1991/12/art3full.pdf.
457. U.S. Congress. House. Home Owner's Loan Act of 1933. HR 5240. 73rd Cong., 1st sess.
458. Seburn, P. (1991). Evolution of employer-provided defined benefit pensions.
459. Kinsella, K. and Gist, Y. (1995). Older Workers, Retirement, and Pensions: A Comparative International Chartbook. Washington, D.C.: U.S. Department of Commerce, Bureau of the Census, p. 68. www.census.gov/prod/1/intnl/ipc95-2/ipc95_2.pdf.
460. Moysich, A. (1997). The Savings and Loan Crisis and Its Relationship to Banking. In: History of the Eighties: Lessons for the Future. Vol. 1, An Examination of the Banking Crises of the 1980s and Early 1990s., 1st ed. Washington, D.C.: Federal Deposit Insurance Corporation, p. 179,187. www.fdic.gov/bank/historical/history/167_188.pdf.
461. Ibid.
462. McFadden, R. (2014). Charles Keating, 90, Key Figure in '80s Savings and Loan Crisis, Dies. The New York Times. www.nytimes.com/2014/04/02/business/charles-keating-key-figure-in-the-1980s-savings-and-loan-crisis-dies-at-90.html.
463. Moysich, A. (1997). The Savings and Loan Crisis and Its Relationship to Banking. In: History of the Eighties: Lessons for the Future. Vol. 1, An Examination of the Banking Crises of the 1980s and Early 1990s., 1st ed.
464. Carlson, M. (2006). A Brief History of the 1987 Stock Market Crash with a Discussion of the Federal Reserve Response. Washington, D.C.: Board of Governors of the Federal Reserve, p. 17. www.federalreserve.gov/pubs/feds/2007/200713/200713pap.pdf.
465. Matthews, C. (2012). 25 Years Later: In the Crash of 1987, the Seeds of the Great Recession. TIME. business.time.com/2012/10/22/25-years-later-in-the-crash-of-1987-the-seeds-of-the-great-recession.
466. Pension Benefit Guaranty Corporation. (1995). Pension Reversion: Removing Pension Dollars. Washington, D.C.: Communications and Public Affairs Department.
467. Williams Walsh, M. (2005). New Tug of War over Excess Pension Cash. The New York Times. www.nytimes.com/2005/03/03/business/new-tug-of-war-over-excess-pension-cash.html.

468. Maynard, M. (2005). United Air Wins Right to Default on Its Employee Pension Plans. The New York Times. www.nytimes.com/2005/05/11/business/united-air-wins-right-to-default-on-its-employee-pension-plans.html.
469. Coronado, J. and Copeland, P. (2003). Cash Balance Pension Plan Conversions and the New Economy. Washington, D.C.: Federal Reserve Board of Governors, p. 7. www.federalreserve.gov/pubs/feds/2003/200363/200363pap.pdf.
470. Oppel Jr., R. (1999). Companies Cash in on New Pension Plan; But Older Workers Can Face Penalties. The New York Times. www.nytimes.com/1999/08/20/business/companies-cash-in-on-new-pension-plan-but-older-workers-can-face-penalties.html.
471. Lichtenstein, J. and Turner, J. (2005). Cash Balance Pension Plans and Older Workers. Washington, D.C.: AARP Public Policy Institute. assets.aarp.org/rgcenter/econ/ib78_pension.pdf.
472. Schultz, E., Auerbach, J. and Burkins, G. (1999). Pension-Plan Controversy Escalates As IBM Gives In to Employee Anger. The Wall Street Journal. www.wsj.com/articles/SB937779366171684213.
473. Schultz, E. (1999). Overfunded Pension Plans Fatten Companies' Earnings. The Wall Street Journal. www.wsj.com/articles/SB929398258967849O3.
474. Sprague v. General Motors Corp. [1994] 843 F. Supp 90-CV-70010 (US District Court for the Eastern District of Michigan), p. 266. law.justia.com/cases/federal/district-courts/FSupp/843/266/2594099.
475. Lowenstein, R. (2008). Long-Term Capital Management: It's a Short-Term Memory. The New York Times. www.nytimes.com/2008/09/07/business/worldbusiness/07iht-07ltcm.15941880.html.
476. Yang, S. (2014). The Epic Story of How a 'Genius' Hedge Fund Almost Caused a Global Financial Meltdown. Business Insider. www.businessinsider.com/the-fall-of-long-term-capital-management-2014-7.
477. Fahey, M. (n.d.). Global Interest Rates: How Does the Fed Stack Up? CNBC. www.cnbc.com/central-banks-interest-rates-around-the-world. Accessed September 30, 2019.
478. Anason, D. (2017). Flashback: The Day Glass-Steagall Died. American Banker. www.americanbanker.com/opinion/flashback-the-day-glass-steagall-died.
479. Kwan, S. (2003). Underfunding of Private Pension Plans. San Francisco: FRBSF Economic Letter. www.frbsf.org/economic-research/publications/economic-letter/2003/june/underfunding-of-private-pension-plans.
480. Schultz, E. (1999). Overfunded Pension Plans Fatten Companies' Earnings.
481. Ibid.
482. Smart, T. (1998). Swollen Pension Funds, Surprise Profits. The Washington Post. www.washingtonpost.com/archive/business/1998/06/14/swollen-pension-funds-surprise-profits/d32ba9af-674a-4328-8b90-0fed030a57f4.
483. Kwan, S. (2003).
484. Posner, W. U.S. Department of the Treasury. Pension Benefit Guaranty Corporation, March 13, 2003. www.treasury.gov/FOIA/Documents/03132003pbgc.pdf.
485. Dolan, J. (2016). The Pension Gap. Los Angeles Times. www.latimes.com/projects/la-me-pension-crisis-davis-deal.
486. Ibid.

487. Alden, C. (2005). Looking Back on the Crash. The Guardian. www.theguardian.com/technology/2005/mar/10/newmedia.media.
488. U.S. Congress. House. Committee on Agriculture. Commodity Futures Modernization Act of 2000. HR 4541. 106th Cong., 2d sess. 2000. H. Rep. 106-711. www.congress.gov/congressional-report/106th-congress/house-report/711/1.
489. Fahey, M. (n.d.).
490. Federal Reserve Bank of St. Louis, Economic Research. (n.d.). S&P/Case-Shiller U.S. National Home Price Index. fred.stlouisfed.org/series/CSUSHPINSA. Graph units shown as "Percent Change from Year Ago, Not Seasonally Adjusted."
491. See Chapter 7 of this book.
492. Angelides, P., Thomas, B., Born, B., Holtz-Eakin, D., Georgiou, B., Murren, H., Graham, B., Thompson, J., Hennessey, K. and Wallison, P. (2011). The Financial Crisis Inquiry Report: Final Report of the National Commission on the Causes of the Financial Economic Crisis in the United States. Washington, D.C., p. 212. www.govinfo.gov/content/pkg/GPO-FCIC/pdf/GPO-FCIC.pdf.
493. Morgenson, G. and Story, L. (2009). Banks That Bundled Bad Debt Also Bet Against It. The New York Times. www.nytimes.com/2009/12/24/business/24trading.html.
494. U.S. Congress, House, Garn-St. Germain Depository Institutions Act of 1982, HR 6267, 97th Cong., 2d sess., Pub. L. No. 97-320, www.fdic.gov/regulations/laws/rules/8000-4100.html.
495. Snowden, K. (2009). The Anatomy of a Residential Mortgage Crisis: A Look Back to the 1930s. Greensboro, NC: Bryan School of Business and Economics, UNC Greensboro, p. 8. sedonaweb.com/attach/schools/NCBEfaculty/attach/chapter-297.pdf.
496. Thompson, S. (2007). Speeches & Testimony. Federal Deposit Insurance Corporation. www.fdic.gov/news/news/speeches/archives/2007/chairman/spmar22071.html.
497. Edmiston, K. (2009). Characteristics of High Foreclosure Neighborhoods in the Tenth District. Federal Reserve Bank of Kansas City, pp. 52,62. www.kansascityfed.org/PUBLICAT/ECONREV/PDF/09q2edmiston.pdf.
498. Money, Banking and Financial Markets. (2017). Looking Back: The Financial Crisis Began 10 Years Ago This Week. www.moneyandbanking.com/commentary/2017/8/6/looking-back-the-financial-crisis-began-10-years-ago-this-week.
499. U.S. Department of the Treasury. (2013). TARP Programs: Investment in American International Group (AIG). www.treasury.gov/initiatives/financial-stability/TARP-Programs/aig/Pages/default.aspx.
500. U.S. Department of the Treasury. (2019) TARP Programs: Housing. www.treasury.gov/initiatives/financial-stability/TARP-Programs/housing/Pages/default.aspx. Accessed September 30, 2019.
501. Jahan, S., Saber Mahmud, A. and Papageorgiou, C. (2014). What Is Keynesian Economics? Finance & Development. 51(3). www.imf.org/external/pubs/ft/fandd/2014/09/pdf/basics.pdf.
502. U.S. Department of the Treasury. (2016). TARP Programs. www.treasury.gov/initiatives/financial-stability/TARP-Programs/Pages/default.aspx.
503. Board of Governors of the Federal Reserve System. (2017). Quarterly Report on Federal Reserve Balance Sheet Developments: Overview. www.federalreserve.gov/monetarypolicy/bsd-overview-201703.htm.

504. Federal Reserve Bank of St. Louis, Economic Research. (2019). Effective Federal Funds Rate. fred.stlouisfed.org/series/FEDFUNDS.
505. National Compensation Survey. (2014). Employee Benefits in the U.S., March 2014. U.S. Department of Labor, Bureau of Labor Statistics. www.bls.gov/ncs/ebs/benefits/2014/ownership/private/table02a.pdf.
506. Ibid.
507. Aiden Byrne, J. (2017). U.S. Companies Spent $4T Buying Back Their Own Stock. New York Post. nypost.com/2017/08/19/us-companies-spent-4t-buying-back-their-own-stock.
508. Milani, K. and Tung, I. (2018). Curbing Stock Buybacks: A Crucial Step to Raising Worker Pay and Reducing Inequality. Roosevelt Institute. rooseveltinstitute.org/curbing-stock-buybacks-crucial-step.
509. Ivanova, I. (2018). GM Bought Back $10 Billion in Stock Since 2015, Double What Job Cuts Will Save. CBS News. www.cbsnews.com/news/gm-bought-back-10-billion-in-stock-since-2015-double-what-job-cuts-will-save.
510. Chiglinsky, K., Kochkodin, B. and Clough, R. (2017). The $31 Billion Hole in GEís Balance Sheet That Keeps Growing. Bloomberg. www.bloomberg.com/news/articles/2017-06-16/ge-s-31-billion-hangover-immelt-leaves-behind-big-unfunded-tab.
511. Egan, M. (2018). GE's $24 Billion Buyback Boondoggle. CNN Money. money.cnn.com/2018/03/23/investing/ge-share-buybacks-immelt/index.html.
512. Lerner, M. (2017). The Mortgage Market Is Now Dominated by Non-Bank Lenders. The Washington Post. www.washingtonpost.com/realestate/the-mortgage-market-is-now-dominated-by-nonbank-lenders/2017/02/22/9c6bf5fc-d1f5-11e6-a783-cd3fa950f2fd_story.html.
513. Gelzinis, G. (2019). Strengthening the Regulation and Oversight of Shadow Banks: Revitalizing the Financial Stability Oversight Council. Center for American Progress. www.americanprogress.org/issues/economy/reports/2019/07/18/471564/strengthening-regulation-oversight-shadow-banks.
514. Kaul, K. and Goodman, L. (2016). Nonbank Servicer Regulation: New Capital and Liquidity Requirements Don't Offer Enough Loss Protection. Washington, D.C.: Urban Institute, Housing Finance Policy Center, p. 7. www.urban.org/sites/default/files/publication/78131/2000633-Nonbank-Servicer-Regulation-New-Capital-and-Liquidity-Requirements-Don%27t-Offer-Enough-Loss-Protection.pdf.
515. Freed, D. (2015). The Next Asset Likely to Blow Up Big Banks' Balance Sheets. TheStreet. www.thestreet.com/story/13145252/1/the-next-asset-likely-to-blow-up-big-banks-balance-sheets.html.
516. Richter, W. (2017). Risk Has Been Abolished in the Markets. Business Insider. www.businessinsider.com/risk-has-been-abolished-in-the-markets-2017-7.
517. Davies, P. (2017). How Risky Loans Are Kept Afloat in Alphabet Soup. The Wall Street Journal. www.wsj.com/articles/how-risky-loans-are-kept-afloat-in-alphabet-soup-1501582788.
518. Mackintosh, J. (2018). There Have Never Been So Many Bonds That Are Almost Junk. The Wall Street Journal. www.wsj.com/articles/there-have-never-been-so-many-bonds-that-are-almost-junk-1537466036.

519. Rochford, J. (2018). The Next Wreck in Junk Bonds Will Be Bigger, Longer and Uglier. MarketWatch. www.marketwatch.com/story/the-next-wreck-in-high-yield-bonds-will-be-bigger-longer-and-uglier-2018-06-04.
520. Sweet, K. (2017). As Americans Take on More Debt, Some Pockets of Concern. AP News. apnews.com/6e0366059f8e434a8b6ea0b0b906786f.
521. Vlastelica, R. (2017). Record Margin Debt May Be a Red Flag, But Analysts Say Don't Worry. MarketWatch. www.marketwatch.com/story/record-margin-debt-may-be-a-red-flag-but-analysts-say-dont-worry-2017-03-16.
522. Sweet, K. (2017). As Americans Take on More Debt, Some Pockets of Concern.
523. Scully, M. (2017). Auto Lender Santander Checked Income on Just 8% in Subprime ABS. Bloomberg. www.bloomberg.com/news/articles/2017-05-22/subprime-auto-giant-checked-income-on-just-8-of-loans-in-abs.
524. Fair Isaac Corporation. (2014). FICO Score 9 Now Available at Equifax. www.fico.com/en/newsroom/fico-score-9-now-available-at-equifax-10-09-2014.
525. Tankersley, J. and Rappeport, A. (2018). 1.5 Million Retirees Await Congressional Fix for a Pension Time Bomb. The New York Times. www.nytimes.com/2018/02/18/business/multiemployer-pension-crisis.html.

CHAPTER 14

526. Triangle: Remembering the Fire. (2011). [film] Directed by D. Pinkerson. New York, NY: Blowback Productions.
527. History. (2009). Triangle Shirtwaist Factory Fire. www.history.com/topics/triangle-shirtwaist-fire.
528. Yaeger, L. (2017). The Lessons of the Triangle Shirtwaist Factory Fire, 106 Years Later. Vogue. www.vogue.com/article/triangle-shirtwaist-factory-106-anniversary.
529. Trattner, W. (1970). Crusade for the Children: A History of the National Child Labor Committee and Child Labor Reform in America. Chicago: Quadrangle Books, p. 41.
530. Leuchtenburg, W. (2005). When Franklin Roosevelt Clashed with the Supreme Court—and Lost. Smithsonian Magazine. www.smithsonianmag.com/history/when-franklin-roosevelt-clashed-with-the-supreme-court-and-lost-78497994.
531. Ruiz, M. (2015). What Sexual Harassment at Work Really Looks Like. Cosmopolitan. www.cosmopolitan.com/career/a36462/sexual-harassment-at-work.
532. Heffernan, M. (2013). Why Is the Finance Industry So Sexist? CBS News. www.cbsnews.com/news/why-is-the-finance-industry-so-sexist.
533. Lewin, T. (2006). At Colleges, Women Are Leaving Men in the Dust. The New York Times. www.nytimes.com/2006/07/09/education/09college.html.
534. Clark, P. (2014). Salary Gap: Most Lucrative Industries Pay Women the Least. Bloomberg. www.bloomberg.com/news/articles/2014-08-18/salary-gap-most-lucrative-industries-pay-women-the-least.
535. Francis, D. (2019). Employers' Replies to Racial Names. The National Bureau of Economic Research. www.nber.org/digest/sep03/w9873.html.
536. Tutton, M. (2018). Modern Slavery in Developed Countries More Common Than Thought. The CNN Freedom Project. www.cnn.com/2018/07/19/world/global-slavery-index-2018/index.html.

537. Sahadi, J. (2014). Labor Trafficking in America: Victims Enslaved in Plain Sight. CNN Money. money.cnn.com/2014/10/21/pf/labor-trafficking.
538. Buckley, C. (2008). Forced Labor in the United States: A Contemporary Problem in Need of a Contemporary Solution. In: K. Bales, ed., Human Rights and Contemporary Slavery. Denver: Graduate School of International Studies, University of Denver, p. 117. www.du.edu/korbel/hrhw/researchdigest/slavery/us.pdf.
539. Kelkar, K. (2016). From Media Cutoffs to Lockdown, Tracing the Fallout from the U.S. Prison Strike. PBS NewsHour. www.pbs.org/newshour/updates/prison-strike-lockdown-fallout.
540. Federal Bureau of Prisons. (2019). BOP Statistics: Inmate Race. www.bop.gov/about/statistics/statistics_inmate_race.jsp. Accessed October 2, 2019.
541. Bonczar, T. (2003). Prevalence of Imprisonment in the U.S. Population, 1974-2001. Bureau of Justice Statistics Special Report, NCJ 197976, p. 1. www.bjs.gov/content/pub/pdf/piusp01.pdf.
542. James, B. (2016). Prisoners All over the U.S. Are on Strike for 'An End to Prison Slavery'. Vice. news.vice.com/article/prisoners-all-over-the-us-are-on-strike-for-an-end-to-prison-slavery.
543. UNICOR: Federal Prison Industries, Inc. (2016). 80 Years of New Beginnings. Petersburg, VA: UNICOR, pp. 4-5. www.unicor.gov/publications/corporate/CATC6500_FINAL_20160114.pdf.
544. Kelkar, K. (2016). From Media Cutoffs to Lockdown, Tracing the Fallout from the U.S. Prison Strike.
545. James, B. (2016). Prisoners All over the U.S. Are on Strike for 'An End to Prison Slavery'.
546. Vongkiatkajorn, K. (2016). Why Prisoners across the United States Have Gone on Strike. Mother Jones. www.motherjones.com/politics/2016/09/prison-strike-inmate-labor-work.
547. Avery, B. (2019). Ban the Box: U.S. Cities, Counties, and States Adopt Fair Hiring Policies. National Employment Law Project. www.nelp.org/publication/ban-the-box-fair-chance-hiring-state-and-local-guide.
548. Sterbenz, C. (2014). Why Norway's Prison System Is So Successful. Business Insider. www.businessinsider.com/why-norways-prison-system-is-so-successful-2014-12.
549. Kvalvaag, H. (2016). Norwegian Prisons Rehabilitate Criminal Offenders. University of Bergen. www.uib.no/en/news/100126/norwegian-prisons-rehabilitate-criminal-offenders.
550. TIME. (n.d.). Inside the World's Most Humane Prison, Photo Essays. content.time.com/time/photogallery/0,29307,1989083,00.html. Accessed October 2, 2019.
551. U.S. Bureau of Labor Statistics (2013). International Comparisons of Hourly Compensation Costs in Manufacturing, 2012. www.bls.gov/fls/ichcc.pdf.
552. Grevatt, M. (2009). The Ford Hunger March of 1932. Workers World. www.workers.org/2009/us/ford_hunger_march_0402.
553. National Labor Relations Board. (n.d.). Employer/Union Rights and Obligations. www.nlrb.gov/rights-we-protect/rights/employer-union-rights-and-obligations. Accessed October 2, 2019.
554. Anonymous. (2017). Information Confirmed through a Phone Call Discussion with the Colorado Branch of the National Labor Relations Board on May 12, 2017.

555. U.S. Congress. Senate. Committee on Foreign Relations. Worker Safety and Labor Rights in Bangladesh's Garment Sector. 113th Cong., 1st sess., 2013. S. Rep. 113–22. www.gpo.gov/fdsys/pkg/CPRT-113SPRT85633/pdf/CPRT-113SPRT85633.pdf.
556. Odhikar. (2013). Broken Dreams: A Report on the Rana Plaza Collapse. pp. 3-5. odhikar.org/wp-content/uploads/2013/06/Fact-finding_RMG_Rana-Plaza_Eng.pdf.
557. U.S. Congress. Senate. Committee on Foreign Relations.
558. International Trade Union Confederation. (2014). ITUC Global Rights Index: The World's Worst Countries for Workers. Brussels: ITUC, p. 38. www.ituc-csi.org/IMG/pdf/survey_ra_2014_eng_v2.pdf.
559. U.S. Environmental Protection Agency. (2016). Advancing Sustainable Materials Management: 2014 Fact Sheet: Assessing Trends in Material Generation, Recycling, Composting, Combustion with Energy Recovery and Landfilling in the United States. Washington, D.C.: EPA, p. 8. www.epa.gov/sites/production/files/2016-11/documents/2014_smmfactsheet_508.pdf.
560. Environmental Defense Fund. (2018). In Demand: Clean Energy, Sustainability and the New American Workforce. Boston: EDF Climate Corps, p. 4. edfclimatecorps.org/sites/edfclimatecorps.org/files/edf_in_demand_clean_energy_sustainability_and_the_new_american_workforce.pdf.
561. Zulinski, J. (2018). U.S. Leads in Greenhouse Gas Reductions, But Some States Are Falling Behind. Environmental and Energy Study Institute. www.eesi.org/articles/view/u.s.-leads-in-greenhouse-gas-reductions-but-some-states-are-falling-behind.
562. Epstein, P., Buonocore, J., Eckerle, K., Hendryx, M., Stout III, B., Heinberg, R., Clapp, R., May, B., Reinhart, N., Ahern, M., Doshi, S. and Glustrom, L. (2011). Full Cost Accounting for the Life Cycle of Coal. Annals of the New York Academy of Sciences, 1219(1), pp. 73-98. www.ncbi.nlm.nih.gov/pubmed/21332493.
563. Union of Concerned Scientists. (2017). Benefits of Renewable Energy Use. www.ucsusa.org/clean-energy/renewable-energy/public-benefits-of-renewable-power.
564. Esty, D. and Charnovitz, S. (2013). Environmental Sustainability and Competitiveness: Policy Imperative and Corporate Opportunity. Harvard Business School, pp. 3-4. www.hbs.edu/competitiveness/Documents/USComp-EstyCharnovitz-Working-Paper.pdf.
565. U.S. Environmental Protection Agency. (n.d.). Benefits and Costs of the Clean Air Act 1990-2020, the Second Prospective Study. www.epa.gov/clean-air-act-overview/benefits-and-costs-clean-air-act-1990-2020-second-prospective-study.
566. Hanna-Attisha, M., LaChance, J., Sadler, R. and Champney Schnepp, A. (2016). Elevated Blood Lead Levels in Children Associated with the Flint Drinking Water Crisis: A Spatial Analysis of Risk and Public Health Response. American Journal of Public Health, 106(2), pp. 283-290. ajph.aphapublications.org/doi/10.2105/AJPH.2015.303003.
567. U.S. Environmental Protection Agency. (n.d.). Learn about Lead. www.epa.gov/lead/learn-about-lead.
568. Maher, K. (2018). Schools across the U.S. Find Elevated Lead Levels in Drinking Water. The Wall Street Journal. www.wsj.com/articles/schools-across-the-u-s-find-elevated-lead-levels-in-drinking-water-1536153522.
569. The New York Times. (1993). COMPANY NEWS; Jack in the Box's Worst Nightmare. www.nytimes.com/1993/02/06/business/company-news-jack-in-the-box-s-worst-nightmare.html.

570. National Law Center on Homelessness & Poverty. (2018). Homelessness in America: Overview of Data and Causes. nlchp.org/wp-content/uploads/2018/10/Homeless_Stats_Fact_Sheet.pdf.
571. vanden Heuvel, K. (2014). Why Is the VA Suffering from a Lack of Resources in the First Place? The Nation. www.thenation.com/article/why-va-suffering-lack-resources-first-place.
572. U.S. Interagency Council on Homelessness. (2018). Home, Together: The Federal Strategic Plan to Prevent and End Homelessness. p. 4. www.usich.gov/resources/uploads/asset_library/Home-Together-Federal-Strategic-Plan-to-Prevent-and-End-Homelessness.pdf.
573. Kesling, B. (2018). More Young Veterans Committing Suicide, VA Data Show. The Wall Street Journal. www.wsj.com/articles/more-young-veterans-committing-suicide-va-data-shows-1537970087.
574. Rostron, A. (2018). The Dickey Amendment on Federal Funding for Research on Gun Violence: A Legal Dissection. American Journal of Public Health, 108(7), pp. 865-867. www.ncbi.nlm.nih.gov/pmc/articles/PMC5993413.
575. Rosell, D. and Siever, L. (2015). The Neurobiology of Aggression and Violence. CNS Spectrums, 20(3), pp. 254-279. www.ncbi.nlm.nih.gov/pubmed/25936249.
576. Ibid.
577. Einstein, K., Palmer, M. and Glick, D. (2018). Who Participates in Local Government? Evidence from Meeting Minutes. Perspectives on Politics, 17(1), pp. 28-46. www.politicsofhousing.com/research/who_participates_in_local_government.pdf.
578. Dougherty, C., 2021. Gavin Newsom signs two laws to ease California's housing crisis. New York Times. www.nytimes.com/2021/09/17/business/newsom-california-housing-crisis.html.
579. Gross, T., 2017. A 'Forgotten History' Of How The U.S. Government Segregated America. National Public Radio. www.npr.org/2017/05/03/526655831/a-forgotten-history-of-how-the-u-s-government-segregated-america.
580. Bloomberg. (2019). How Singapore Helped 90% of Households to Own Their Homes. [video] www.bloomberg.com/news/videos/2018-08-30/how-singapore-helped-90-of-households-to-own-their-homes-video.
581. Los Angeles Times. (1985). Murdoch Becomes U.S. Citizen, Can Buy TV Network. www.latimes.com/archives/la-xpm-1985-09-04-mn-23112-story.html.
582. Graves, L. (2017). Donald Trump and Rupert Murdoch: Inside the Billionaire Bromance. The Guardian. www.theguardian.com/us-news/2017/jun/16/donald-trump-rupert-murdoch-friendship-fox-news.
583. Fletcher, D. (2009). A Brief History of the Fairness Doctrine. TIME. content.time.com/time/nation/article/0,8599,1880786,00.html.
584. McCabe, D. (2016). Bill Clinton's Telecom Law: Twenty Years Later. The Hill. thehill.com/policy/technology/268459-bill-clintons-telecom-law-twenty-years-later.
585. Lutz, A. (2012). These 6 Corporations Control 90% of the Media in America. Business Insider. www.businessinsider.com/these-6-corporations-control-90-of-the-media-in-america-2012-6.
586. Media Violence. (2001). Pediatrics, 108(5), pp. 1222-1226. pediatrics.aappublications.org/content/108/5/1222.

587. Park, A. (2014). Little By Little, Violent Video Games Make Us More Aggressive. TIME. time.com/34075/how-violent-video-games-change-kids-attitudes-about-aggression.
588. Huesmann, L. R., Moise-Titus, J., Podolski, C., & Eron, L. D. (2003). Longitudinal Relations between Children's Exposure to TV Violence and Their Aggressive and Violent Behavior in Young Adulthood: 1977-1992. Developmental Psychology, 39, 201-221. www.apa.org/pi/prevent-violence/resources/tv-violence.
589. Haynes, T. (2018). Dopamine, Smartphones & You: A battle for Your Time. Harvard University. sitn.hms.harvard.edu/flash/2018/dopamine-smartphones-battle-time.
590. Lee, D. (2018). The Tactics of a Russian Troll Farm. BBC News. www.bbc.com/news/technology-43093390.
591. Roettgers, J. (2019). Facebook Took Down 2.2 Billion Fake Accounts in Q1. Variety. variety.com/2019/digital/news/facebook-took-down-2-2-billion-fake-accounts-in-q1-1203224487.
592. Allcott, H., and M. Gentzkow. (2017). Social Media and Fake News in the 2016 Election. Journal of Economic Perspectives 31 (2): 211–236. doi: 10.1257/jep.31.2.211.
593. "Dissemination of False Advertisements," Title 15 U.S. Code, Sec. 52. www.law.cornell.edu/uscode/text/15/52.
594. Brennan Center for Justice. (2019). Automatic Voter Registration, a Summary. www.brennancenter.org/our-work/research-reports/automatic-voter-registration-summary. Accessed October 3, 2019.
595. Grossman, I. (2014). Transforming Elections: Changes in State Law Have More People Registering Online, Voting Early and Casting Ballots in Central Locations. The Council of State Governments, Midwest. www.csgmidwest.org/policyresearch/0614-state-election-laws.aspx.
596. U.S. Constitution. Art. 2, Sect. 1.
597. DeSilver, D. (2018). U.S. Voter Turnout Trails Most Developed Countries. Pew Research Center. www.pewresearch.org/fact-tank/2018/05/21/u-s-voter-turnout-trails-most-developed-countries.

Made in the USA
Monee, IL
04 November 2026

67384575R00105